Bread and Beauty

Historical Materialism Book Series

The Historical Materialism Book Series is a major publishing initiative of the radical left. The capitalist crisis of the twenty-first century has been met by a resurgence of interest in critical Marxist theory. At the same time, the publishing institutions committed to Marxism have contracted markedly since the high point of the 1970s. The Historical Materialism Book Series is dedicated to addressing this situation by making available important works of Marxist theory. The aim of the series is to publish important theoretical contributions as the basis for vigorous intellectual debate and exchange on the left.

The peer-reviewed series publishes original monographs, translated texts, and reprints of classics across the bounds of academic disciplinary agendas and across the divisions of the left. The series is particularly concerned to encourage the internationalization of Marxist debate and aims to translate significant studies from beyond the English-speaking world.

For a full list of titles in the Historical Materialism Book Series
available in paperback from Haymarket Books, visit:
https://www.haymarketbooks.org/series_collections/1-historical-materialism

Bread and Beauty

The Cultural Politics of José Carlos Mariátegui

Juan E. De Castro

Haymarket Books
Chicago, IL

First published in 2021 by Brill Academic Publishers, The Netherlands
© 2021 Koninklijke Brill NV, Leiden, The Netherlands

Published in paperback in 2021 by
Haymarket Books
P.O. Box 180165
Chicago, IL 60618
773-583-7884
www.haymarketbooks.org

ISBN: 978-1-64259-597-0

Distributed to the trade in the US through Consortium Book Sales and
Distribution (www.cbsd.com) and internationally through Ingram
Publisher Services International (www.ingramcontent.com).

This book was published with the generous support of Lannan
Foundation and Wallace Action Fund.

Special discounts are available for bulk purchases by organizations and
institutions. Please call 773-583-7884 or email info@haymarketbooks.org
for more information.

Cover art and design by David Mabb. Cover art is a detail of *Construct
39, Morris, Daisy / Rodchenko, Triple Peaks* (2006).

Printed in the United States.

10 9 8 7 6 5 4 3 2 1

Library of Congress Cataloging-in-Publication data is available.

Contents

Acknowledgements

As has been the case with my recent books, Ignacio López-Calvo and Nicholas Birns read the manuscript and made many valuable suggestions. Additionally, Marc Becker commented on early drafts of some of the chapters. The book is infinitely better thanks to them. Obviously, all remaining flaws are my responsibility.

I am particularly grateful to Anthony Arnove, from Haymarket Press, for his enthusiasm for this project, and Danny Hayward, from Historical Materialism, for his careful editing. My former research assistant Alberto Quintero was of great help during the writing process.

This book, like everything worthwhile I do, is only possible thanks to the support of my wife Magdalena.

Introduction

In the midst of overgrown grass and flanked by shrubs and trees, six mostly well-dressed men – only one is missing his tie – and two more informally attired women – one is wearing a vest and a tie – posed for a photograph in January 1928. Near the centre, a man is sitting in a wheelchair. He is the magnetic centre of the photograph. One's gaze is pulled by his figure, and not because he is the only one wearing a bow tie.

He is looking straight at the camera; his head is resting on his hand; his hair, a bit long for the time, seems to be a throwback to the nineteenth century or, perhaps, foreshadows the 1960s, when his work would be rediscovered. While one can see that his right leg has been amputated, his body, held in a some-what serpentine pose, seems to oddly defy his physical infirmity. His gaze and posture are not those of a defeated man. He is clearly somebody who believes in himself and in his capacity to overcome any physical or, for that matter, any other kind of adversity. He is José Carlos Mariátegui, the subject of this study. Of all his photographs, this is the one where his iron will is best evidenced.

He is surrounded by his friends. Behind him, from left to right, are three painters: the Peruvian impressionist Ricardo Flórez, the Argentine José Malanca, and the also Peruvian Jorge del Prado; the latter two post-impressionists. Sitting on the grass, to his left (our right) is Ricardo Martínez de la Torre, his closest collaborator and co-editor of *Amauta*, the innovative magazine Mariátegui had founded in 1926 and that had already included articles by Sigmund Freud and Miguel de Unamuno. To his right – our left – three figures are sitting on the grass. The one nearest Mariátegui is the poet Blanca del Prado, Jorge's sister. Next to her are Mariátegui's dearest friends – Noemí Milstein and Miguel Adler, two Jewish immigrants, originally from Ukraine, who edited a magazine *Repertorio Hebreo*, in which Mariátegui collaborated.[1]

The photograph can be interpreted as representing Mariátegui's personal and intellectual world. His simultaneous interest in art and politics, his cosmopolitanism, his intense belief in friendship, his refusal to let physical or any

---

1 Miguel Adler and Noemí Milstein left Peru in 1929, when the regime of President Augusto B. Leguía began to harass Mariátegui's associates. Adler studied anthropology with Paul Rivet. Adler and Milstein would become the parents of the well-known French-born Mexican anthropologist Larissa Adler Milstein and grandparents of the Chilean born Mexican anthropologist and historian Claudio Lomnitz.

FIGURE 1   Mariátegui and friends at the Bosque de Matamula. Image courtesy of the
              Archivo José Carlos Mariátegui.

other limitations strangle his thought and creativity, can all be inferred from the
image. Looking at the photograph one is not surprised that Mariátegui would
theorise Latin American socialism as 'neither copy or imitation' but as 'heroic
creation';[2] or that he claimed that 'the universal, ecumenical roads we have
chosen to travel ... take us ... ever closer to ourselves'.[3] The cosmopolitanism
of his friends – Peruvians, Argentines, European Jews – and the absence of any
explicitly political figure hint at the preeminence given in his thought to culture and aesthetics and at the transcultural matrix within which he understood
the world.

Writing in the Lima of the 1920s, a margin of margins of Western culture
if there ever was one, Mariátegui did not see as foreign the cultural and political innovations of that headiest of decades, when it seemed that utopia was
around the corner, and when a new art was being born from the ashes of realism. Instead he deemed them as necessary for the understanding of Peruvian
indigenous traditions. (One must remember that even if Lima prided itself in its
Hispanic colonial glory, the country as a whole was, as Mariátegui often noted,
four-fifths indigenous). It is thus not surprising that his enemies would call him

---

2   This sentence comes from 'Anniversary and Balance Sheet', a key editorial from *Amauta*, the
    magazine he directed, Mariátegui 2011, p. 130.
3   Mariátegui 1971, p. 287.

an 'Europeist', despite Mariátegui being the first to see in indigenous culture and its institutions a bridge to modernity.

The passage that inspires the title of this study makes clear what is unique about the Peruvian socialist: 'The revolution will be for the poor not only the conquest of bread, but also of beauty, of art, of thought, of all the accessories of the spirit'.[4] Just like he saw nationalism and cosmopolitanism as necessarily imbricated, for Mariátegui, the material and the spiritual, politics and aesthetics, could not nor should be separated.

This passage, moreover, implicitly establishes connections between the two main and often antagonistic anti-systemic political philosophies: Marxism, the current to which Mariátegui subscribed, and anarchism, greatly influential among the Peruvian working-class at the time. The phrase 'the conquest of bread' is the title to one of Pyotr Kropotkin's best-known works.

This conjunction of aesthetics and life, and of art and politics, so characteristic of his writings, was, of course, not unknown in Mariátegui's time. The artistic movement he most admired – surrealism – reacted to the separation of the aesthetics from life that was characteristic of nineteenth-century and early modernist high art by attempting, in Peter Bürger's words, to 'organize a new life praxis from the basis in art'.[5] Moreover, Soviet Russia in the 1920s was seen, perhaps naively, not only as a society experiencing changes that would lead the poor to have bread, it was hoped in perpetuity, but also as the land of Mayakovsky, Pudovkin and Eisenstein. Art and revolution were, for a short but fruitful time, seen as two sides of the same avant-garde coin.

What makes Mariátegui different from these artists and politicians – even from those who like Leon Trotsky actually produced theorisations of the aesthetic – is that this weaving between art and politics, so often preached, informed his politics. The new life praxis he proposed – egalitarian, potentially anti-racist, in other words, socialist – was to be nourished by the development of a new art and thought free from the taint of colonialism.

What was perhaps his major political intervention was also a major cultural event: the founding of the magazine *Amauta*, named for the legendary wisemen of the Incas, in 1926. (The name Amauta has become associated with Mariátegui. It is, indeed, used as his sobriquet). As he wrote in 'Presentación de *Amauta*' (Introducing *Amauta*), the first editorial of his magazine: 'In Peru one feels for some time a current, each day more vigorous and defined, of renov-

---

4 Mariátegui 1980c, p. 158. This statement is part of his article on 'Henry Barbusse', a French writer Mariátegui greatly admired. In this case, as in that of all non-English-language texts in the Bibliography, the translation is mine.

5 Bürger 1984, p. 49.

ation. The proponents of this renovation are called avant-gardists, socialist, revolutionaries'.[6] In its first issue, *Amauta* included a translation of Freud's 'Resistance to Theory'; 'Tempestad en los Andes' (Tempest in the Andes), a preview of Luis Valcárcel's book of the same name, a near mystical celebration of the rebirth of indigenous Quechua culture; a poem by the Peruvian symbolist José María Eguren; as well as more expected political fare, such as articles on the Spanish dictatorship of the 1920s or on the relationship between church and state in post-revolutionary Mexico. Thus, not only were Western and local knowledge considered as complementary, but poetry and prose, and art and analysis, were all seen by Mariátegui as the means necessary to procure the kind of ideological change that would support a more just society. As Fernanda Beigel has argued, Mariátegui promoted an 'aesthetic and political avant-garde' that had, among its major goals, the elimination of neocolonial structures and discrimination in the Andes,[7] and, at the same time, developed editorial and publishing networks that would help disseminate new ideas and new art.[8] He started the publishing house Editorial Minerva, which put out books by progressive and avant-garde writers and thinkers, and established connections with presses and journals throughout the world, including *The Nation, Der Sturm*, and *L'Esprit*.[9]

Of course, he also founded the (Peruvian) Socialist Party, which would, after his death, be transformed into just another cookie-cutter Communist Party, by those subservient to the Stalinist Communist International. He also helped start a labor union – the Confederación General de Trabajadores del Perú (General Federation of Workers of Peru) – which was particularly active in organising the mostly indigenous miners who worked for US mining corporations. He therefore believed in a holistic politics in which persuasion, debate, and dialogue were synonymous with organising and proselytising. His refusal to toe dogmatic lines is evidenced by the fact that even as Mariátegui approached the Third International, he violated the famous eleven points mandated for any and all of its members by not calling the party he founded Communist. More significant is the fact that the phrase dictatorship of the proletariat is not mentioned once in the new party's platform. Revolution, for him, was as much a change of spirit – indeed, this was one of his favourite words – as political

---

6   Mariátegui 1981c, p. 237.
7   See Beigel 2003.
8   See Beigel 2006. Valcárcel's *Tempestad en los Andes* was among the books put out by Mariátegui's publishing house.
9   See Beigel 2006.

action. But, at the same time, a revolution would not be a real revolution if it did not lead to a more just and equal world.

When his declining health, the growing rigidity of the Peruvian government, the rise of populist nationalism – which divided the Peruvian left – and the troubles with the ever more stringent Comintern, put his political and cultural praxis into question, Mariátegui decided to relocate and continue his magazine in what he expected to be a more welcoming Buenos Aires. Tragically, he died in April 1930, a month before his expected move.

1   Mariátegui's Reception in the English-Speaking World

While Mariátegui's *Seven Interpretive Essays on Peruvian Reality* (1928) – henceforth *Seven Essays* – is one of the undisputed masterpieces of the Latin American critical canon, read in part or in whole in colleges – and beyond – throughout the region, the Peruvian Marxist has been relatively ignored in the English-speaking world. It is true that, as was the case with many Latin Americans of his time, Mariátegui was particularly attentive to the latest trends in French literature and art. Moreover, for partly personal reasons, he was deeply influenced by Italian writers and thinkers. However, despite the fact that he had only a limited command of the English language,[10] Mariátegui was extremely interested in the cultures, literatures, and especially politics of the United Kingdom (which then included Ireland) and the United States. Although his relative lack of fluency in English may help explain certain omissions in his criticism of Anglophone writers – for instance, there is no mention of T.S. Eliot, Ezra Pound, or Virginia Woolf in his writings – Mariátegui's personal canon includes such noted British, Irish, and US cultural figures as George Bernard Shaw, James Joyce, Charles Chaplin, and Waldo Frank, the latter considered in the Latin America of the 1920s as a major novelist and critic.[11] Moreover, Mariátegui followed closely the political evolution of both the United Kingdom and the United States. As one would expect, the vicissitudes of the British Labour Party caught his interest; but he also studied the political manoeuvres of Lloyd George during the Paris Peace Conference, and John Maynard Keynes's analysis of the consequences of the Versailles treaty.[12] The figure and ideas of

---

10   When as asked by Argentine editor Samuel Glusberg whether he would be interested in translating Waldo Frank's novel *Holiday*, Mariátegui responded 'My knowledge of English is too limited to attempt the translation of a literary work' (Mariátegui 1994, p. 305).

11   See Mariátegui 1981b.

12   See Mariátegui 1980c.

Woodrow Wilson, then seen primarily as the idealistic proponent of an ethical international system, caught his analytical eye.[13] He may very well be the only major Latin American thinker to write on William Jennings Bryan, the late nineteenth-century US populist and recurring Democratic Party candidate, today best-known for his role in the Scopes 'Monkey' Trial that helped give rise to modern right-wing Christian fundamentalism.[14] Moreover, for him, one of the central characteristics of his period was precisely the passing of the torch of capitalist hegemony from the United Kingdom to the United States. As he wrote in 1928 in his 'On Explaining Chaplin':

> Chaplin entered history at a moment when the axis of capitalism was silently shifting from Great Britain to North America. The disequilibrium of the British machine, recorded early on by his ultrasensitive spirit, acted on his centrifugal and secessionist impulses. His genius felt the attraction of the new capitalist metropolis.[15]

As a Marxist critic, Mariátegui felt it necessary to always keep in mind the evolution of the world economy, not only when considering political and economic affairs, but as the example just quoted proves, also when analysing cultural matters. In the 1920s, this meant always keeping track of the developments in the Anglophone world. Despite his vehement opposition to the imperialist policies of the United States, Mariátegui admired the vitality and energy he believed characterised North American society. In an article significantly titled 'National Progress and Human Capital' (1925), he writes: 'The wealth of the United States is not in its banks or in their markets; it is in its people'.[16] No one was further from the reductive caricatures of North America as the land of materialistic Calibans, so common among Latin American intellectuals during the first decades of the twentieth century, than Mariátegui.[17] For him, the US was not only an aggressive economic, political, and military hegemon, it also served as a

---

13   See Mariátegui 1980c.
14   See Mariátegui 1979.
15   Mariátegui 2011, p. 438.
16   Mariátegui 2011, p. 155.
17   The identification of the United States with Shakespeare's Caliban and of Latin America
     with Ariel, which surely must strike the Anglophone reader as puzzling, originated in the
     region's response to the Spanish American war (1898). Writing in 1898, Rubén Darío, one
     of the greatest poets to ever write in Spanish, described New York City's population in
     these pejorative terms: 'The ideals of those Calibans is limited to the stock market and
     industry. They eat, eat, calculate, drink whisky, and make millions' (Darío 1998, p. 451).
     Uruguayan essayist José Enrique Rodó's *Ariel* (1900) developed Darío's idea into a book

counterpoint – in both negative and positive terms – that helped better explain the twists and turns of Latin American history. Mariátegui wrote for a major magazine of the US left, *The Nation*. There he published in 1929 'The New Peru', a historical survey of the situation of the country's indigenous population.[18] One year later, Waldo Frank, one of his closest friends, wrote a deeply felt obituary note, 'A Great American', for the same publication.[19] This would, however, be the last significant reference to Mariátegui in English for a few decades.

The list of books published in English on Mariátegui is surprisingly brief. It is tempting to see in this omission a consequence of the anti-communism that has defined US culture and cultural industry into the present. However, this was not the case, at least to the same degree, in the United Kingdom. There may, therefore, be other reasons for Anglophone indifference towards the writings of Mariátegui. One answer may be found in that, as Hosam Aboul-Ela notes, 'comparative literary studies in the United States often takes primary texts – novels, poems, plays, and films – from the global south and then processes them via Western theoretical models'.[20] In culture, as in the world economy, Latin America is often seen primarily as a source for raw materials, even if instead of guano, cooper, or tropical lumber, they be named Pablo Neruda, Jorge Luis Borges, or Gabriel García Márquez. This disregard for the theoretical and critical interpretations produced in Latin America (and other regions of the global south) is based on an implicit belief, as again Aboul-Ela notes, in 'Europe and Anglo-America's status as the exclusive domain of ideas and theory'.[21] While occasionally Latin American essayists and critics are translated into English – as was the case with the works of the earlier Peruvian intellectual Francisco García Calderón, Mexican philosopher José Vasconcelos, and the later Brazilian sociologist Gilberto Freyre, to only mention authors active during the first half of the twentieth century –[22] their insights have almost no influence outside the cultural ghettoes of Spanish and Portuguese departments, if at all.

---

length defence of Latin America's Ariel-like spirituality against North America's putative crass materialism.

18   This article is generally included as a footnote in the Spanish editions of *7 ensayos* (see Mariátegui 2007). It is also available in English in a standalone form in Vanden and Becker's 2011 *José Carlos Mariátegui; An Anthology* (Mariátegui 2011).

19   Frank 1930.

20   Aboul-Ela 2007, p. 11.

21   Aboul-Ela 2007, p. 11.

22   The geographical proximity of Mexico, as well as the interest generated by the country's revolution, and the traditional US interest in Brazil, as the other hemispheric giant, may help explain the relatively rapid translations of texts by Vasconcelos (*Aspects of Mexican*

Be that as it may, the English language *Seven Essays* was published in 1971. Mariátegui's more vitalistic writings, including those on aesthetic topics, only began to be translated in 1996 with Michael Pearlman's anthology *The Heroic and Creative Meaning of Socialism*. Harry Vanden's and Marc Becker's 2011 *José Carlos Mariátegui: An Anthology*, the most recent collection of the Peruvian's essays, appropriately includes writings on social, political, and cultural topics.

Perhaps in response to the publication of *Seven Essays*, the first monograph on Mariátegui published by a major academic press only came out in 1972: John M. Baines's *Revolution in Peru: Mariátegui and the Myth*. Written from a perspective wholly aligned with Cold War US foreign policy, Baines sees in the Peruvian Marxist a muddled thinker, of interest only as an early example of a nationalist moderniser of the ilk of Gamal Abdel Nasser or the Peruvian General Juan Velasco, in power when the book was published. Curiously, the book does not explore, as one would have expected, the possible connection between the Peruvian Marxist's ideas and the Cuban Revolution, then still near its peak influence and reputation.

Fortunately, the next work published in English, Jesús Chavarría's *Jose Carlos Mariátegui and the Rise of Modern Peru, 1890–1930* (1979) is a major study of the Peruvian's life and thought, as well as of the historical context in which he developed and wrote his works. Based on thorough research – including interviews with Mariátegui's former collaborators – it presents a solid introduction to the Peruvian's thought and the society that helped shape him and that, in turn, he analysed and tried to change. The book's sins, if one can call them that, are those of omission: understandably, given that Chavarría was a historian, it does not study Mariátegui's writings on literary or aesthetic matters in any depth.

The next academic books published in the US responded with surprising delay to the political effervescence in the Latin America of the 1960s and 1970s and that continued, even if in a residual manner, in the Nicaraguan Revolution (1979–90) and the Salvadorean Civil War (1979–82). It is true that one could argue that Baines was implicitly studying the genealogy of 1960s leftism, or that Chavarría, who was a leader in the Chicano movement before going on

---

Civilization: Lectures on the Harris Foundation, also includes lectures by Manuel Gamio, 1926) and Freyre (*The Masters and the Slaves*, 1946). The case of García Calderón is exceptional. His *Latin America: Its Rise and Progress* (1915) is the translation of *Les Démocraties latine de l'Amerique* (1912), a book only translated into Spanish in 1987. The fact that it was published in France, received critical accolades, and bore a preface by Raymond Poincaré, a major intellectual of the time, surely played a major role in its inclusion in Scribner's 'Latin American Series,' as the only book written by an author from the region.

to found *Hispanic Business Inc.*, a media company, may have been interested in Mariátegui precisely as part of a search for precursors for *La Causa*. However, it is only with Harry Vanden's *National Marxism in Latin America: José Carlos Mariátegui's Thought and Politics* (1986) that the Peruvian's fusion of nationalism and Marxism is presented as predicting the revolutionary ideas that fuelled the insurgencies and revolutionary governments in Cuba, Nicaragua (in power, at the time) and elsewhere. Perhaps following Vanden's lead, Marc Becker in his *Mariátegui and Latin American Marxist Theory* (1993) foregrounds the influence and confluence of the Peruvian's ideas with other radical movements in the region. And then silence – only partly broken in 1996 by Pearlman's anthology – until the publication of Vanden's and Becker's important anthology in 2011.

In addition to *José Carlos Mariátegui: An Anthology*, the 2010s have seen the publication of two books on Mariátegui, both written by British academics. Melissa Moore's 2014 *José Carlos Mariátegui's Unfinished Revolution: Politics, Poetics, and Change in 1920s Peru* brings to the study of the Peruvian Marxist the arsenal of postmodern theory and poetics. This highly innovative work stresses the textual level of Mariátegui's writings and, in particular, their interpellative character, as well as his connections with other writers of the period, such as the poet Magda Portal. However, numerous omissions – there is, for instance, barely a mention of anarcho-syndicalist Georges Sorel's influence – limit the achievement of the work. But perhaps what is most unexpected in Moore's study is her antipathy towards Mariátegui's politics.[23] Though one should, perhaps, not be surprised. The turn towards textuality has often implied a retreat from politics.

Unlike Moore, Mike González's *In the Red Corner: The Marxism of José Carlos Mariátegui* (2019) presents a sympathetic and informed introduction to the life and writings of the Peruvian socialist. Addressed primarily to a general, though potentially leftist, reader, the British Latin Americanist and activist cor-

---

23   An example of Moore's antipathy towards Mariátegui's actual political proposals is evidenced in her reading of 'Anniverary and Balance Sheet', from which the phrase 'heroic creation' comes: 'Mariátegui's attempt to raise and channel political consciousness and, through this, to direct change along party-political lines, through a particular kind of language, perhaps one more political than poetic, or politico-poetic, may thus undermine the interpretive, transformative, poetic, and personal value of this language' (Moore 2014, p. 89). As the passage makes clear, Moore sees an opposition between politics and poetics. For the British academic, when Mariátegui – as we will see, forced by circumstance – becomes concerned with political ideology and organisation, his work loses its transformative power to become nothing more than communist propaganda, seen by Moore in the most stereotyped terms possible.

rectly stresses the originality of Mariátegui's attempt at grounding his socialist policies and proposals on the analysis of his country's specific political and social realities, as well as lucidly noting the points of contact between the Peruvian's interpretation of Marxism and that developed by Antonio Gramsci.[24] Perhaps what is most noticeable about González's study is that it is framed by the rise of 'the new movements', including resurgent indigenous movements, in Latin America and beyond, as well as by the acknowledgement of the failure of the South American Pink Tide to establish successful and long-term movement towards greater equality and prosperity.[25] However, despite the study's overall excellence, one cannot but be surprised by González's concern with defending the Leninist (though not Marxist-Leninist) bona fides of the author of *Seven Essays*.

2   Mariátegui in (Mostly) Latin America

As previously mentioned, the position of Mariátegui in Latin America as a classic has implied a continuous interest in his writings, even if not unaffected by the ups and downs of the region's political evolution. Mariátegui's uniqueness, at least within the Latin American context, may help explain the quality of the studies dedicated to his writings. In my opinion, these are second only to the work on Jorge Luis Borges, one of the contemporaries most admired by the author of *Seven Essays*. Monographs such as Alberto Flores Galindo's *La agonía de Mariátegui* (Mariátegui's Agony, 1980), perhaps the masterpiece of the whole corpus of *mariáteguista* scholarship, written by the author closest in spirit and, tragically, in life to Mariátegui,[26] *Discutir Mariátegui* (To Discuss Mariátegui, 1985), Óscar Terán's philosophical study of Mariátegui's ideas and life, and, more recently, Fernanda Beigel's diptych *La epopeya de una generación y una revista* (The Epic of a Generation and a Magazine, 2006) and *El itinerario y la brújula* (The Itinerary and the Compass, 2003), are the equal in creativity and insight to the best-known critical works produced in Latin America by the likes of Octavio Paz (*Sor Juana or the Traps of Faith*, 1988), Beatriz Sarlo (*Borges:*

---

24   The connections between Gramsci and Mariátegui are analysed in the first chapter of this book, 'José Carlos Mariátegui: The Making of a Revolutionary in the Aristocratic Republic'.

25   According to González, 'The recent experience of the "pink tide" and the Bolivarian revolution have once again confirmed that the petty bourgeoisie cannot represent or lead an "integrated nation" by compromising with imperialism' (González 2019, p. 110).

26   Flores Galindo (1949–90) also died prematurely, in his case of a brain tumor.

A Writer on the Edge, 1993), or Roberto Schwarz (*Machado de Assis: A Master in the Periphery of Capitalism*, 1990). To the previously mentioned masterworks of 'Mariátegui studies' one can add a panoply of shorter works by critics such as Antonio Melis, Ophelia Schutte, Mabel Moraña, José Aricó, Antonio Cornejo Polar, Javier Sanjinés, Michael Löwy, and Sara Castro-Klarén, among many others. The excellence of so much of the work on the Peruvian Marxist is one of the reasons why writing about Mariátegui is such a daunting endeavour.

This proliferation of first class works, which could be expanded by a brilliant second line of monographs including those by Vanden, Robert Paris, Becker, Melis, and Roland Forgues, is some sort of minor miracle when one takes into account the fact that Mariátegui's unorthodoxy, from the perspective of Soviet communism, led to the marginalisation of his works after his death. For instance, *Seven Essays* was reprinted only once, with limited distribution, between 1928, its original date of publication, and 1950, when the by then grown-up children of the author decided to begin publishing the totality of their father's writings. In fact, immediately after his death in 1930, the Peruvian Communist Party, led by his former associates and putative friends, such as Eudocio Ravines, had embarked on a policy of *desmariateguization* that identified Mariátegui's ideas as intrinsically opposed to those of Marxism-Leninism. The first Peruvian books on Mariátegui, such as Jorge del Prado's *Mariátegui y su obra* (Mariátegui and His Opus, 1946), predate by a few years the death of Stalin in 1953, and respond to a partial reclaiming of Mariátegui on the part of Communism as a way of distancing the national party from then recently expelled and discredited leaders, such as Ravines. This first political appropriation of the author of *Seven Essays* strategically minimises his deviations from Marxist-Leninist orthodoxy and presents his intellectual trajectory as moving from heterodoxy to Stalinist orthodoxy, though one cut short by his early death. However, no effort was put into reprinting his two books or at recovering his uncollected articles, a task later taken up exclusively by Mariátegui's heirs. The full political rediscovery of Mariátegui will have to wait for Stalin's death and the de-Stalinisation of international communism, which created an opening for the return of previously marginalised radical voices.

But an even greater boost to this unearthing of Mariátegui's work and reputation came from the success of the Cuban Revolution in 1959. The apparently original nature of Cuban socialism led to the search for precedents both within and without the island. The revolutionary government thus published a collection of Mariátegui's essays in 1960, *El problema de la tierra y otros ensayos* (The Problem of the Land and Other Essays), and four years later a complete edition of *Seven Essays*. While, as seen in the chapter 'Mariátegui and Che', the often asserted influence of Mariátegui on Ernesto 'Che' Guevara, though plausible, is far from certain, there is no doubt that the Cuban Revolution served to renew interest in the Peruvian Marxist's works and ideas.

The search for a revolutionary genealogy for the Cuban Revolution and, more generally, the radical movements of Latin America involved critics and writers throughout the world. Melis's work, together with that of Paris, who at the same time was also researching the Peruvian Marxist, helped set the basis for the birth of *mariateguismo* not only as a political concern, but also as an academic one – although, as was the wont of the new left that came of age in the 1960s, politics and intellectual pursuits were closely interwoven. Melis's epithet for Mariátegui, 'First Marxist of America', which provided the title for his seminal article published in 1967, would rightly become representative of the new esteem in which the Peruvian socialist was held by the Latin American and, to a lesser degree, European new left. Among the many topics deftly introduced by Melis was the study of the influence of Italian culture and politics on Mariátegui. The presence of Italian and, to lesser degree, of French cultures in Mariátegui's work would be examined at length by Paris in his doctoral dissertation defended in 1969, though bits and pieces had begun to be published in influential French journals, such as the legendary *Annales. Éco-nomies, Sociétes, Civilisations*, beginning in 1966. (It would only be translated into Spanish in 1981 as *La formación ideológica de José Carlos Mariátegui*). Perhaps as a response to this stress on European sources, Peruvian scholars, such as literary critic Antonio Cornejo Polar, sociologist Aníbal Quijano, and historian Flores Galindo, would emphasise the impact of Peruvian society and culture on the author of *Seven Essays*. Cornejo Polar, for example, developed his ideas about heterogeneity in literature – the cultural breaks among the author, the world described in the literary work, and the intended readership – through an analysis of Mariátegui's discussion of *indigenismo* (the literature about the indigenous world written by mestizo authors). Along these lines, Quijano, in his *Introducción a Mariátegui* (Introduction to Mariátegui, 1982),[27] saw in the author of *Seven Essays* a profound social analyst whose writings, despite the presence of irrationalist influences, such as those of Sorel, prefigured the theory of dependency, central to the global macro-economic understandings of the 1960s and 1970s. Finally, Flores Galindo analysed Mariátegui's 'agony', that is,

---

27   Though published in 1982 in a standalone book, *Introducción a Mariátegui* was a version
       of his lengthy 1979 'Prólogo' to the (first) edition of *7 ensayos* by the Biblioteca Ayacucho
       (see Quijano 2007a). I will examine Quijano's 'Prólogo' later in this study in 'Epilogue: A
       Tale of Two Quijanos'.

his struggles with the APRA (Alianza Popular Revolucionaria Americana [Popular Revolutionary American Alliance]) – the anti-imperialist alliance founded by Víctor Raúl Haya de la Torre – that became a political party in 1928, and also with the Comintern (the world-wide alliance of Communist parties, led by the Soviet Union) that had then recently opened an office in Buenos Aires. For Flores Galindo, Mariátegui's opposition to both nationalist populism and Stalinism helped define an original vision of politics that was simultaneously non-dogmatic and revolutionary. Thus Mariátegui's activism and thinking prefigured the kind of progressive politics Flores Galindo believed should lead the struggle for justice in Peru.

A similar process of reinterpretation of Mariátegui from the perspective of the present (1970s) was also being proposed by Argentine Gramscian José Aricó. Although someone like Flores Galindo saw in Mariátegui's implicit anti-Stalinism the potential for a different kind of revolutionary politics, Aricó, undoubtedly responding to the brutal dictatorship experienced by Argentina between 1976 and 1983, found in the anti-hierarchical aspects of the Peruvian's thought a source for the development of a socialist and democratic, if not social democratic, politics.

This phase of rediscovery of Mariátegui culminated in the 'Congress at the University of Sinaloa' in Mexico (1980), which brought many of the new *mariateguistas* together. According to Beigel, this congress led to three key conclusions regarding Mariátegui:

1. The development of a 'lay view' on the author of *Seven Essays* 'less conditioned by the need to separate the "good" from the "bad", the true from the false'.[28] In other words, Mariátegui was no longer judged according to an a priori set of values – obviously the Soviet interpretation of Marxism – but rather on the basis of his own blindness and insights.

2. 'The recuperation of the historicism of Mariátegui's works';[29] in addition to Flores Galindo's *La agonía de Mariátegui*, the reconstruction of Mariátegui's library in Vanden's seminal *Mariátegui, influencias en su formación ideológica* (1975), though predating the Congress, represents this aspect of the new consensus achieved in Sinaloa.

3. 'The legitimisation of Mariátegui's thought as properly Marxist', even if there was division about his relationship to a Leninism understood as distinct from Stalinism.[30]

---

28   Beigel 2003, p. 17.
29   Beigel 2003, p. 17.
30   Beigel 2003, p. 17.

One can add to Beigel's summary of the conclusions of the 'Sinaloa Congress' that Mariátegui was often seen as a necessary predecessor and, sometimes, influence not only on the Cuban Revolution, but also on the socialist political movements in Central America. Even though one can object to their stress on the, in my opinion, untenable orthodox Leninism of Mariátegui, Vanden's *National Marxism in Latin America* (1986) and Becker's *Mariátegui and Latin American Marxist Theory* (1993), both previously mentioned, are the main studies of the possible relationship between the Peruvian Marxist and later revolutionary movements in the region. While the interpretation of Mariátegui's writings solidified during the conference still holds, though not without significant wrinkles, his actual reputation will be put to the test by the changing political realities of the decade. 1980 was also the year when the Shining Path, which originally claimed to be inspired by Mariátegui, began its first, rather timid, public actions: the burning of ballot boxes. Before the capture of its leader Abimael Guzmán in 1992, it would unleash a total war on Peruvian society, including the mainstream left, which led to the largest bloodbath in the country since the Spanish conquest.[31] The brutality and irrationality of the Shining Path led many in Peru to question not only radical versions of Marxism, but also even the notion of social change itself. Needless to say Mariátegui's standing took a hit. After all, if socialism led to the apocalypse, what honour is there in being the 'First Marxist'?

Not only the disappearance of the left, but also the Peruvian support of the free market, among the political and economic elites, middle classes and even the poor, can be attributed to a great degree to the effect of the Shining Path. For instance, Alan García, the only Peruvian president from the APRA party founded by Haya de la Torre, had been an economic populist during his first term 1985–90. However, by his second non-consecutive term (2006–2011), he had become a staunch defender of neoliberal policies. Moreover, the fact that perhaps the two most prominent promoters and popularisers of neoliberal ideas in Latin America, the novelist Mario Vargas Llosa, winner of the Nobel Prize for Literature in 2010, and Hernando de Soto, the author of the influential manifesto *The Other Path*, are Peruvian, may itself be related to the epochal impact of the Shining Path on the country's life. The relative economic success of neoliberal policies – the country's economic growth rate has been among the highest in the world for the last decade – has reinforced this commitment to the free market.

---

31   The Comisión de la Verdad y de la Reconciliación estimated that 69,280 people died during the conflict.

It is therefore not surprising that even though the connections between Mariátegui and the Shining Path were only nominal, the characteristic recent response to the author of *Seven Essays* by Peruvian scholars has consisted of saying, as in the case of former left-Hegelian José Ignacio López Soria, *Adiós a Mariátegui* (Goodbye to Mariátegui), or arguing for a breaking of intellectual and critical links, as is the case with Marcel Velázquez Castro's 'Mariátegui Unplugged' (2004).[32] Obviously, this rejection of Mariátegui has also much to do with the need felt by intellectuals and scholars to acclimatise themselves to the hegemony of neoliberalism. Nevertheless, it is a sign of the continued significance of Mariátegui that this retooling for neoliberal rationality often implies a coming to terms with his legacy and figure.

This neoliberal hegemony, which is obviously not limited to Peru, even if the Andean country has embraced free markets in a more uncritical manner than most,[33] is also the result of the fall of the so-called socialist block. The impact of 1989, at least temporarily as significant as 1789, led many among the left to come to the conclusion, sometimes rueful, sometimes euphoric, as in the case of former radical Robert Heilbroner, that 'capitalism organizes the material affairs of humankind more satisfactorily than socialism'.[34] In fact, this remolding of once leftists to positions acceptable to the new consensus, such as postmodernism, if not outright neoliberalism, would become common throughout Latin America.

However, interest in Mariátegui seems to have survived this social transformation. New interpretations, now frequently rejecting or deemphasising the more radical passages in Mariátegui's writings, have been proposed. For Forgues, in *Mariátegui: la utopía realizable* (1995), the Peruvian's writings, in particular his concept of the 'feasible utopia', becomes the means to imagine a socialism free of the many deficiencies that characterised the Soviet system. A similar description of Mariátegui's work as reconciling socialism with the

---

32   The full title of López Soria's 2007 work is *Adiós a Mariátegui. Pensar el Perú en perspectiva postmodernia*.

33   In an article significantly titled '¿Reemplazó Perú a Chile como baluarte del neoliberalismo en América Latina?' ('Did Peru Replace Chile as the Bastion of Neoliberalism in Latin America?'), well-known Latin Americanist Cynthia McClintock states: 'The majority of Peruvians believe that the market-oriented policies have worked. In the last election the left only received 19% of the vote' (quoted in Fajardo 2016). Pace McClintock, one must note that this is the largest vote received by the left since the 1980s, even if, obviously, the vast majority of Peruvians voted for politicians who, regardless of their differences, all proposed the continuation of the neoliberal policies first put in place by Alberto Fujimori in 1990.

34   Heilbroner 1989, p. 98.

truest democratic impulses, including the democratisation of the workplace, is presented by César Germaná in his *El socialismo indoamericano de José Carlos Mariátegui* (José Carlos Mariátegui's Indo-American Socialism, 1995). Argentine critic Beigel has studied Mariátegui as the privileged example for alternative political praxes. In *El itinerario y la brújula* (2003), she analyses his role as a central historical figure in the development of the temporary alliance between artistic and political 'vanguards' in Latin America. In her second book on Mariátegui, *La epopeya de una generación y una revista* (2006), she studies his use of journalism and the creation of editorial networks as a means to promote political goals and partnerships.

Not surprisingly, given the adoption of recent theoretical trends among debunkers of Mariátegui mentioned above, some of the post-1989 revisions have been attempts at streamlining his thought for our postmodern, postcolonial, post-everything period. For instance, in *Vigencia de Mariátegui* (Relevance of Mariátegui, 1995), Francis Guibal associates Mariátegui with Jacques Derrida's deconstruction. Diverse critics, such as Aníbal Quijano ('Prólogo', 1979/2007; 'Modernity and Identity in Latin America', 1995), Sara Castro-Klarén ('Posting Letters,' 2008), and Javier Sanjinés ('Mariátegui and the Andean Revolutionarism,' 2012), have argued that Mariátegui's writings embody an Andean rationality different from Western thought. Moreover, both Castro-Klarén, who sees this Andean rationality as corrective rather than opposed to that of the West, and Hosam M. Aboul-Ela, in the surprising *The Other South: Faulkner and the Mariátegui Tradition* (2007), find in Mariátegui's work an alternative to the stress on textuality found in academic postcolonial thought.

In February 2019, an event took place in Madrid, Spain, that, perhaps, augurs a new spurt of interest in Mariátegui. At the Reina Sofia Museum, best-known for housing Pablo Picasso's masterpiece *Guernica*, the exposition *The Avant-garde Networks of Amauta/Redes de vanguardia. América Latina 1926–1930*, curated by the Blanton Museum of Art (in Austin) and the Museo de Arte de Lima, opened to widespread critical and popular acclaim. (*The Avant-garde Networks* was scheduled to travel to Lima, Mexico City and then to close in Austin). While by stressing *Amauta*'s promotion of the avant-garde visual arts, the exposition participated in this process of reinterpreting Mariátegui delineated above, it brought his praxis and ideas to a public that had previously not known of him. Not surprisingly, the catalogue, edited by curators Beverley Adams and Natalia Majluf, includes in addition to two key texts by Mariátegui – 'Presentación de *Amauta*' (Introducing Amauta) (1926) and 'Anniversary and Balance Sheet', over one hundred and fifty pages of essays by such major scholars as

Beigel, Horacio Tarcus, and the curators.[35] More unexpectedly, at least for those not fully acquainted with Mario Vargas Llosa's writings, during the opening of the exposition the Peruvian Nobel Prize-winner heaped praise on *Amauta* and Mariátegui. Vargas Llosa who, in addition to being one of the most important novelists in Spanish, is also an unabashed neoliberal, argued that the exhibition proved that 'Peru was once a great cultural center. And not only by assimilating culture from abroad but also by producing it'. He ascribed much of this creativity of the 1920s to the activity of the Peruvian Marxist, noting that 'with the death of Mariátegui, Peru suffered a cultural blackout'.[36] Vargas Llosa's participation can be credited with further bringing attention to Mariátegui's work and writings.

Responding to the success of the exhibition, and perhaps influenced by Vargas Llosa's enthusiasm, in what amounts to the first presence of Mariátegui in mainstream Anglophone media, *The Economist* and *The Financial Times* took note of the exhibition and its subject. Rachel Spence in *The Financial Times* celebrated the 'brief chapter in Latin American culture that saw politics, art and literature come together in a burst of creativity and openness thanks to the obsessive passion of one man, José Carlos Mariátegui'.[37] Despite claiming that 'Mariátegui was wrong about big things. It is capitalism, not communism, that has freed billions from poverty', Michael Reid in *The Economist* celebrated 'The wisdom of José Carlos Mariátegui' and argued that 'The Latin American left should rediscover the Peruvian thinker's pluralism and creativity'.[38] However, while both Spence and, despite his explicitly neoliberal position, Reid provide useful overviews of Mariátegui and *Amauta*, they present a domesticated version of Mariátegui as primarily an ethical and aesthetic example, while downplaying his actual political analyses and proposals. Therefore, it is not surprising that the best recent short English-language introduction to the Peruvian Marxist is to be found in the brief but very substantive interview of Michael Löwy by Nicolas Allen, published in the leftwing journal *Jacobin* in late 2018.[39] Both Löwy and Allen are not only knowledgeable of Mariátegui's life and works, but also able to relate the latter's ideas to the urgent problems of today.

---

35   Faithful to the transnational nature of the exposition, the contributors to *Redes de van-guardia. Amauta y América Latina 1926–1930* include scholars from Argentina (Beigel, Horacio Tarcus), Mexico (Natalia de la Rosa), Peru (Ricardo Kusunoki and Majluf), and the United States (Adams). See Adams and Majluf 2019.
36   Quoted in Planas 2019.
37   Spence 2019.
38   Reid 2019.
39   Löwy 2018.

To conclude this survey of *mariateguismo*, I would like to quote from Vanden's and Becker's 'Introduction' to their 2011 *José Carlos Mariátegui: An Anthology*. Writing after the onset of the 'great recession' in 2008, the editors argue:

> world capitalism is suffering one of its worst setbacks in a century, and the very theoretical foundations on which neoliberal capitalism is based are being called into question as they prove inadequate to guide the world system.[40]

As they had earlier noted (in their 'Acknowledgements'), 'Mariátegui's writings have much to say in the crisis period through which we are living'.[41]

Most readers of the 1930s and 1940s interpreted Mariátegui through the prism of Stalinism, those of the 1960s and 1970s through the naive certainty of an imminent socialist Latin America, and those of the 1990s and early twenty-first century from a triumphalist or tragic belief in the ultimate efficiency of the free market. We, however, have seen the ruins created by earlier attempts at violent political change and have learnt that the 'triumph of Capitalism' has ultimately led to greater inequality, poverty, systemic economic instability, as well as environmental catastrophe. Rather than biding Mariátegui farewell or unplugging him, I propose to return to his work and see what he has to offer us as citizens of this world in crisis. His thought is, after all, one of the roads not taken by radicalism.

3   On This Book

This study attempts to provide an interpretation of Mariátegui's writings that, as the book's title indicates, foregrounds the intertwining in his thought between aesthetics and politics. Thus, certain traditional topics stressed in earlier studies on the author of *Seven Essays* – for instance, the importance he gave to national reality, or his belief in the need to relate socialism and modernity with indigenous cultures – are discussed throughout the book rather than being assigned a specific chapter. This is both an acknowledgement of the centrality of these issues to the thought of Mariátegui and of the fact that the exclusive stress on them has, on occasion, served to create a distorted image of the Peruvian as being exclusively an *indigenista* (supporter of indigenous cul-

---

40   Vanden and Becker 2011c, p. 11.
41   Vanden and Becker 2011a, p. 9.

tures, populations, and causes). Needless to say, this image of Mariátegui as a rabid regionalist is contradicted by his consistent concern with cosmopolitan topics, as well as with the interrelationship in his works of local and global histories. Of course, this change in emphasis should not be taken as denying the importance of Peruvian reality for Mariátegui or his belief in the modernizing and liberating potential found in indigenous cultures and institutions.

The first chapter, 'José Carlos Mariátegui's Life and Times: The Making of a Revolutionary in the Aristocratic Republic', situates his life and the general tendencies of his work within the context of the Peruvian cultural tradition, as well as of the international trends and political contexts of his day. Mariátegui was born in relative poverty, and made the jump from print shop assistant in a newspaper to becoming a celebrated journalist and pundit, to major intellectual, without the benefit of a formal education. His journalistic background – most of his texts, including the two books he published during his lifetime, *La escena contemporánea* (The Contemporary Scene, 1925) and *Seven Essays*, began as magazine articles – helps explain the fragmentary character of his writing and the eclectic nature of his influences.

'Mariátegui, Sorel, and Myth', the following chapter, continues the study of the relationship of his ideas with those of his predecessors, in this case Georges Sorel, the French prophet of political violence and of irrationality who, in the Peruvian's works, occupies a position on occasion equal to that of Marx. Mariátegui's esteem for Sorel has been a cause for scandal for both Soviet-style Communists and new leftists of the 1960s and 1970s. However, rather than joining Sorel in the uncritical celebration of revolutionary violence, the Peruvian finds in his French predecessor the means with which to attempt to understand the subjective aspect of radical politics.

The third chapter, 'José Carlos Mariátegui: From Race to Culture', examines the concept of race in his work. Writing in the 1920s, when the hierarchisation of the races was seen as an established scientific fact, Mariátegui's occasional recourse to ethnic stereotypes has led some to describe him as a racist. Without minimising the disturbing nature of some of his comments, I argue that the core of his arguments is predicated on the rejection of race as a meaningful classificatory concept. In fact, the 'rebirth' of Asian nations such as China, Japan, or Turkey in the early twentieth-century, is often presented by Mariátegui as proof that Peru's indigenous population can embrace modernity and modify it in response to their traditions and needs.

While the chapter 'Mariátegui's Cosmopolitan Nationalism' acknowledges the importance of national reality and indigeneity in the Peruvian's thought, it analyses, in particular, the manner in which he sees these as imbricated with world cultural and social developments. I present his defence of feminism, against both Hispanic and indigenous patriarchal traditions, as an example of the manner in which international influences are central to the development of a local radical position. The fifth chapter, 'José Carlos Mariátegui and the Politics of Literature', studies the role the Peruvian assigns to literature and, more generally, cultural products in promoting progressive political change. Mariátegui, who had early in his life been a creative writer, in addition to a journalist, never fully abandoned literature. Among his last completed works was *La novela y la vida. Siegfried y el profesor Canella* (The Novel and Life. Siegfried and Professor Canella), an experimental novel set in Italy. (Published serially in 1929, it only came out in book format in 1955). Moreover, even though political considerations were central to Mariátegui's evaluation of literary works, he delinks the political valence of a work from its explicit content, instead stressing the role literature and the arts play in developing, maintaining, and undermining ideological and political consensuses. 'José Carlos Mariátegui and the Culture of Politics' traces the attempts of the Peruvian Marxist to create a political movement suited to the specificity of Peruvian reality. This is done against the background of his former friend Haya de la Torre's transformation of the APRA, till then a loose alliance of individuals opposed to the burgeoning US imperialism in the region, into a political party, together with the growing intervention of the Stalinist III International.

The seventh chapter, 'Mariátegui and Argentina: Defending Buenos Aires, Criticising Communism' examines the personal and ideological contexts of the Peruvian socialist's planned relocation to Buenos Aires, which was frustrated by his death in 1930. In this chapter, I also analyse Mariátegui's perhaps excessively optimistic evaluation of Argentine culture and society as a bastion of liberalism and his decision to publish *Defensa del marxismo* (Defence of Marxism), a surprisingly Sorelist text, as his Buenos Aires calling card. The final chapter is 'Mariátegui and Che: Reflections on and around Walter Salles's *The Motorcycle Diaries*'. The chapter uses a brief, but significant, mention of the Peruvian Marxist in this well-known film, in order to investigate the putative connection between the two revolutionaries. While both attempted to construct a revolutionary politics suited to the region's specific reality, they ultimately represent significantly divergent positions regarding the role of culture and of violence in political praxis. However, Salles's film also shows the manner in which Mariátegui has influenced the way Latin Americans think about radical political change. 'Epilogue: A Tale of Two Quijanos' concludes the book. The 'Epilogue' analyses the 'Prólogo' to the Biblioteca Ayacucho edition of *Seven Essays* written by the perhaps most influential Peruvian social scientist of the last fifty years, the late Aníbal Quijano (1930–2018). Composed of two sections written nearly thirty years apart – 'José Carlos Mariátegui: reencuentro y debate'

(José Carlos Mariátegui: Reencounter and Debate) (1979) and 'Treinta años después: otro reencuentro. Notas para un debate' (Thirty Years Later: Another Reencounter. Notes for a Debate) (2007) – the changes in the theoretical and political perspectives evidenced by the noted sociologist are, I believe, representative of those experienced by the region's radical intelligentsia. In addition to examining the insights and weaknesses found in the different interpretations of Mariátegui's works, the epilogue attempts to look at the cultural and social frames that partly explain the evolution of radical ideas in the region.

Mariátegui's open, incomplete, and fragmentary thought continually invites us to develop it. This book is my attempt at doing so.

CHAPTER 2

José Carlos Mariátegui: The Making of a Revolutionary in the Aristocratic Republic

Born in the small southern town of Moquegua in 1894,[1] José Carlos Mariátegui was the son of soon to be absent father Javier Mariátegui, a member of a prominent liberal family that had played a major role in Peru's independence from Spain in 1821,[2] and of Amalia La Chira, a seamstress. Some have wanted to see in Mariátegui's mother a descendant of an indigenous chieftain named La Chira who led the first revolt against Francisco Pizarro during the early days of the Spanish conquest.[3] If this were the case, one could, therefore, find through his mother's line a premonition of the mature José Carlos's *indigenismo* – defence of indigenous peoples and traditions – and, from both his parents, of his political radicalism.

Be that as it may, in 1902, the eight-year-old José Carlos Mariátegui was brought to Lima, the capital of the country, by his mother to be treated for a mysterious swelling of the leg and for fever. It was the very first sign of the osteoarticular tuberculosis that would prematurely kill him in 1930. The child Mariátegui was hospitalised for three months in the Maison de Santé, an institution ran by French nuns. Although he recovered from the crisis, he walked with a limp from then on. He would never be able to return to school.

---

1   Mariátegui believed he had been born in 1895 in Lima. It was only in the 1972 that Guillermo Rouillón discovered the birth certificate and corrected the date of birth (Rouillón 1975, pp. 35–6). Most of the information on Mariátegui's early life is taken from Rouillón's *La edad de piedra*.

2   Humberto Rodríguez has argued that the father of José Carlos Mariátegui, as well as of his younger brother Julio César Mariátegui and sister Amanda Mariátegui was actually Julio César Chocano, a relative of the poet José Santos Chocano (see Rodríguez 1995, p. 70).

3   On the possible descent of José Carlos from La Chira, see Rouillón 1975, p. 18. In addition, to Mariátegui's maternal surname La Chira, the strongest evidence of this connection resides in that his mother's ancestor came from Piura, in northern Peru, where the heroic *cacique* had resided back in the sixteenth century.

1 Lima in the Early 1900s

Although a metropolis compared to Moquegua, where he was born, or to the small sea-port of Huacho, in which he had been partly raised, the Lima to which the child José Carlos, then known under his legal name of José del Carmen Eliseo, arrived was, in many ways, a backwater of the Hispanic world. While Lima had once been the capital of a vice-royalty that stretched from Panama to Patagonia, it had long been superseded by Buenos Aires and even Santiago de Chile as a regional cultural and economic centre. If Buenos Aires had 950,891 inhabitants as of 1904, Lima in 1903 only had 130,289.[4] Lima was, in many ways, a city of the past. Its latticed balconies, narrow winding streets, and the religiosity of its inhabitants – Catholic processions were a daily occurrence – harkened back to its colonial glory days. Physically and culturally, Lima reflected Peru's unchanged colonial social structures and mores. However, a process of modernisation had slowly begun. The same year Mariátegui moved to Lima, the first electric tramways started to replace streetcars pulled by beasts of burden. 1902 was also the year when films began to be regularly exhibited, with the first permanent movie theatres being built in 1908. Newspapers, which throughout the nineteenth century had shamelessly represented the points of views of specific political groups and sectors, began to think of themselves as purveyors of objective information and were reorganised as – for the time – modern corporations.[5] In one of these newspapers, *La Prensa*, founded in 1903, the fifteen-year-old Mariátegui would rise from apprentice typesetter in 1909, to style corrector, to one of the best-known chroniclers of Lima's high society, publishing in 1911 his first article, under the Franco-Hispanic pseudonym Juan Croniqueur.[6]

Furthermore, the political reality of Peru had also experienced significant changes beginning soon after the birth of Mariátegui. The 'Revolution of 1895', led by 'the diminutive but persistent adventurer, Nicolás de Piérola',[7] had

---

4 The information on the population of Buenos Aires comes from Nouwen 2013, p. 210; the information on population of Lima from Hunefeldt 2001, p. 21. Santiago de Chile had a population of 332,734 in 1907 (Walter 2005, p. 3).

5 According to Fernanda Beigel 'during the second half of the nineteenth century, newspapers oriented towards providing information had begun to spread, replacing "a journalism of opinion" dominant until then. With this change a new dimension of the press took place, one that expanded progressively the circulation of information, a good demanded by ever growing social sectors' (Beigel 2006, p. 48). She adds that, in the case of Peru, this transformation would arrive 'only in the twentieth century' (Beigel 2006, p. 49).

6 See Rouillón 1975, pp. 92–3.

7 Chavarría 1979, p. 13.

deposed the last of the military governments that had plagued the country since its defeat at the hands of Chile in the War of the Pacific (1879–81), in which Peru lost in perpetuity the provinces of Tarapacá and Arica and temporarily that of Tacna. (The province of Tacna would be returned to Peru in 1929 under the terms of a new 'Treaty of Lima' signed between both countries). Piérola's administration was to be followed by civilian governments led by the conservative Civilista Party. He thus inaugurated a period designated by historians as the Aristocratic Republic. As Alberto Flores Galindo notes: 'The Aristocratic Republic had represented, between 1895 and 1919, the achievement at the level of the state of the confluence of interest between the oligarchy and the land owners, on the basis of the political marginalisation of the vast majority'.[8] However, this period was also characterised by the beginnings of a slow, but constant, industrial expansion. According to Peter Blanchard, 'the numbers of factories continued to grow: from 264 in 1902, to 291 in 1905, and 505 in 1918'.[9] This moderate economic growth led to an expansion of the working and middle classes, as well as to a breakdown of the geographical isolation of Lima from the provinces. Despite peasant uprisings in the countryside and the beginnings of an anarchist labor movement – in 1905 the bakers' union Federación de Obreros Panaderos 'Estrella del Perú' (FOPEP) was founded – this was a period of relative social stability and growth.[10]

These years also saw what could be called an attempt at a conservative cultural modernisation that, despite its personal and ideological ties with the neocolonial Aristocratic Republic, served as the template against which Mariátegui's generation would rebel. This 'Generation of 1900', as the intellectuals who came of age during the first decade of the twentieth century are called, had among its paladins the historian José de la Riva Agüero, who, according to Flores Galindo, 'founded modern historical analysis in the country';[11] the social analyst Francisco García Calderón, according to the Nobel Prize winning poet Gabriela Mistral, 'the effective and, perhaps, only inheritor' of the legendary Uruguayan thinker José Enrique Rodó;[12] and Víctor Andrés Belaúnde, legal scholar and social critic, who would later become the Peruvian represent-

---

8   Flores Galindo 1980, p. 19.
9   Blanchard 1982, p. 8.
10   Flores Galindo writes about these rebellions: 'those indigenous masses, apparently resigned to their fate and defeated, rebel, and, within the grey world of the Aristocratic Republic, they raise a demand that seems absurd or incomprehensible: they want to go back in time, they reject the history they have had to bear since the Conquest and they attempt to recover an idealized Inca Empire' (Flores Galindo 1980, p. 41).
11   Flores Galindo 1988, p. 43.
12   Quoted in Rodríguez Monegal 1985, p. 167.

ative at the United Nations, and whose best known work, *La realidad nacional* (The National Reality), is a riposte to Mariátegui's *Seven Essays*. The international reputation acquired by this group of intellectuals is exemplified by the postulation of Francisco García Calderón, together with his brother, the writer Ventura García Calderón, to the Nobel Prize in literature in 1934 by such literary luminaries of the time as Jules Romains and Jean Giraudoux.[13]

Traumatised by the country's military defeat in 1879, the 'Generation of 1900' turned to scholarship as a means of modernising not only the university but implicitly also the country as a whole. Francisco García Calderón's dictum 'Peru will be saved beneath the dust of a library' exemplifies the centrality that academic research, though understood primarily as archival, had for this group of scholars, thinkers, and, on occasion, politicians.[14] García Calderon's *Le Pérou Contemporain* (1907) is the first comprehensive analysis of Peruvian society and, therefore, a significant precedent for Mariátegui *Seven Essays*. Despite his belief in racial and geographical determinism, Riva Agüero, perhaps the most brilliant of the group, would gain national and international acclaim with his bachelor's thesis *El carácter de la literatura del Perú independiente* (1905). Miguel de Unamuno, arguably the most important intellectual writing in Spanish at the time, and Marcelino Menéndez y Pelayo, Spain's main literary scholar, both praised this work published when Riva Agüero was only nineteen. His doctoral dissertation, *La historia en el Perú* (1910), is generally considered the country's first modern historical study.[15] The 'Generation of 1900', however, never questioned the basic colonial social structures – such as the latifundia – or the racist hierarchies that both justified and supplemented them. Despite the criticisms they, on occasion, levelled at the Spanish colony, they were ultimately both Hispanist and Eurocentric.[16] They never looked at the indigenous

---

13   Flores Galindo 1988 p. 41. By 1934, when nominated for the Nobel Prize, the García Calderón brothers were long ensconced in the Parisian literary elites. Ventura would, in fact, be offered a seat in the French Academy, but refused to renounce his Peruvian citizenship, a requirement for the position. According to Flores Galindo: '[Francisco] was the true leader of the Latin Americans in Paris, which included Rubén Darío. In 1933, Francisco and his brother Ventura would be postulated for the Nobel Prize by a diverse group of European intellectuals including Jean Giraudoux and Jules Romains' (Flores Galindo 1988, p. 41).

14   Quoted in Sánchez 1970, p. xi.

15   On the centrality of Riva Agüero to literary studies, see José Jiménez Borja 2005. On both Riva Agüero's and García Calderon's achievements, see Flores Galindo 1988.

16   The treatment of what was then called the 'Indian Problem' in García Calderón major work is exemplary of the limitations of the analysis and solutions presented by the Generation of 1900. He concludes *Le Pérou Contemporain*, written in French – the lingua franca of the world's intelligentsia – and published in Paris – still the capital of modernity – by

population as anything but civilisational dead weight. As Flores Galindo notes, for them, 'Indians were the other, condemned to silence and expressionless as stones'.[17]

Mariátegui, after his embrace of Marxism, and, to a lesser degree, his contemporaries, like the political leader Víctor Raúl Haya de la Torre, the *indigenista* historian and social scientist Luis Valcárcel, the literary critic Luis Alberto Sánchez, the historian Jorge Basadre, and others, attempted to come to terms with Peru's neocolonial reality – as they continued the process of intellectual modernisation began by the Generation of 1900. This so-called 'Generation of the Centenary' – in reference to the one hundred years elapsed since the battle of Ayacucho in 1824 which marked the final defeat of the Spanish armies during the wars of independence – cut through the emotional and personal Gordian knot that tied earlier Peruvian intellectuals to the Colony. The fact that Mariátegui and many of these later intellectuals came from the provincial middle, if not lower, classes also played a central role in the different structures of feeling that characterised both groups. Unlike Riva Agüero, who was actually a Spanish noble (the Marquis of Montealegre de Aulestia), or the García Calderón brothers, the children of a former President of the Republic, Mariátegui and his contemporaries did not have an affective connection to the aristocratic or oligarchic past. Though descended from one of the founders of the Peruvian republic, Mariátegui had experienced hardship when growing up.

For some, the break with the Generation of 1900 implied the classic gesture of turning their ideas and values on their head. Luis Valcárcel, perhaps

---

writing about the poverty and depressed social conditions experienced by the (majority) indigenous population. Described as 'aged infants' and as characterised by a 'sad and profound atavism' García Calderón argues that 'the indigenous race demands a secular protector, in the religious sphere against the priest; in the social order, against the cacique, the owner of the hacienda, feudal lord of the political and local life' (García Calderón 1907, p. 328). To his credit, he believed in the need to respect and revitalise the indigenous community – 'respect their traditions, in [land] property and family [structure]' (García Calderón 1907, p. 328). But his solution to the injustice experienced by Peru's indigenous population is to 'govern this race through a wise guardianship, make of the Indian a worker or a soldier, promote emigration in the same territory to liberate the Indian of his local traditions, familial superstitions, of his monotonous and depressing environment' (García Calderón 1907, p. 328). He believed that education (in the Spanish language) would lead to the 'forming of an indigenous elite that will help the government in its civilizing work' (García Calderón 1907, p. 328). Supervision, education, and the creation of Hispanophilic indigenous elites – subordinated to *real* Hispanic elites – are for the author of *Le Pérou Contemporain* the solutions to social inequality.

17   Flores Galindo 2010, p. 160.

the best-known of the indigenistas, is a case in point. Reversing the valuations characteristic of earlier Peruvian thought, he wrote about the 'femininity of the [Hispanic] coast, masculinity of the Andes'.[18] Given the patriarchal values of the time, he thus misogynistically praises the mostly indigenous Andean Peru over the mainly Hispanic coast. Against the Eurocentric and Hispanist tradition, he declared that 'the sierra [highlands] is the nation'.[19] He even celebrated racial essentialism – 'Races do not die. Cultures can die'[20] He inverted traditional racial and cultural hierarchies when, after describing the Inca as civilizing agents, he predicts that 'culture will again descend from the Andes'.[21] Mariátegui went beyond this reversal of binaries. Although he occasionally resorted to the racial stereotypes or essentialist views characteristic of his times, he reframed the 'indigenous question', not as a racial, moral, or cultural issue, but as an economic and social one.[22] For Mariátegui, social problems require social answers: reform and/or revolution. The administrative and educational measures proposed by García Calderón and other members of the Generation of 1900 are, if not rejected, at best seen as supplements to the true solution of the problem based on economic and social change and empowerment.

However, the relationship between both generations was not only one of opposition. The case of Valcárcel, the most vehement of the indigenistas in his belief in the existence of an indigenous renaissance and in his celebration of the Andes over the Hispanic coast, can serve as an example of the occasionally surprising connections between both groups. One of his main mentors was Riva Agüero. Luis Alberto Sánchez, later the foremost intellectual associated with Haya de la Torre's APRA party, was also a student and friend of Riva Agüero. Even Mariátegui sent his *Seven Essays* to Francisco García Calderón, who surprisingly declared in a note to be 'almost always in agreement ... when you [Mariátegui] study the diverse aspects of the indigenous problem and offer solutions'.[23] There were communicating vessels between both generations.[24]

---

18   Valcárcel 1972, p. 114.

19   Valcárcel 1972, p. 115.

20   Valcárcel 1972, p. 21.

21   Valcárcel 1972, p. 21.

22   'The problem of the Indian is rooted in the land tenure system of our economy. Any attempt to solve it with administrative or police measures, through education or by a road building programme, is superficial and secondary as long as the feudalism of the gamonales continues to exist' (Mariátegui 1971, p. 22).

23   Mariátegui 1994, p. 272.

24   Chavarría notes about the Generations of 1900 and of the Centenary: 'Not only did Mariátegui live during an era of exceptional dynamism and change, but he was also part of

2   Manuel González Prada and the Radicals

The intellectual flowering that began with the Generation of 1900 and reached
its full fruition with Mariátegui and his contemporaries had an important precedent in the work of Manuel González Prada (1844–1918), poet, essayist and
the first major radical Peruvian thinker and activist.[25] Reacting to the country's military defeat, González Prada rejected both the colonial past and the
neocolonial present. In his celebrated and influential 'Speech at the Politeama
Theater' (1888), the Peruvian radical stated:

> The real Peru isn't composed of the groups of American-born Spaniards
> and foreigners living on the strip of land situated between the Pacific and
> the Andes; the nation is made up of the masses of Indians living on the
> eastern slopes of the mountains.[26]

One thus finds in this speech the rejection of colonial legacies and neocolonial
structures. Even more importantly, González Prada proposes the revaluation of
indigenous cultures and populations and the belief in the need to incorporate
the latter within a new Peruvian nationality that would later characterise the
writings of Mariátegui and his contemporaries. One is, therefore, not surprised
when one reads in the *Seven Essays* that 'he [González Prada] represents the
first lucid instant ... in the conscience of Peru'.[27]

The political impact of González Prada's speeches and writings was diluted
by his decision to relocate to Paris a month after he had founded the Partido
Radical (Radical Party) in 1891.[28] After his return from Europe, in 1898, Gonzá-

---

    an extraordinary intellectual tradition, rich in other individuals of high talent. His own
    generation of 1919 and the preceding generation of 1900 are considered the two leading
    generations of intellectuals during the whole of Peru's national history' (Chavarría 1979,
    p. 3).

25   González Prada had liberal, verging on radical, precursors. Among these one can mention
    Francisco de Paula González Vigil, on whom González Prada wrote an important essay
    'Vijil'. (González Prada spelled Vigil's name following his own phonetic orthography).

26   González Prada 2003b, pp. 49.

27   Mariátegui 1971, p. 204. Later in life, González Prada became Peru's foremost anarchist
    and was a well-known presence among Lima's workers. Within in this context, he met
    the young Mariátegui, when he was an apprentice typesetter. José Carlos would become
    a friend of Alfredo González Prada, the master's son, and would often borrow books from
    the great intellectual (Rouillón 1975, pp. 80–3). In 1928, Mariátegui dedicated an issue of
    his magazine *Amauta* to his former mentor.

28   'The Literary Circle was the origin of the National Union Party, whose political program

lez Prada evolved ideologically in the direction of anarchism. From then on, he wrote mainly in worker publications, no longer a presence in mainstream cultural circles, but, on the other hand, becoming a major influence on the radical movements of the 1920s.[29]

If the Generation of the Centenary found in González Prada a mentor and example, the Generation of 1900, while they admired González Prada's nationalism and his skill as a poet and writer, rejected his proposals to solve Peru's problems. Riva Agüero's and García Calderon's project of a conservative modernisation can be seen as a response to González Prada's radical liberal and, later, anarchist vision of modernity.[30]

3   Colónida

The first literary reaction against the social vision of the Generation of 1900 – as distinct from the political response implicit in González Prada's and the nascent worker movement's turn towards anarchism – was presented by the Colónida literary group to which the young Mariátegui belonged. (They are known after the literary journal Colónida, which published four issues in 1916, before it folded).[31] This group of poets and narrators was led by Abraham Valdelomar. As would be the case with the slightly younger Mariátegui, Valdelomar had come to Lima from the southern provinces of the country, in his case Ica. In his Seven Essays, Mariátegui wrote about the group:

---

was published in May 1891. According to Prada it ought to have been a "radical party" and named that, but the timidity of its followers caused its character to be blurred under the other name' (Sobrevilla 2003, p. xxvii).

29   Partially contradicting González Prada's marginality is the fact that he was named head of the Peruvian National Library in 1912, after Ricardo Palma quit the post. He himself would quit 1914 in protest against a military coup and was reappointed after the return to democracy in 1916. (He died in 1918). While there is little doubt that this was a prestigious position, it arguably responded to his earlier literary and cultural achievements, rather than being an acknowledgment of his anarchist ideas (see Sobrevilla 2003, p. xxxvii).

30   I return to the relationship between González Prada (and his group), the Generation of 1900 and Mariátegui and his contemporaries in the chapter 'José Carlos Mariátegui and the Politics of Culture'.

31   Other members of the group were: Alfredo González Prada (Manuel's son), Federico More (on whom Mariátegui wrote in Seven Essays), and the novelist Augusto Aguirre Moráles, whose description of the Incas in his historical novel El pueblo del sol (1924, 1927) is criticised in Seven Essays; see Mariátegui 1971.

> *Colonida* represented not so much a revolution ... as an insurrection against academicism and its oligarchies, its emphasis on rhetoric, its conservative taste, its old-fashioned gallantry, and its tedious melancholy.[32]

Moreover, in contradistinction to the Hispanism of the Generation of 1900,

> Valdelomar ... brought cosmopolitan elements from abroad, was attracted by *criollo* and Inca elements. He relived his childhood in a fishing village and he discovered, albeit intuitively, the quarry of our autochthonous past.[33]

This description, with its stress on the fusion of the cosmopolitan, the local, and the indigenous is, in principle, also applicable to the mature Mariátegui, and with some qualifications, to other members of his generation. However, the *Colónidas* also 'tended to have a rather morbid taste for the decadent, the elite, the aristocratic'.[34] In fact, Valdelomar used the Cervantine nom de plume 'Conde de Lemos'[35] and affected a fake aristocratic behaviour that parodied the airs of nobility put on by many intellectuals at the time – as in the case of Riva Agüero. These aristocratic gestures distanced Valdelomar and the other *Colónidas* from their lower- and middle-class origins. They, but especially Valdelomar, were also given to witticisms, epigraphs, dressing à la Oscar Wilde, visiting opium dens, etc. The behaviour of Valdelomar and the *Colónidas* was meant to both shock the staid Peruvian upper and middle classes and, at the same time, to bring attention to their persons and art.

This decadentism is exemplified in the *Colónida* celebration of opiates – Mariátegui even wrote a poem titled 'Morfina' – and in an editorial in the journal that, in addition to defending the value of opium, also defended the 'right to pleasure and the freedom of committing suicide'.[36] In this manner, they, again, contradicted the intellectual seriousness and the Catholic ethos seen by Generation of 1900 as constitutive of Hispanic and Peruvian tradi-

---

32   Mariátegui 1971, p. 229.
33   Mariátegui 1971, p. 231.
34   Mariátegui 1971, p. 229.
35   Miguel de Cervantes dedicated the second part of *Don Quixote*, as well as other works, to Pedro Fernández de Castro y Andrade, Conde de Lemos (Count of Lemos). However, Valdelomar's appropriation of the Conde Lemos name may have also been a reference to another holder of that nobiliary title, Pedro Antonio Fernández de Castro (1632–72), the nineteenth viceroy of Peru.
36   Quoted in Sánchez 1969, p. 213.

tion. However, despite their break with the values of Riva Agüero et al, the *Colónida* group refrained from a full questioning of the neocolonial social structures or the culture that justified it.[37]

The limitations of this 'insurrection' are already implicit in the name *Colónida* given by Valdelomar to their journal. The name derives from 'Colón', the Spanish version of Columbus. In fact, what may be the first iteration of the word Colónida was part of a proposal by a Venezuelan newspaper, *El Cruzado*, in 1892, to rename the American continent in honor of Columbus.[38] Underlying the coinage of the neologism was, therefore, a Hispanist attempt at redressing what was felt to be an injustice to Columbus. One here must remember that Christopher Columbus is traditionally seen in the Hispanophone world as one of the highest representatives of Spain's culture and colonising efforts, rather than, as is often the case in the United States, as a hero of Italy.

4   A Sublime Dance

One can argue that the most representative event of this period of bohemia and decadence in Mariátegui's life took place in 1917, when he was jailed for organising a dance performance in, of all places, a cemetery.

Mariátegui and his friend and fellow journalist César Falcón convinced Norka Rouskaya, a Swiss imitator of modern dance icons Isadora Duncan and Tórtola Valencia, to dance in the Lima cemetery. (They were following the example set by Duncan who had previously danced at the cemeteries of New York and Paris). After gaining permission for the dancer to visit the cemetery after hours, Rouskaya, Mariátegui, Falcón, a few friends, and a violinist entered the cemetery at 1 a.m. on 4 November 1917. While the violinist played Chopin's 'Funeral March' – part of her theatrical routine – the very lightly dressed

---

37   Nevertheless, it may not be surprising that Valdelomar, despite his dandyism and decadentism, participated actively in the short-lived presidency of Guillermo Billinghurst – 1912–14. Politically Billinghurst represented an attempt at appealing to the artisan underclass and the nascent working class cut short by a military coup. (Valdelomar was first named director of the official newspaper *El Peruano* and later was given a minor diplomatic post in Rome). Like the *Colónida* group, the Billinghurst presidency represented a kind of insurrection that did not question the foundations of the oligarchic republic – the President had been a successful mayor of Lima and was a very wealthy businessman – but that, at the same time, expressed the winds of cultural, political, and even populational change that were beginning to impact the till then immobile structures of the capital and the nation. On Valdelomar's collaboration with Billinghurst, see Sánchez 1969, pp. 88–92.

38   Febres 1894, p. 330.

Rouskaya danced next to the tombstone of President Ramón Castilla,[39] generally considered the greatest Peruvian president of the nineteenth century. Before the dance ended, the authorities arrived and took the participants to jail. They would all be freed a few days later.[40]

Not surprisingly given the fervent Catholicism of Lima's population, the event was a major scandal.[41] Perhaps the most unusual aspect of the whole incident was Mariátegui's indignation at being jailed. He claimed that the performance had 'reverence and purity' and 'religiosity'.[42] However, as a devout Catholic he must have known that cemeteries, like churches, were hallowed ground. During the scandal, Mariátegui mentioned as part of his defence his attendance earlier that year at a spiritual retreat in a Carmelite monastery. In fact, according to Canon Law,

> Only those things which serve the exercise or promotion of worship, piety, or religion are permitted in a sacred place; anything not consonant with the holiness of the place is forbidden.[43]

It is difficult to characterise Rouskaya's dancing as either 'exercising' or 'promoting' the Catholic religion.

Given the relative mildness of the penalties levelled against the participants and spectators, much of the discussion of the event – which has attempted to psychoanalyse the societal response – can be seen as exaggerated. Unlike New York or even Paris, where Duncan had danced in cemeteries, the overwhelming majority of the population, including most of the elite, was Catholic. Moreover, Catholicism was the official religion of the state and freedom of religion had only been established two years earlier. Therefore, Rouskaya, Mariátegui, and the others participated in an act that for both Canon Law and general Catholic opinion was literally sacrilegious. One could even argue that the fact that the

---

39   Abraham Valdelomar who, surprisingly, did not attend the dance in the cemetery, wrote a review of Rouskaya's performance in which he describes her version of Chopin's 'Funeral March': 'Intelligent and understanding spectators will never forget the beginning of the 'Funeral March', when Norka, with her tunic with folds, immobile like a Hellenic statue, as slender as the very Minerva with bronze eyes, appears on a vague background where stand the erect and striated columns of a Greek temple' (Valdelomar 2011, p. 3).

40   According to Rouillón, 'After a few days, Mariátegui, Falcón, the artist Rouskaya, and the musician Cáceres were given their freedom' (Rouillón 1975, p. 196).

41   One here cannot but wonder whether a similar event today – involving well-known journalists and an international celebrity – would not also cause a scandal.

42   Quoted in Rouillón 1975, p. 195.

43   [Canon Law] Can. 1210.

dance took place next to the tomb of President Ramón Castilla adds to the sac-rilege of the event. The political 'religion' of the Republic was also being desec-rated by Rouskaya's dance. Nevertheless, the limited response by the state – according to Rouillón while they were in jail for a few days, 'the prison regime was not rigorous' – reflects concern with public and ecclesiastic opinion, as well as the limitations the state felt it had when it came to punishing a well-known journalist and an international performer.[44]

The dance at the cemetery is congruent with the *Colónida* group's Romantic and post-Romantic explorations of the sublime, as evidenced in their interest in drug experimentation and their defence of suicide. As Michel Deguy notes:

> The mortal condition and the moment of perishing are always at stake when the sublime appears. The sublime is the concentration, the start of the startling that weighs in speech against death.[45]

Even if not 'speech' – Deguy's text is a commentary on Longinus – the dance and the music performed can be interpreted as symbolic statements 'against death'. Given its setting and the actual musical composition played, Nourkaya's dance reflected the 'ephemeral immortality of the point gained ... snatched from death'.[46] In 1917, Mariátegui was still in thrall to *Colónida*'s post-Romantic aesthetics. However, the fact that the dance took place in a cemetery, a sacred space in a Catholic country, and, as we have seen, near the tomb of President Castilla,[47] one of the republic's forefathers, can be taken to imply an embryonic questioning of political and religious hierarchies and structures that were still imbricated.

The whole incident gains additional importance by the fact that it coin-cided with the ten days that shook the world, when Lenin and the Bolshev-iks took over the Russian government. On 7 November 1917, three days after

---

44   Rouillón 1975, p. 195.
45   Deguy 1993, p. 9.
46   Deguy 1993, p. 9.
47   Mariátegui did not have a negative opinion of Castilla. In *Seven Essays*, he writes:
      'Castilla was the military caudillo at his best. His shrewd opportunism, slyness, crude-ness, and absolute empiricism prevented him from adopting a liberal policy until the very end. Castilla realised that the liberals of his time were a literary group, a coterie, not a class. Therefore, he cautiously avoided any act that would seriously oppose the interests and principles of the conservative class. But the merits of his policy lie in his reformist and progressive leanings. His acts of greatest historic significance – the abolition of Negro slavery and of forced tribute from the Indians – expressed his liberal attitude' (Mariátegui 1971, p. 50).

Rouskaya donned – or dropped – her clothes and danced on hallowed ground, the Bolsheviks took power. Shortly after, Mariátegui was accused by the then Major of Lima, Luis Miró Quesada, of being a bolsheviki. (The divergence from the current standard spelling of the word in Spanish – bolchevique – is a sign of how novel the Russian Revolution was for Peruvians). On 30 December 1917, Mariátegui responded in a phrase that could be taken as predicting his own intellectual development, 'Very bolshevikis and very Peruvian! But more Peruvian than bolsheviki'.[48] The transition from bohemian to revolutionary was beginning.

It is tempting to see in Mariátegui's embrace of politics the substitution of one mode of the sublime for another. The sublime aesthetisation of death was exchanged for the revolutionary sublime. In fact, for some radicals of the time, and after, the working class were a heroic, dangerous, and ultimately uplifting natural force that would create a new world. The fear of death and its implicit supersession became associated with political activity, with a specific social class, and with a particular event – the revolution, which could be seen as threatening with death and promising its overcoming.

What makes this facile generalisation problematic is the fact that Mariátegui's later political praxis, while aimed at making the revolution and socialism possible was in itself not immediately revolutionary. Unlike, for instance, Ernesto 'Che' Guevara, for whom the primary goal of politics was the direct realisation of revolutionary activity, Mariátegui was concerned with the forging of consent, the education of the masses, and the construction of commonalities, that is generational and class goals that ultimately make political change possible.[49] Absent from Mariátegui's writings and political action is, however, a specific discussion about how to transform this radical commonality into revolution. Perhaps this is a limitation; yet it may also be an expression of the realistic streak that one finds in Mariátegui even at his most utopian.

Nevertheless, one can still see Mariátegui's turn towards socialism as connected to the Rouskaya incident. Precisely as he manifests his loss of faith in Peru's political and even religious institutions, a new faith and goal becomes available. As we will see, Mariátegui often emphasised the spiritual and even religious aspects of Marxism and socialism.[50] Mariátegui, the mystic of monk-

---

48   Qtd. in Rouillón 1975, p. 202.
49   Mariátegui's political proposals are studied in the chapter 'José Carlos Mariátegui and the Culture of Politics'. I contrast Guevara and Mariátegui in the chapter 'Mariátegui and Che'.
50   Mariátegui's view on the relation between religion and politics is studied in the chapter 'Mariátegui, Sorel and Myth'.

ish spiritual retreats, the heretic of sensual cemetery dances, finds a way of expressing those apparently contradictory emotions in his embrace of socialism.

5   Turn Left

In the case of Mariátegui, it is not easy to separate the political from the literary, and the litterateur from the revolutionary. After all, the longest of his *Seven Essays* is on Peruvian literature. Moreover, his *Colónida* period coincided with his becoming a political journalist as he left *La Prensa*, where he had made the unusual jump from apprentice typesetter to star journalist in just a few years, to *El Tiempo* in 1916, a newspaper critical of the government of then president José Pardo, where he started a satirical political column, 'Voces'. Paradoxically, this period also saw him writing in, of all things, a horse racing magazine *El Turf* and a 'woman's journal' *Lulú*. But, despite becoming entangled in Lima's upper-class hobbies and activities, Mariátegui never broke with his former fellow workers. Instead, his journalism became a conduit though which working-class and anarcho-syndicalist organisations could publish notices about union activity.[51]

While anarchism and its anarcho-syndicalist offshoot were hegemonic among workers, and, of course, González Prada was himself an important disseminator of these anti-systemic ideas, beginning in 1918, as, in his words, he became 'nauseated with criollo politics', Mariátegui 'resolutely took the direction of socialism'.[52] He, as well as other Peruvian would-be radicals, found a surprising mentor in Víctor Maúrtua. Maúrtua, a central figure of Peru's political and cultural establishment, was a professor of law, senator and not much later minister of foreign relations.[53] According to Rouillón,

> The maestro Maúrtua, reader of Hegel, Marx, Engels, Bergson, Sorel, Labriola, Unamuno, Alomar, Araquistáin, Barbusse, Romain Rolland, Jack London, and other humanists ... preached that, in this difficult hour for the world, the writer, the artist and the scientist had to join the struggles of workers and students.[54]

---

51   Rouillón 1975, p. 168.
52   Mariátegui 1994, p. 331.
53   Rouillón 1975, p. 204.
54   Rouillón 1975, p. 205.

The importance of Maúrtua for Mariátegui is particularly evident in that the writers previously mentioned were to remain among his main influences.[55] In addition to Marx, Henri Barbusse, Rolland, Unamuno and Georges Sorel will be among the handful of references to which Mariátegui will return again and again in his attempt at understanding Peru and the world.[56]

This is also the period when Mariátegui began to consider how he as a writer and journalist could contribute to the social and political changes taking place in Lima and the world. He thus began to develop in an embryonic form what Fernanda Beigel has called his 'editorialist praxis'. Moving beyond the previous journalistic models existing in Peru – those that saw journalism as unmediated representations of the views of specific political parties, or, later, as presenting an objective view of reality – the creation of magazines and newspapers became for Mariátegui a way to intervene in Peruvian society by helping coalesce inchoate insurgent groups and ideas into more coherent proposals and movements that could ultimately replace the aristocratic republic and its institutions.

Thus, in 1918, he created *Nuestra Época*, a short lived literary and social journal inspired by the Spanish socialist magazine *España*. (It only published two issues before folding the same year). Mariátegui's continuing radicalisation was further evidenced when he founded with Falcón a radical newspaper, *La Razón*, in 1919. Coinciding with one of the first major and longest strikes in Peru – for the lowering of prices and the extension of the eight-hour workday to the totality of Lima workers – *La Razón* became the venue through which workers could disseminate their demands. When the strike, which had begun in January 1919, reached its highpoint on 22 July, the striking workers visited the newspaper's locale, thanking *La Razón* for its support.[57] Its commitment to the strike evidenced the political aspect of Mariátegui's editorialist praxis, just as *Nuestra Época*'s stress on literature served as proof of his belief in the political value of literature and culture.

---

55   In *Seven Essays*, Mariátegui writes about 'the philosophy of Víctor Maúrtua, whose impact on the Socialist orientation of some of our intellectuals is almost unknown' (Mariátegui 1971, p. 229).

56   One must note, however, that it is not clear when Mariátegui actually became acquainted with Sorel's work. For instance, Chavarría argues that the Peruvian first read Sorel in Italy (Chavarría 1979, p. 70 and p. 207 n. 24). On Sorel's influence, see the chapter 'Mariátegui, Sorel, and the Myth'.

57   Rouillón 1975, p. 283.

6   A Polemical Exile

The political turmoil of 1919 coincided with presidential elections. Former President (1908–12) Augusto B. Leguía, the putative winner of the contest, suspected that Congress would refuse to swear him in as required by law. Therefore, he led a coup that made him President for the next eleven years. His government ushered in a period of economic modernisation linked to the influx of U.S. investment. However, after a period of concessions during which he tried to appropriate progressive political demands, the government became repressive towards political dissent.[58] *La Razon*'s success in representing and promoting the worker's movement led to, perhaps, the most controversial event in Mariátegui's life: his exile to Europe, together with Falcón.[59] According to Falcón 'a relative [referring to Alfredo Piedra, a minister in the government, who was a relative of Leguía] came to see us and spoke in private with Mariátegui and myself. At the end, we both clearly understood this phrase "Either outside the country, or in jail"'.[60] Moreover, both Falcón and Mariátegui would (sporadically) receive a small stipend from the government for their activity as 'propaganda agents' for Peru.

For critics of Mariátegui, this apparent accommodation with a ruler who came to be seen by the end of his government as the epitome of tyranny is a sign of the limits of his rebellion. After all, there were others who were later exiled without the fig leaf cover and financial support that Mariátegui received, including his later collaborator, and even later rival, Haya de la Torre. (However, Haya's exile came in 1924, when Leguía's government had hardened its repres-

---

58   Soon after Augusto Leguía had been toppled by a military coup led by Lieutenant Colonel Luis Miguel Sánchez Cerro, 'Ya Ha Firmado', the cover article in *Time Magazine* (9 September 1930) stated: 'Continuously since 1919, off and on since 1908, Augusto Bernardino Leguia has ruled Peru. In that time he has raised Peru to a position in South American affairs only second to the potent ABC powers, Argentina, Brazil, Chile. A network of railways, fine roads have been built. The oil and copper industries have been developed. Peru (not all his compatriots regard this as a blessing) has been opened up for foreign capital. With the aid of US diplomats, the 46-year-old Tacna-Arica boundary dispute with Chile has been settled. The disadvantages of the Leguía regime are the disadvantages of any dictatorship. Peruvians have a very great fondness for personal liberty. But in the past 20 years they have had little of it. Hundreds have been exiled, thousands imprisoned, not a few shot for small cause' (Anonymous 1930).

59   I have generally followed Rouillón's account (Rouillón 1975, pp. 306–10). However, as is generally the case with this author, the solidity of his version of events is undermined by the interpolation of imagined dialogues, etc.

60   Rouillón 1975, p. 310.

sion of potential antagonists and no longer cared about giving the appearance of magnanimity). That said, one has to wonder what conceivable reason would Mariátegui have had to prefer jail to Europe, in particular given his already fragile health. However, he never published any text supportive of the Leguía regime.[61]

7   Italy and Gramsci

His sojourn in Europe between 1919 and 1923 permitted Mariátegui to travel throughout the continent and meet prominent figures of the time, such as writers Barbusse – who declared him 'the prototype of a new type of American man'[62] – and Rolland in Paris, and Maxim Gorky in Berlin. However, it was in Italy where he stayed longest and 'espoused a wife and some ideas'.[63] Italy thus represents a key fork in his personal and intellectual life.[64]

During Mariátegui's stay in Italy, he witnessed dramatic social and political events that left an imprint on his thinking. The *biennio rosso* (red biennium) of 1919 and 1920 seemed to announce the revolution, even if it only prepared the ground for the rise of fascism out of the ashes of socialism. (The March on Rome, which led to Benito Mussolini and the fascists taking power, took place in 1922). Turin was in a state of insurrection, racked by strikes, while the political radicalisation of the Italian Socialist Party gave rise to a Maximalist wing that directed by, among others, Antonio Gramsci, then became the Italian Communist Party in 1921.

But not only were society and politics affected by the radical upsurge of the biennio rosso, a radical left-wing culture also developed. Marxism became if not hegemonic, to use a terminology Gramsci developed years later while in

---

61   Cecilia Ferrer Mariátegui, the granddaughter of José Carlos, quotes fragments of unpublished letters from the exiled journalist to his former companion Victoria Ferrer that indicate the haphazard nature of the payments received by Mariátegui from the Leguía government (Ferrer Mariátegui 2013, pp. 3–4).

62   According to Armando Bazán in his biography of Mariátegui, Barbusse told the biographer 'Vous ne savez pas qui est Mariátegui? Et bien ... c' est une nouvelle lumiere de Amerique; un specimen nouveau de l' homme americain' (Bazán 1982, p. 54).

63   Mariátegui 1994, p. 331.

64   His Italian wife, Anna Chiappe, proved to be particularly supportive of her husband as his health waned later in the decade, particularly after the amputation of a leg in 1924. In a moving 'prose poem' from 1926, 'La vida que me diste' ('The Life you Gave me'), dedicated to her, Mariátegui wrote: 'And now that you are a bit musty, a bit pale ... I feel that the life you've lost is the life you've given me' (Mariátegui 1980f, p. 94).

prison, then at least a cultural force all intellectuals had to grapple with. Piero Gobetti, a radical liberal, and Gramsci collaborated in *L'Ordine Nuovo*, a journal that attempted to promote the Maximalist line against the more reformist tendencies prevalent in the Socialist Party. Earlier, Benedetto Croce, the dean of European philosophy at the time, had written a book on Marx quoted on more than one occasion by Mariátegui.

The particular impact of Italian thought on Mariátegui was probably due to the obvious affinity of his embryonic vision of politics with that developed by the more radical figures in the Italian left. This congruence has as much to do with the peculiar talents of Gramsci or Gobetti as with the fact that Italy was itself a peripheral country in Europe. Moreover, like Peru, Italy was a Catholic, mostly agrarian country. The correspondences between the two countries facilitated Mariátegui's incorporation of Italian socialist ideas and practices. As Oscar Terán perceptively argues, Mariátegui's incorporation of Italian and, more generally, European ideas, took place within an intellectual framework shaped by his Peruvian experiences and by his sense of the peculiarities of his native country's social structures which he, as a journalist, had gotten to know so well.[65] For personal and intellectual reasons, Italian culture became a central and permanent influence on the author of *Seven Essays*. Mariátegui even spoke Italian at home.[66]

The peculiar constellation of authors that one finds as influences in Mariátegui's work has a strong Italian bent. Sorel, a central figure in the Peruvian's thought, and whom he probably read in Lima thanks to Maúrtua, was a significant presence in Italy during (and before) Mariátegui's stay. Other authors who became permanent influences include the previously mentioned Gobetti, for whom Mariátegui claimed to 'feel great spiritual affinity';[67] Croce, who family lore claims as a personal friend of the family of Anna Chiappe, Mariátegui's wife; and Luigi Pirandello, who would influence his one mature literary endeavour, *La novela y la vida. Siegfried y el profesor Canella* (The Novel and Life: Siegfried and Professor Canella). The personal interaction of Mariátegui with key figures in Italian culture was noted by Chiappe in 1969: 'Mariátegui spoke several times with Pirandello ... He was also a friend of Gobetti ... Croce was

---

65   See Terán 1985, pp. 11–12.

66   Italian and French were the two foreign languages in which Mariátegui was fluent. He also read in German and, with some difficulty, English. As Harry Vanden shows in his study of Mariátegui's library, he owned many of the Marxist classics, including Marx's *Capital* and Lenin's *State and Revolution*, in their Italian versions. See Vanden 1975.

67   Mariátegui 1971, p. 183.

fond of him'.[68] The recurrent echoes of these authors in Mariátegui's works evidence the depth with which Italian culture became etched in his mind.

In particular, the extent of the influence of Gramsci on Mariátegui has long been a topic of discussion. Despite the proto-theoretical nature of Gramsci's writings that contrasts with the 'anti-academic' character of Mariátegui's texts,[69] critics have identified significant points in common between both thinkers. These include the iconoclastic nature of their interpretation of Marx, their common rejection of the positivism of the European Social Democracy of the time, the importance both assign to political praxis, the stress on winning the consent and support of the majority of the population, and the centrality of cultural production in the achievement of what Gramsci would later call hegemony, being among the most significant.[70] Given these common intellectual concerns, many will even call Mariátegui 'the Latin American Gramsci'.[71]

Rouillón, for one, presents Mariátegui as 'fully identified with the revolutionary line agitated by Gramsci', becoming a member of the Socialist Party, and even meeting his supposed hero and exchanging ideas with the Italian master during a visit to Turin.[72] According to Rouillón, 'when the leader of the Turinese socialists was informed that he was in front of a young Peruvian who supported his cause and was a member of one of the neighborhood groups in Rome, he welcomed the members of the group [including Falcón] as if he had known them for a long time'.[73] Likewise, his wife, Anna Chiappe, remembered that during the congress of Livorno, she and her husband 'met there Antonio Gramsci and Palmiro Togliatti [another Socialist, later Communist, leader]. Mariátegui held friendly conversations with both'.[74] (Mariátegui visited the congress as a correspondent for the Lima newspaper *El Tiempo*).

---

68   Chiappe 2012. One must note that it has been impossible to determine, apart from the anecdotes recounted by his wife and descendants, the extent of Mariátegui's actual relationship with these and other key Italian cultural figures.

69   Mariátegui 1994, p. 332.

70   On the points in common between Mariátegui and Gramsci, see Melis 1979, pp. 13–14; Löwy 2018; and González 2019, pp. 66–7.

71   Obviously the phrase is generally intended as high praise. Some examples are Munck 2013, p. 212; Céspedes 1995, 417; Viñas 2000, p. 52.

72   Rouillón 1984, p. 57. Rouillón supposedly based his description of Mariátegui's admiration for Gramsci on testimony by his friends César Falcón and Palmiro Machiavello, who spent time together in Italy. In fact, according to Rouillón, the three friends went to Turin in order to meet the Italian Marxist.

73   Rouillón 1984, p. 72.

74   Chiappe 2012.

Although Rouillón bases his information on the testimony of Falcón and especially of Palmiro Machiavello, a Peruvian diplomat who became friendly with Mariátegui in Italy and shared in his socialist beliefs, one cannot avoid being sceptical regarding his description of Mariátegui as a follower of Gramsci. In fact, there are other sources, such as Hugo Pesce, a close collaborator of Mariátegui during the late 1920s, who have noted that the author of *Seven Essays* never referred to Gramsci in personal conversation.[75] Moreover, the references to Gramsci in Mariátegui are very few and superficial.[76] Could Mariátegui have gone from admiration to indifference in just a few years? Be that as it may, the Gramsci presented by Rouillón is not the theorist of hegemony and the subaltern who would later become so influential among the new left, as well as later postmodern and postcolonial thinkers. Instead, Rouillón presents Gramsci not only as an Italian Maximalist, but also as a representative of Leninist orthodoxy. In this manner, by associating him with the Italian Marxist, Rouillón describes Mariátegui already from his socialist beginnings as 'following the thought of Lenin and Gramsci ... that the class struggle inevitably leads to the dictatorship of the proletariat'.[77] Likewise, one cannot but doubt the testimony of Falcón, who will later become an active member of the Comintern and, therefore, after the rediscovery of Mariátegui in the 1950s and 1960s, develop

---

75 Chavarría 1979, 206 n. 13.

76 The explicit mentions of the Italian theorist in Mariátegui's writings are limited to four brief instances that, generally, seem to follow Beigel's description of the Gramsci of the 1920s as 'an important militant who formed part of the Communist/Ordinovist faction' (Beigel 2006, pp. 106–7). In Mariátegui's description of 'Socialist Politics in Italy' from 1925 he includes 'the writer Gramsci' among the 'Communist leaders', together with 'the engineer Bórdiga, the lawyer Terracini, and the professor Grazidei' (Mariátegui 1980c, p. 141). In his 1928 essay 'La influencia de Italia en la cultura hispano-americana' (The Influence of Italy in Spanish American Culture), he mentions Gramsci as part of his list of names of authors, places, and artistic movements he associates with his own experience of Italy, together with the La Scala theater, Croce, the city of Milan, and even the Café Aragno, among others (Mariátegui 1981b, p. 156). In what is, perhaps, his most substantial reference to the author of *The Prison Notebooks*, Gramsci is mentioned as an influence on Piero Gobetti's interest on the economic background of historical fact: 'His investigation was transported to the field of actual and direct experience, thanks to his growing closeness to Gramsci and his collaborations with *L'Ordine Nuovo*' (Mariátegui 1981b, p. 139). (This essay is from 1929.) In his posthumously published *Defensa del marxismo*, he mentions the imprisonment of Gramsci (together with that of Terracini) (Mariátegui 1981a, p. 115). Given Mariátegui's open acknowledgment of his intellectual sources – from Sorel, to Unamuno, to Freud, to Gobetti, to Croce – this paucity of references and the relatively informal manner in which the Peruvian refers to Gramsci serve as evidence of a lack of influence.

77 Rouillón 1984, p. 92.

an interest in promoting the image of his former friend as a mainstream Communist. (Falcón had kept silent about Mariátegui during the decades after his death). As we will see in 'José Carlos Mariátegui and the Culture of Politics', this presentation of the author of *Seven Essays* as a strict Leninist contradicts the bulk of Mariátegui's writings, as well as his political activity.

But if the lack of textual evidence undermines the case for the influence of the Leninist Gramsci, it also makes the influence of the later Gramsci of hegemony and subalternity even less plausible. This is not surprising since 'The Gramsci who became known world wide after the publication of his notebook entries was not – even accepting the most optimistic speculations about a personal encounter – the one Mariátegui knew'.[78] *The Prison Notebooks*, Gramsci's miscellaneous texts written in prison between 1928 and 1935, only began to be published in 1948. (The Italian Marxist leader had died in 1937). However, even informed *mariateguistas* have assumed a factually impossible direct influence of the mature Gramsci on Mariátegui.

Hosam Aboul-Ela has written on this supposed influence of Gramsci on Mariátegui:

> the imagined relationship between Mariátegui and Gramsci demonstrates the way global spatial inequalities reflect the reception and distribution of ideas and thinkers. Gramsci's primacy in the pairing – that is his being made a central influence on the Peruvian – comes partially from the Italian's greatest propinquity to the core. Given the current emphasis in canons of theory, it would be ridiculous to call Gramsci 'the Italian Mariátegui'.[79]

One can add to Aboul-Ela's comments that these 'global spatial inequalities' are made even more evident by the fact that, for all practical purposes, Mariátegui's main writings – *Seven Essays* was published in 1928 – are chronologically anterior to Gramsci's.

---

78   Beigel 2006, p. 106.
79   Aboul-Ela 2007, pp. 29–30. A similar point regarding this imagined relationship between Mariátegui and Gramsci has been made by Walter Mignolo, one of the most influential Latin Americanists today: 'The two great thinkers have been placed in relation several times. The general tendency is to underline the influences of Gramsci on Mariátegui. There are few who have doubts about it, although they do not radically contest the idea. The assumption here is that Gramsci could have influenced Mariátegui; never that Mariátegui could have influenced Gramsci. And the underlying presupposition under the assumptions is that "influence" goes from the center to the periphery of the modern/colonial world, never the other way around' (Mignolo 2012, p. 191).

However, there was a significant, though less direct, Gramscian presence in Mariátegui through the example of *L'Ordine Nuovo*. More than the explicit content found in this journal – though it undoubtedly was read by Mariátegui – the influence of the Italian periodical was exercised on the Peruvian's use of journalism and book publishing as a way of disseminating radical perspectives and agglutinating public opinion around these. Mariátegui, who had already attempted to develop a radical 'editorialist praxis' in Peru through the short-lived *Nuestra Época* and *La Razón*, found a new model in *L'Ordine Nuovo*, the journal, as well as the books it published and promoted. But Gramsci was not an exclusive influence on what Beigel calls Mariátegui's 'editorialist praxis'. The *ordinovista* fellow-traveller Gobetti and his journal *La Rivoluzione Liberale* and its independent publishing house were also major influences on the Peruvian socialist.[80] Following the examples of Gramsci and Gobetti, Mariátegui would, on his return to Lima, create a progressive press (Editorial Minerva) that not only published political works, such as his disciple Ricardo Martínez de la Torre's *El movimiento obrero en 1919* ([The Worker's Movement in 1919] 1928), a study of the 1919 strikes in Lima, but also 'pure' literature like a collection of José María Eguren's symbolist poetry, *Poesías* ([Poetry] 1929). He also started the seminal cultural magazine *Amauta* and the short-lived working class journal *Labor*.

8   Back to Peru and Death

Despite his now explicit radicalism, and the Leguía regime's near dictatorial repression of any political activity that it saw as threatening, Mariátegui regained his position as a prominent journalist after his return to Lima in 1923. Yet now instead of writing on the day to day of political events, he became a pundit who published in the main magazines of the time – *Variedades* and *Mundial* – on the principal contemporary political, social, and cultural issues. In 1926 he founded the journal *Amauta*, named after the (proto-intellectual) class of wise men of the Inca Empire, which welcomed collaborations not only from noted Peruvian writers and intellectuals – such as César Vallejo or Haya de la Torre – but also included texts by such major world cultural figures as Sigmund Freud or Miguel de Unamuno. The two books he published during his lifetime – *La escena contemporánea* (The Contemporary Scene 1925) and *7 ensayos de interpretación de la realidad peruana* (*Seven Interpretative Essays*

---

80   On *L'Ordine Nuovo's* influence, see Beigel 2006, pp. 105–14; on Gobetti's, see Beigel 2006, pp. 115–30; and Melis 1979, pp. 14–16.

on Peruvian Reality 1928) – were compilations or, in the case of the latter, re-workings of articles published in these journals and *Amauta*. Both books, as well as *Amauta*, established Mariátegui's reputation as a major literary and social critic throughout the Spanish-speaking world. At the time of death, he also left the finished manuscripts of *Defensa del marxismo* (Defense of Marxism) and *La novela y la vida* and a nearly complete manuscript of *El alma matinal* (The Morning Soul). The manuscript of *Ideología y política* (Ideology and Politics), a book-length 'essay on the political and ideological evolution of Peru' was lost in mysterious circumstances.[81] At a personal level, Mariátegui would in 1924 face another health crisis which, as mentioned in the 'Introduction', led to the amputation of what had till then seemed his healthier right leg. From then on, until his death in 1930 from the disease he contracted as a child, he was confined to a wheelchair. However, Mariátegui responded to his lack of mobility by creating what Beigel has called editorial networks. He thus exchanged magazines, articles, and became commercial representative for numerous journals and presses that, for instance, connected the Peruvian thinker with Barbusse's *Monde* and the Trotskyist *Lutte de Classes*, and, among book publishers, the British Macmillan and the Italian Mondadori.[82] His work reached readers throughout Peru and Latin America.

He also became the focus of correspondence and personal networks that formed the kernels from which his cultural and political projects grew. As Beigel notes:

> Another mode of insertion into [his social] environment began in June 1925, when he moved into the house located on Washington Izquierda, and the meetings of the salon began. The Amauta's [Mariátegui's] role as the agglutinating axis for diverse intellectual sectors – that transformed

---

81 On the 'lost book', see Basadre 1971, p. xxxv. In his 'Author's Note' to *Seven Essays*, Mariátegui wrote: 'I intended to include in this collection an essay on the political and ideological evolution of Peru. But as I advance in it, I realize that I must develop it separately in another book. I find that the seven essays are already too long, so much so that they do not permit me to complete other work as I would like to and ought to; nevertheless, they should be published before my new study appears. In this way, my reading public will already be familiar with the materials and ideas of my political and ideological views' (Mariátegui 1971, p. xxv). Mariátegui announced in his correspondence the completion of *Ideología y política* which was to be published by César Falcón in Spain. However Falcón, who had become a member of the Spanish Communist Party, claimed not to have received the manuscript. This lost book should not be confused with a book of the same title published by Mariátegui's heirs, comprised of some of the Peruvian Marxist's explicitly political texts.

82 See Beigel 2006, pp. 288, 290.

the 'red corner' into a permanent center of [intellectual] exchange – and his ability as cultural organizer contributed to the process of his becoming the spokesperson for the 'new Peruvian' generation.[83]

(In addition to its possible political connotations, the corner of the room where Mariátegui usually sat was called the 'red corner' because of the colour of the tapestry that adorned its walls).

As we will see in 'Mariátegui and Argentina', his decision to move to Buenos Aires responded to his desire to continue and expand these networks, which had been undermined by the hardening of the Leguía regime, which jailed him in 1927 and later in 1929 placed him under house arrest. The government also intercepted his correspondence and questioned anyone who dared visit his home. His planned relocation to Argentina was also a reaction to the political isolation Mariátegui experienced towards the end of his life as what could be called his political networks, which he had built throughout the 1920s, began to crumble. The breakup of the Peruvian left in 1928, due to Haya's decision to turn the Alianza Popular Revolucionaria Americana (Popular Revolutionary American Alliance [APRA]) into a political party and Mariátegui's opposition to this transformation – studied in 'José Carlos Mariátegui and the Culture of Politics' – began to isolate him from many former comrades. Likewise, despite his having helped found the Partido Socialista [Socialist Party] in 1928, and the labour union Confederación General de Trabajadores del Perú [General Federation of Workers of Peru] in 1929], his disagreements with the Comintern – the Soviet-led confederation of international communist parties and movements – threatened his future within the Communist movement. Unfortunately, Mariátegui's trip to Buenos Aires was frustrated by his death at only 35 years of age. His funeral in 1930 was the occasion of, in the words of historian Marc Becker, 'one of the largest processions of workers ever seen in the streets of Lima'.[84]

9   After-Death and After-Life

Mariátegui's iconoclastic Marxism rapidly became anathema for the ever-hardening Stalinist Third International. Almost immediately after his death, Eudocio Ravines, who represented the Comintern, changed the name of the

---

83   Beigel 2006, p. 178.
84   Becker 2015.

Party from Socialist to Communist.[85] Already in December 1933–January 1934, the Ravines-led Peruvian Communist Party published a communiqué titled 'Bajo la bandera de Lenin' ('Under Lenin's Flag'). A blistering attack, probably by Ravines, it argued that:

> Mariateguismo is a confusion of ideas ... He had not only theoretical but practical errors. There are, in reality, few points of contact between Leninism and mariateguismo ... Mariateguismo confuses the national problem with the indigenous problem; attributes to imperialism and capitalism a progressive function in Peru; [and] substitutes debate and discussion, etc. for revolutionary tactic and strategy.[86]

In fact, Ravines, or the author authorized by Soviet Communism, concludes the text by stating 'Our position regarding mariateguismo is and must be one of implacable and irreconcilable combat'.[87] Mariátegui, who was misleadingly acknowledged as the founder of the Peruvian Communist Party – as we have seen, he had actually founded the (Peruvian) Socialist Party – was also presented as a flawed thinker whose ideas had to be combatted, in an incredible irony, in his name: 'The first to recognize this [non-Communist] essence of *mariateguismo*, and, therefore, to mercilessly fight against it, was the same Comrade Mariátegui'.[88]

Given this dismissal of Mariátegui by international Communism, it is not surprising that it was only among the margins of Latin American political and cultural life that his memory survived. Horacio Tarcus notes how his influence in Argentina was limited to 'ignored Trotskyists'.[89] This began to change in 1950 when Mariátegui's widow and now grown-up sons decided to revitalise Editorial Minerva and Editorial Amauta and republish his works. In addition to *La escena contemporánea* and *Seven Essays*, they published texts previously not available in book form. However, even into the 1950s he seemed to be at best an occasional memory for some of his contemporaries, such as Jorge Basadre,

---

85   Eudocio Ravines would eventually abandon the communist movement, becoming an activist for the hard right in Peru and internationally. Despite his political evolution and his role in eradicating *mariateguismo* from the Peruvian Communist Party in the 1930s, he presents a sympathetic portrayal of Mariátegui in his *The Yenan Way* (1951), written with the help of William F. Buckley.

86   Anonymous 1980, p. 21.

87   Anonymous 1980, p. 21.

88   Anonymous 1980, p. 21.

89   Tarcus 2011, p. 80.

or a subversive reading for heretical Apristas, such as Hilda Gadea, Ernesto 'Che' Guevara's first wife. It was only with the Cuban Revolution that interest in Latin American Marxism and in Mariátegui became widespread throughout the region. A classic, to be sure, Mariátegui remains a resource for thinking anew the history and reality of Latin America.

CHAPTER 3

Mariátegui, Sorel and Myth

Despite having been dismissed by Lenin as 'a notorious muddlehead',[1] French thinker Georges Sorel is not only a recurrent reference in José Carlos Mariátegui's writings, but is also presented by him as one of the major figures in the history of Marxism. In *Defensa del marxismo*, the Peruvian writes: 'By clarifying the historical role of violence, he is the most vigorous continuator of Marx in that period [late nineteenth/early twentieth century] of social-democratic parliamentarism'.[2] Disregarding Lenin's characterisation, Sorel is described by the Peruvian as having 'decisively influenced' the Russian revolutionary's 'mental formation',[3] arguably by his rejection of social meliorism.[4]

Not surprisingly, given Lenin's opinion of Sorel and even more given his role as one of the intellectual sources of fascism,[5] mainstream Marxists have frequently felt queasy about the Peruvian's consistent praise for the French thinker.[6] Most members of the 1960s Latin American New Left did not admire Sorel or, for that matter, approve of his influence on the thought of the author of *Seven Essays*. In 1979, Aníbal Quijano, the prominent Peruvian social scient-

---

1 Lenin 1927, p. 249.
2 Mariátegui 1981a, p. 21. Harry Vanden and Marc Becker provide only a partial translation of *Defensa del marxismo* in their *José Carlos Mariátegui: An Anthology*. Whenever convenient, I will use their translations, but here I am providing my own.
3 Mariátegui 1981a, p. 21.
4 The source for this belief in Sorel's influence on Lenin is probably the French author's 'In Defense of Lenin'. After citing a newspaper article that makes the case for this influence, Sorel, however, writes: 'I have no reason for believing that Lenin made use of some of the ideas in my books; but if that were the case, I would be uncommonly proud' (Sorel 1972, p. 279).
5 Mariátegui was aware of the links between Sorel and Mussolini: '*Reflections on Violence* seem to have decisively influenced in the intellectual formation of two leaders as antagonistic as Lenin and Mussolini' (Mariátegui 1981a, p. 21). Mussolini himself acknowledged his admiration for Sorel, calling him 'notre maitre' (quoted in Falasca-Zamponi 1997, p. 31).
6 But not only has Mariátegui's 'Sorelism' been an object of negative criticism by scholars. The presence in his thought of other non-Marxist influences, such as Benedetto Croce or Friedrich Nietzsche, has also been criticised. As Patricia D'Allemand notes: 'With a few exceptions such as Antonio Melis and Alberto Flores Galindo, Mariátegui's critics have not been disposed to engage in a positive reading of the unorthodox aspects of his writings, which have thereby been ignored or discounted as "irrational" or "idealist" deviations within his Marxism. This reticence on the part of Mariátegui's critics to approach what in fact constitutes one of the creative aspects of the Peruvian's Marxism has led to an incomplete reading of his proposals, which to a large extent distorts them' (D'Allemand 2000, p. 80).

ist of the second half of the twentieth century, admitted his discomfort with Sorel's influence on Mariátegui:

> Fifty years later, it is surprising to find in someone like Mariátegui such unabashed admiration for ideas as confused and predictable as those of Sorel. It is even more surprising that he believed in Sorel's influence on Lenin, despite knowing and citing the latter's *Materialism and Empiriocriticism*, in which Sorel is mistreated as a 'notorious muddlehead'.[7]

Marxism was seen as the continuation and development of the rationalism of the Enlightenment. Sorel's rejection of any type of determinism, of historical progress, his celebration of myth and irrational emotion, his celebration of violence as a virtue in itself – among other traits – contradicted the building blocks of Marx's intellectual system and his political and social predictions.

However, the fall of the Soviet Union and the concomitant loss of prestige of the critical and political canon established by the official Communist movement, as well as the parallel rise of postmodern criticisms of Eurocentrism, reason, and grand narratives, has led some to a reappraisal of Sorel's influence. The French thinker's rejection of historical rationality and progress prefigure aspects of contemporary postmodern and post-structuralist thought. Moreover, Sorel's closeness to the anarchist tradition – Proudhon was one of his intellectual sources – has led some, like Renzo Llorente to describe his thought as 'anarcho-Marxism'.[8] The rebirth of anarchism as the main anti-systemic ideology of the early twenty-first century has rekindled interest in the French *syndicaliste*. Not surprisingly, recent critics have shown greater appreciation for the presence of Sorel in Mariátegui's writings. Already in the 1990s, Adolfo Sánchez Vázquez had seen in Mariátegui's borrowing of the Sorelian notion of the myth the means of overcoming the rigid materialist determin-

---

7 Quijano 2007a, p. lxxxi.

8 Llorente 2012, p. 78. Mariátegui was fully aware of Proudhon's influence on Sorel: 'Proudhon, of whom all know the iconoclastic phrase, but not the careful work, based his ideals on a thorough analysis of institutions and social customs ... And Sorel, in whom Marx and Proudhon reconcile, was not only deeply concerned with the formation of the legal conscience of the proletariat, but also with the influence of family organization and moral stimuli on the mechanism of production, as well as the whole social equilibrium' (Mariátegui 1981d, p. 118). According to Llorente: 'While there are many factors that account for Sorel's controversial status in the history of Marxism, one reason is undoubtedly his debt to Pierre-Joseph Proudhon, whose works had a profound and lasting influence on Sorel's thought' (Llorente 2012, p. 79). Despite Sorel's 'controversial status', as Llorente notes, 'his idea strongly influenced some major Marxist thinkers including Antonio Gramsci, Georg Lukács, José Carlos Mariátegui and Antonio Labriola' (Llorente 2012, p. 78).

ism and bureaucratisation of action that the Hispano-Mexican philosopher felt characterised the Marxism of the pro-Soviet Communist parties.[9] More recently, others, including the well-known Bolivian subalternist theorist Javier Sanjinés, find in Mariátegui's use of the myth a means for the linking of Marxism with indigenous traditions and thus, implicitly, as presenting in his work an anti-racist decentring of political thought and action.[10] Undoubtedly, Mariátegui finds in Sorel's concern with the subjective and irrational side of political action the means to supplement the still flat materialist Marxism hegemonic in his day, which, one must note, saw Latin America as condemned to repeating European social developments with a notable time-lag. Mariátegui's ability to find valuable resources for the radical reconstruction of Peruvian society in indigenous cultural customs and institutions, as well as his stress on local reality as a necessary component of social interpretation, were both furthered by the disregard for the strictures of Eurocentric scientificist Marxism he learned from Sorel.

1   Mariátegui and Sorel

As we have seen, Mariátegui probably came into contact with Sorel's writings before he travelled to Europe in 1919. However, the French thinker only became a central and constant reference after the Peruvian started self-identifying as a Marxist in 1923.[11] Despite his lack of conventional academic credentials – he

---

9   In his brief 'El marxismo latinoamericano de Mariátegui', Sánchez Vázquez notes: 'Precisely as a revolutionary, Mariátegui looked in these philosophies for what he could not find in the vulgar, scientistic, determinist Marxism: the acknowledgment of the role of the activity of a subject moved by her desire for transformation. This does not imply that he becomes ... a representative of irrationalism and subjectivism. Mariátegui criticizes – with Sorel – the illusions of progress, that is, the progressiveness of bourgeois modernity' (Sánchez Vázquez 2011, p. 158).

10   See Sanjinés 2012.

11   Mariátegui probably read Sorel in Lima before his exile. As we have seen, according to biographer José Luis Rouillón, Víctor Manuel Maurtúa, journalist, professor, and politician, who was interested in the radical thought of the time, played a role in bringing Sorel to Mariátegui's attention: 'From Mariátegui's contacts with anarchist agitators, with Maúrtua, with international life, comes the period when he had a predilection for Georges Sorel' (Rouillón 1975, p. 208). The Italian immigrant artist Remo Polastri Bianchi may also have played a role in bringing Sorel to Mariátegui's attention, lending him Italian translations of his essays (Rouillón 1975, p. 211). Moreover, as Robert Paris has noted, Sorel was a reference even for conservative authors such as Francisco García Calderón (Paris 1973, p. 129). In fact, Sorel, together with Antonio Labriola, rather than Marx, or, for that matter, Lenin, were probably among the first socialists read by Mariátegui. As Rouillón writes: 'José Car-

was an engineer – and his distance from established political parties, Sorel had a significant presence in intellectual circles during the first decades of the twentieth century. An example of the pervasiveness of Sorel's influence can be found in the fact that, as Michael Löwy has noted, Mariátegui was not alone in his interest in the French thinker:

> As did European revolutionaries such as Lukacs, Gramsci, and the 1917–1920 Benjamin, all of whom sought to break away from the asphyxiating grip of the Second International's Marxist positivism, Mariátegui found Sorel fascinating. Despite his ambiguities and ideological regressions, Sorel was the Romantic socialist par excellence.[12]

However, as Löwy also points out, Mariátegui differs from other Bergsonian and Sorelian Marxists of the 1917–23 period who, with Lukács, Gramsci, Bloch, and Benjamin, drew away from Sorel as they came closer to official communism in the 1920s. The Peruvian Marxist is the only one who, despite his devotion to the Third International, continues to employ Sorelian themes.[13]

One must ask then why Mariátegui remained faithful to Sorel even as official Communist cultural politics began to marginalise the French thinker. One imagines that aspects of Sorel's life and writings resonated with Mariátegui. The young autodidact must have seen himself – or better said, an image of a possible future self – reflected in Sorel's self-description near the start of *Reflections of Violence*:

> I am neither a professor, a populariser of knowledge, nor a candidate for party leadership. I am a self-taught man exhibiting to other people the notebooks which have served for my own instruction.[14]

Mariátegui, who would later begin his *Seven Essays* by claiming that his masterpiece had been written by 'one whose thoughts formed a book spontaneously and without premeditation',[15] must have also identified with these following comments by Sorel: 'I did not write with the intention of composing a book:

---

los's first contacts with Marx were made indirectly through interpreters' (Rouillón 1975, p. 205). For Mariátegui's first socialist and radical influences, also see 'José Carlos Mariátegui: The Makings of a Revolutionary in the Aristocratic Republic', in this study.

12   Löwy 2008, p. 73.
13   Löwy 2008, p. 77.
14   Sorel 1972, p. 27.
15   Mariátegui 1971, p. 2.

I simply wrote down my reflections as they came to my mind'.[16] Mariátegui's 'Sorelism' may additionally be explained by the independent manner in which the Peruvian developed his own brand of Marxism. Self-taught when it comes to socialism, as well as other topics, he was free of any direct Soviet influence and from the canon and ideas it promoted. Even his stay in Italy, which saw him reporting for the Peruvian press on the break-up of the Italian Socialist Party and the founding of the Italian Communist Party, did not necessarily lead him down the road of orthodoxy. Not only were his main Italian influences on the margins of the Communist Party – Benedetto Croce, the idealist philosopher who wrote on Marx, and especially Piero Gobetti, the radical liberal – but Italian Communism was the most heterodox of all the European Marxist movements. This independence was not only intellectual. As Alberto Flores Galindo has convincingly shown, contact between Mariátegui and the Third International only began after he was jailed in 1927, during the anti-left raid implemented by the Augusto Leguía government.[17] Given this intellectual and political isolation from 'official' Communism during most of the 1920s, the decade in which he developed his socialist ideas and activism, he probably did not feel, at least until late in his short life, any pressure to modify his ideas.

He, of course, read the classics by Marx and Engels, and the then-contemporary works by Lenin, Trotsky, and Bukharin, as well as other leaders of the Russian Revolution. After going over the Peruvian's library, Harry Vanden notes:

> Mariátegui's esteem for Marxism-Leninism, and his dedication to this doctrine, as it had developed during the third decade of the [twentieth] century, derived fundamentally from the Peruvian writer's direct contact with the texts of Marx, Engels and Lenin.[18]

However, the Bolshevik influence on Mariátegui was mainly on his thinking about practical politics, rather than on his social and historical theories.[19]

---

16   Sorel 1972, p. 26. As is well-known, Mariátegui associates the idea of spontaneously composing a book with Nietzsche, also one of the influences on Sorel.

17   According to Flores Galindo, governmental persecution 'began in June 1927, when the police confiscated *Amauta* [Mariátegui's magazine], jailed José Carlos Mariátegui and had him placed in hospital arrest in San Bartolomé Military Hospital ... In a letter published in La Prensa ... Mariátegui did not hesitate to confess his self-definition as a Marxist ... but ... clearly denied any connection with the Russian Communist Central' (Flores Galindo 1980, p. 20).

18   Vanden 1975, p. 63.

19   In *Seven Essays* there are five mentions of Lenin and in *Ideología y política* (the collection of political articles compiled by his children) four, but no reference to any of his

Even if Mariátegui's own activism is distant from central Leninist principles, such as democratic centralism or the vanguard role of the party, Lenin and other Bolsheviks serve as examples of true revolutionary action rather than as guides to understanding social and psychological reality. Mariátegui writes about Lenin in *Defensa del marxismo*:

> Lenin appears, incontestably in our epoch as the most energetic and pro-found restorer of Marxist thought ... the Russian Revolution constitutes the dominant accomplishment of contemporary socialism. It is to this accomplishment, of which the historical reach cannot yet be measured, that one must go in order to find the new stage of Marxism.[20]

Despite claiming that Lenin was a restorer of 'Marxist thought', it is clear that the stress is on the impact of the revolution, rather than on any specific Leninist idea, even if in this late text occasional references to the Russian leader's *Imperialism: Highest Stage of Capitalism* crop up.[21] In fact, in 1929, looking at the 'doctrinal crisis of socialism' which he believed afflicted the international left at the time, he makes his opinion on Lenin crystal clear: 'Lenin has disap-peared from the scene prematurely. The tasks of the Russian Revolution did not leave him enough time or energy, moreover, for the scholarly examination of the world situation. Lenin was placed in the position of a historical actor rather than that of an ideologist'.[22]

It is thus not accidental that in *Seven Essays*, a book in which the Russian revolutionary is only mentioned in passing, the modern world is described as the civilisation of 'Marx and Sorel', not 'Marx and Lenin'.[23] Sorel, not Lenin, had the greater theoretical influence on Mariátegui's Marxism, even if the Russian leader is the yardstick against which revolutionary leadership and action is measured.[24] Mariátegui's description of modern industrial civilisation as that

---

writings. Only in *Defensa del marxismo*, written after he had established contact with the Comintern, does Mariátegui refer to a specific text by Lenin: *Imperialism*. There is, however, an indirect reference to *Imperialism* in Mariátegui's 1926 article 'El nuevo estat-uto del imperio británico' (The New Statutes of the British Empire): 'Imperialism defined by Lenin as the last stage of capitalism, stands in open contrast to the new human con-science' (Mariátegui 1980d, p. 123). On Mariátegui's divergences from Lenin, see 'José Carlos Mariátegui and the Culture of Politics' in this study.

20   Mariátegui 2011, p. 190.
21   In *Defensa del marxismo*, Mariátegui quotes twice from Lenin's *Imperialism*, describing this work as 'perhaps, the most foundational of his books' (Mariátegui 1981a, p. 158).
22   Mariátegui 1980e, p. 142.
23   Mariátegui 1971, p. 74.
24   With, from our perspective, anachronistic irony, Robert Paris, in one of the foundational

of 'Marx and Sorel' can also be read as implying a kind of division of labour ascribed to his two intellectual heroes. Marx represents the hard-nosed interpretation of economic reality, exemplified by many of the best pages in *Seven Essays*, while Sorel informs the study of the subjective aspects of reality, including the psychological basis for political change. In *Defensa del marxismo*, he writes: 'The theory of the revolutionary myths, which applied to the socialist movement the experience of religious movements, establishes the basis for a philosophy of revolution profoundly impregnated by psychological and sociological realism'.[25] Sorel is associated with what would later be called social psychology or mass psychology. One could thus argue that not only is Sorel seen as a supplement to Marx, but also to Freud, another of the Peruvian's intellectual heroes.[26] Freud would, then, provide the explanation for individual behaviour, while Sorel would be relevant to understanding that of collectivities.[27] Moreover, as we have mentioned, Sorel gave Mariátegui a theoretical basis from which to sidestep Eurocentric determinisms and find potential for shoots of modernity in Peru's indigenous traditions and institutions. For instance, in *Seven Essays*, Mariátegui refers to Sorel precisely when revaluing the indigenous community as 'not only an economic institution but also, and more important, a social institution, one that defends the indigenous tradition, maintains the function of the rural family, and reflects the popular legal

---

studies of the Peruvian Marxist, writes: 'Although it is true that the British Parliament may have all powers, except that of making a man into a woman, one would need a similar power to transform Mariátegui into a Leninist' (Paris 1973, p. 10). It may be symptomatic that Sorel is mentioned 12 times in *Seven Essays*, including references to his ideas and specific texts, while Lenin is named 5 times, with no reference to any text or theoretical proposition whatsoever.

25   Mariátegui 1981a, p. 21.

26   It is thus only a slight exaggeration when Enrique Krauze writes about Mariátegui: 'He would put Freud on a par with Marx and incorporate this discovery into his political vision' (Krauze 2011, p. 111). Paris notes that Mariátegui's Sorelism 'has an evident relation with his curiosity and also sympathy for psychoanalysis' (Paris 1973, p. 139).

27   In his *Defensa del marxismo*, Mariátegui argues: 'Through Sorel, Marxism assimilates the substantial elements and acquisitions of philosophic currents after Marx. Overcoming the rationalist and positivist bases of the socialism of his time, Sorel finds in Bergson and the pragmatists ideas that reinvigorate socialist thought, reinstituting its revolutionary mission from which the *embourgeoisement* of its parties and parliamentarians, who were satisfied philosophically with the flattest of historicisms and the most timid evolutionism ... The theory of revolutionary myths, that applies to the socialist movement the experiences of religious movements, establishes the basis for a philosophy of revolution deeply impregnated by psychological and sociological realism' (Mariátegui 1981a, p. 21). (With the exception of the first sentence, which I've borrowed, the passage has been omitted from Vanden's and Becker's 'Defense of Marxism' [Mariátegui 2011, p. 190]).

philosophy so prized by Proudhon and Sorel'.[28] Sorel thus helps Mariátegui find justification for one of his most important intellectual gestures, even if, to a degree, the celebration of indigenous culture was characteristic of his 'generation' in Peru.

The mention above of 'Proudhon and Sorel' directs us to another aspect of Sorel's influence on Mariátegui: as a mediator for some of the ideas characteristic of the anarchists and anarcho-syndicalists. In fact, the concern with subjectivity and moral elevation has been intrinsic to the anarchist tradition, while the analysis of class and mode of production was developed by Marx and his followers. One wonders if Mariátegui's privileging of Sorel over Engels or Lenin, in phrases such as 'the civilization of Marx and Sorel', and throughout his works, does not, in addition to reflecting his high valuation of Sorel, also help Mariátegui acknowledge his links to this other radical tradition, and to present his ideas to the anarchist and anarcho-syndicalist sectors of his working-class audience and readership. It is clear, for instance, that Mariátegui shared in the anarchist disdain for electoral politics. And, as we have already seen, Mariátegui referred to Kropotkin's anarchist classic *The Conquest of Bread*, when he wrote in his article on Henri Barbusse: 'And the truth is ours is an age of revolution. The revolution will be for the poor not only the conquest of bread, but also of beauty, of art, of thought, of all the accessories of the spirit'.[29] It may be useful now to add that the passage also paraphrases the central ideas of the Russian anarchist who, like Mariátegui, believed that the purpose of revolutionary politics was not limited to material improvement – a position he ascribed to the Social Democracy of the Second International and beyond. Kropotkin writes, precisely in his *The Conquest of Bread*:

> we expect more from the Revolution. We see that the worker ... is reduced to ignorance of these higher delights, the highest within man's reach, of science, and especially of scientific discovery; of art, and especially of artistic creation. It is in order to obtain these joys for all, which are now reserved to a few; in order to give leisure and the possibility of developing intellectual capacities, that the social revolution must guarantee daily bread to all.[30]

Mariátegui could have subscribed to Kropotkin's every word. Personal moral and aesthetic development were also for Mariátegui among the ultimate goals of the revolution.

28   Mariátegui 1971, p. 61.
29   Mariátegui 1980c, p. 158.
30   Kropotkin 1906, p. 135.

2   The Myth in Sorel

Sorel develops his ideas on the myth in the best-known of his works, *Reflections on Violence* (1908). There Sorel argues:

> men who are participating in a great social movement always picture their coming action as a battle in which their cause is certain to triumph. These constructions ... I propose to call myths, the syndicalist 'general strike' and Marx's catastrophic revolution are such myths. As remarkable examples of such myths, I have given those which were constructed by primitive Christianity, by the Revolution and by the followers of Mazzini.[31]

The myth is thus an attempt to explain why individuals are willing to sacrifice current well-being for hypothetical future collective achievement – whether the Kingdom of Heaven, the French and Italian Republics, or socialism.[32] In other words, Sorel seeks to understand why behaviour irrational from an individualist perspective, but seen as having a future positive social and political impact, has frequently taken place. Early Christians, nineteenth-century nationalists, twentieth-century socialists, all share in this willingness to believe and to sacrifice for ultimately unverifiable results. He is dealing here with 'images' – heaven, a unified republic, a future world of equals – not with rational argumentations.[33] Sorel thus notes: 'A myth cannot be refuted'; and 'myths are not descriptions of things but expression of a determination to act'.[34] The centrality of the myth to the possibility of revolutionary activity is made clear: 'As long as there are no myths accepted by the masses one may go on talking about revolts indefinitely, without ever provoking any revolutionary movement'.[35] Myths, according to Sorel, give a clear, though unverifiable, goal for collective action. In fact, given their agglutinative quality, collective identity is necessarily based on the existence of myths. Irrational and, as he notes, constructed, myths are one of the motors, perhaps the main one, of historical change in *Reflections on Violence*. Given the centrality of myths, history becomes a narrative of irrational moments.

---

31   Sorel 1972, p. 42.
32   'The intellectualist philosophy finds itself unable to explain phenomena like the following – the sacrifice of his life which the soldier of Napoleon made in order to have had the honour of taking part in "immortal deeds" and of living in the glory of France knowing all the time "he would always be a poor man"' (Sorel 1972, p. 43).
33   Sorel 1972, p. 42.
34   Sorel 1972, p. 50.
35   Sorel 1972, p. 49.

Moreover, there is the clear implication in *Reflections on Violence* that it is only by believing in myths that the individual achieves any sense of personal completion. Inspired by Henri Bergson's notion of the 'two selves' – one exterior, 'social representation'; the other interior, 'inner states as living things, constantly becoming, as states not amenable to measure'[36] – Sorel clearly sees the myth as permitting one to come into contact with the inner self, and thus live a fuller, more satisfactory life: 'It is very evident that we enjoy this liberty preeminently when we are making a new individuality in ourselves, thus endeavoring to break the bonds of habit which enclose us'.[37] Belief in myths, not only in the revolutionary 'general strike', thus becomes central to historical development, as well as to the achievement of individual psychological integrity and fullness. If the presence of myths is the key to social and individual development, then not only is there no clear sense of historical progress – fallow mythless periods may follow heroic ones when there are active myths – but the existence rather than the actualisation of the myth is what is significant. Despite his putative socialism, neither improvement in workers' lives, nor a communist utopia, are for Sorel myths or even goals to be accomplished. He is ultimately not interested in the construction of a new society – this, obviously, a main difference with Lenin, Mariátegui, and, in fact, most socialists. While Sorel sympathises with 'revolutionary movements', he does not celebrate or promote socialist revolution itself – whether catastrophic or not.

Instead, what matters to Sorel is the myth of the general strike and the fact that 'the normal developments of strikes is accompanied by an important series of acts of violence'.[38] For him this violence is not something to be decried.[39] For Sorel, the value of the myth of the general strike is that it renders any politics based on compromise – supported by many socialists at the time – impossible: 'they [socialist politicians] feel in a vague way that the whole socialist movement might easily be absorbed by the general strike, which would render useless all the compromises between political groups in view of which the parliamentary regime has been built up'.[40] According to Sorel, myths and compromise, the latter necessarily based on rational considera-

---

36   Quoted in Sorel 1972, p. 47.

37   Sorel 1972, p. 48.

38   Sorel 1972, p. 57.

39   Hannah Arendt is therefore mistaken when she writes: 'Georges Sorel … thought of class struggle in military terms; but he ended by proposing nothing more violent than the famous myth of the general strike, a form of action which we today would rather think of as belonging to the arsenal of nonviolent politics' (Arendt 1970, p. 12). Sorel values the 'general strike' as a myth because, according to him, it is intrinsically linked to violent actions.

40   Sorel 1972, p. 129.

tions, are incompatible. Paradoxically, for Sorel, proletarian violence, fuelled by the belief in the 'general strike', leads concomitantly to a radicalisation of the class conflict and, therefore, to a rebirth of the mythic beliefs of the bourgeoisie: 'It is here that the role of violence in history appears to us as singularly great, for it can in an indirect manner, so operate on the middle class as to awaken them to a sense of their own class sentiment'.[41] It would seem that this heightened opposition – ruthless capitalists firmly believing again in their own bourgeois myths, workers believing blindly in the value of class violence, and acting accordingly – leads to a better functioning society: 'if a united and revolutionary proletariat confronts a rich middle class, eager for conquest, capitalist society will have reached its historical perfection'.[42] As Isaiah Berlin has noted about Sorel:

> Creative vitality cannot exist where everything gives, where it is too soft to resist. Unless the enemy – not the parasitic intellectuals and theorists, but the leaders of the capitalist forces – are themselves energetic and fight back like men, the workers will not find enemies worthy of their steel, and will themselves tend to degenerate. Only against a strong and vigorous opponent can truly heroic qualities be developed. Hence Sorel's characteristic wish that the bourgeoisie might develop stronger sinews. No serious Marxist could begin to accept this thesis, not even the mildest reformist.[43]

Sorel is thus not really concerned with the creation of a classless society or even of one more just, but rather his ideal society is one in which myths are embraced by a majority. Thus, his putative simultaneous admiration for Lenin and Mussolini is not as incongruous as would apparently seem.[44] Both the Russian revolutionary and the Italian leader helped to sharpen the rejection of bland compromise and proposed violence, whether repressive or revolutionary, as political instruments. For the French theorist, the main political goal is the entrenchment of class violence and, therefore, of the possibility for individuals of all classes to live heroic lives.

---

41   Sorel 1972, p. 90.
42   Sorel 1972, p. 92.
43   Berlin 2013, p. 395.
44   Sorel seems to have expressed great admiration for Mussolini after the latter had begun his evolution from socialism to fascism. According to his disciple Jean Variot, Sorel stated: 'Our Mussolini is not an ordinary Socialist. Believe me: one day you may see him at the head of a sacred battalion saluting the Italian flag with his sword. He is a fifteenth century Italian, a condottiere! It is not known yet, but he alone has enough energy to restore power to the government' (quoted in Meisel 1950, p. 14 n. 2).

3   Sorel in Mariátegui

As we have seen, Mariátegui lived in Italy from 1919 to 1922. This was a period
of near revolutionary turmoil. On the one hand, these years were characterised
by strikes, worker takeover of factories, and the birth of Italian communism as
a splinter from the Socialist Party. On the other, fascism took hold and marched
to Rome and power. The fact that fascists and many socialists seemed pos-
sessed by certainty in the unbending truth of their ideas and victory of their
cause seemed to give social validity to Sorel's ideas. Moreover, the hesitancy
he found among the defenders of parliamentary democracy is the reason why
the Peruvian, like Sorel, no longer found mythic power in liberal democracy.
In an essay significantly titled 'Man and Myth', he writes that 'The bourgeoisie
no longer has any myths. It has become incredulous, skeptical, nihilistic. The
liberal myth, which originated in the Renaissance, has aged too much'.[45] In the
turbulent Italy of the 1920s, it seemed as if socialism and fascism were the only
options available. However, unlike Sorel, who died before the March on Rome
of 1922, Mariátegui clearly took the side of socialism.

There are moments in his writings when Mariátegui seems to be on the
verge of falling into a full-blown Sorelism, praising the unthinking embrace of
the myth and the action it justifies over 'intellectualist' analysis. In 'The Final
Struggle', an essay that borrows in its title an image dear to Sorel,[46] Mariátegui
writes:

> Illiterate people do not care about the relativity of the myth. It would not
> even be possible for them to understand it. But generally they do a better
> job than the writer or philosopher. Because they must act, they act. Since
> they must believe, they believe. Since they must fight, they fight.[47]

This is a profoundly irrationalist moment in Mariátegui's writings. The learned
man, even if an autodidact, envies the illiterate person's unproblematic will
to act. In 'The Final Struggle', the author of *Seven Essays* implicitly rejects
the Marxist teleology that saw history as ultimately exploring the possibilit-

---

45   Mariátegui 2011, p. 387. I have corrected Becker's and Vanden's translation.
46   We have already seen Sorel use the militaristic imagery: 'men who are participating in a
      great social movement always picture their coming action as a battle in which their cause
      is certain to triumph' (Sorel 1972, p. 42). Another of the many passages where he resorts to
      apocalyptic military imagery is: 'each time they come to blows the strikers hope it is the
      beginning of the great Napoleonic battle (that which will definitely crush the vanquished)'
      (Sorel 1972, p. 78).
47   Mariátegui 2011, p. 392.

ies implicit in class oppositions until in socialism the proletariat would usher in a classless society in which, as Marx and Engels put it: 'In place of the old bourgeois society, with its classes and class antagonisms, we shall have an association, in which the free development of each is the condition for the free development of all'.[48] For Mariátegui this goal, presented as the necessary end of historical evolution by the founders of Marxism and believed to be such by the 'illiterate' militants, is but another myth that fuels unblinking action. Mariátegui parts way with the mainstream of Marxian – as well as Hegelian – thought that saw the dialectical unfolding of history as necessarily coming to an end. One must add that this teleology – which has often been seen as a secular version of that found in Christianity – would give rise to a near religious certainty in many Marxists. As Mariátegui himself noted in his *Seven Essays*:

> We know that a revolution is always religious. The word 'religion' has a new value and it no longer serves only to designate a ritual or a church. It is of little importance that the Soviets write on their propaganda posters that 'religion is the opium of the people'. Communism is essentially religious, but not in the old sense of the word, which still misleads so many.[49]

As we have seen, this new meaning of religion is the myth.

One can identify a performative contradiction at the core of Mariátegui's appropriation of the Sorelian myth. The Peruvian Marxist yearns for what he cannot be – an uncritical believer – as he provides the kind of clear 'intellectualist' analysis the illiterate enthusiast can never achieve. Moreover, his analysis undermines the myth. In addition to noting the necessity of myth for political change, he also notes its relativity: 'People have a need for certainty. What difference does it make if the certainty people feel today is not the certainty of tomorrow?'[50] There is in this text a tension between the endorsement of the myth, with the celebration of irrationality it implies, and the practice of rational analysis that necessarily leads to the undermining of all myths. However, one must remember that the influence of Sorel helped Mariátegui break with the Eurocentric determinism characteristic of both the Marxism of Europe's Social Democracy and the ever more rigid Stalinism of the Communist movement. As Óscar Terán notes, 'it is evident that these [Mariátegui's] texts feel strongly attracted – as the tides towards the moon – to an anti-intellectual matrix. This [attraction] implied in itself a break with the canonical version of Marxism,

---

48   Marx and Engels 2012, p. 62.
49   Mariágegui 1971, p. 212.
50   Mariátegui 2011g, p. 392.

but from which, in our opinion, he would extract much potential productivity precisely where others, closer to the scientistic model of Marxism, failed'.[51]

4   Rational Irrationalism

As we have seen, Sorel's writings also aided Mariátegui in foregrounding the non-rational, even religious, dimension of social events. He thus notes, 'As Sorel predicted, the historical experience of recent years has proven that present revolutionary and social myths can occupy man's conscience just as fully as the old religious myths'.[52] Mariátegui is thus able in his analysis to look beyond the economic infrastructure to the impact of emotional, religious, and, more generally, irrational subjective dimensions that he, quoting Sorel, calls 'the spiritual part of the economic environment'.[53] But his stress on the religious dimension of socialist politics can be seen as heightening the anti-rational pull found in this writings.

One of his attempts at solving this tension between irrationalism and rationalism is found in his essay 'Pessimism of the Reality, Optimism of the Ideal'. The titular phrase is a dictum coined by Mexican man of letters José Vasconcelos. It is seen by Mariátegui as representing in other terms the tension between the analysis of reality, necessarily pessimistic, and the blind optimism of the myth. In this essay Mariátegui deepens the comparison of myth to religious belief which he adopted from Sorel.[54] For the Peruvian Marxist, religion, which combines a negative appraisal of reality with optimistic activity propelled by irrational belief, provisionally provides an answer to the contradiction between a necessary intellectual relativism and the belief in myth, which, he argues, is necessary for action.[55] Thus:

---

51   Terán 1985, 14.
52   Mariátegui 1971, p. 152.
53   Mariátegui 1971, p. 61. The homology between this aspect of the Peruvian's thought and his defence of surrealism as precisely providing insight into the subconscious and, therefore, into reality itself should be evident. On Mariátegui's defense of surrealism, see 'José Carlos Mariátegui and the Politics of Culture'.
54   As we have seen, Sorel makes this case throughout *Reflections on Violence*, but, perhaps, nowhere more explicitly than when he states: 'Bergson has taught us that it is not only religion which occupies the profounder region of our mental life; revolutionary myths have their place there equally with religion' (Sorel 1972, p. 52).
55   One can add that this aspect of Mariátegui's thought seems to foreshadow, even if in a less theoretically sophisticated manner, Walter Benjamin's reflections in his 'Theses on History'. In this text, the German thinker presents a reappraisal of religion and messianic feelings within radical thought and politics. After mentioning the story of an invincible

All great human ideals have started with a denial, but they also have been an affirmation. Religions have always perpetually represented this pessimism of reality and optimism of the ideal that this Mexican writer is now preaching to us.[56]

Mariátegui, who had a mystical streak, as evidenced in his going on a spiritual retreat in 1916, thus breaks with the traditionally anti-religious bias characteristic of the left.[57] In *Seven Essays*, he goes as far as arguing 'The revolutionary critic no longer disputes with religion and the church the services they have rendered to humanity or their place in history'.[58] While obviously incorrect as an evaluation of the relationship between religion and socialist politics at the time, it is not surprising that he has, on occasion, been seen as an ancestor and influence of Liberation Theology; a movement first fully formulated by Gustavo Gutiérrez, who is also Peruvian.[59] It may, however, be symptomatic that rather than finding in religion, or in a religious version of Marxism, the solution to the dichotomy between a necessarily sceptical rational analysis and an unavoidably irrational faith in the myth, Mariátegui ultimately adopts the philosophical pragmatism of the 1920s:

> This philosophy, therefore, does not call us to abandon action. It only seeks to deny the Absolute. But it recognizes in human history the relative truth, the temporal myth of each time, the same value and the same effectiveness as an absolute and eternal truth. This philosophy proclaims and confirms the need of the myth and the usefulness of the faith.[60]

Even if Mariátegui's appeal to pragmatism may not solve the tensions previously mentioned, it also shows how, regardless of the importance he ascribes

---

chess playing automaton that, in reality, hid a little person inside, Benjamin writes: 'The puppet called "historical materialism" is to win all the time. It can easily be a match for anyone, if it enlists the services of theology, which today, as we know, is wizened and has to keep out of sight' (Benjamin 1985, p. 253).

56   Mariátegui 2011, p. 396.
57   Despite descending, on his father's side, from a family of free thinkers, Mariátegui was raised by a very religious mother. In 1916, Mariátegui went on a spiritual retreat to a Catholic monastery. See Rouillón 1975.
58   Mariátegui 1971, p. 124.
59   Gutiérrez quotes from precisely this essay – 'Pessimism of the Reality, Optimism of the Ideal' – singling out Mariátegui's comment that 'Pessimism comes from reality, optimism from action', when writing about 'the conviction that that reality can and must be transformed by the action of the popular classes' (Gutiérrez 1996, p. 99).
60   Mariátegui 2011, p. 398.

to the myth, or the praises made to mindless action, he was, for himself, unable to wholly give in to the putative pleasures of not thinking.

According to the well-known Bolivian subalternist theorist Javier Sanjinés, Mariátegui had the 'unprecedented idea of creating a "cultural field" where rationality and myth might meet'.[61] *Seven Essays* is a case in point. It provides both a sharp objective analysis of material reality – for instance, evaluating land property systems according to their agricultural productive yield – as well as keeping an eye on 'mythic' aspects of society, such as religion. Terán has summed up the manner in which Mariátegui's masterpiece reconciles the contradictory aspects of the Peruvian's thought:

> *Seven Essays* appeals to the 'economic data' under the inspiration of Marxist theory and this surprisingly works as limit and control of any spiritualist voluntarism. Socialism had taught him that the Indian problem was not moral, but economic, social and political, and that, therefore, it was necessary to take into account the weight of these materialities to achieve a change that was not only desirable, but possible.[62]

One must add, however, that, at his best, this concern with material reality is enhanced with a parallel preoccupation with the 'spiritual', what today we would call cultural and psychological, and which, to a great degree, developed from Mariátegui's encounter with Sorel.

5   Indigenous Cultures and the Myth

Sanjinés has analysed the relevance of Mariátegui's borrowing of the myth to the Peruvian's vindication of Andean indigenous culture and its necessary role in the modernisation of his native country:

> With his conceptualization of the indigenous community, Mariátegui was simply arguing that the mobilizing power of myth transcended that of liberalism, and became one with the power of the indigenous masses. In sum, Mariátegui called for a total revolution in Peru. To achieve this, he called on the strength and influence of messianic sentiments and argued that it was imperative to incorporate them into his revolutionary pro-

61   Sanjinés 2012, p. 415.
62   Terán 1996, pp. 22–3.

ject. Aware that Marxism could only have a chance for success in Peru if it first joined together with Andean culture, Mariátegui introduced the mystical wager of the indigenous community into his thinking. Indeed, the defense of community strengthened their rejection of capitalism. Due to the non-contemporaneity of this contemporaneous structure, Peru could follow a different historical evolution from that of Europe.[63]

The struggle for socialism could, therefore, incorporate the emotional and even religious feelings that underlay indigenous culture's resistance to latinfundist expansion into their communal lands and, by doing so, made it conceivable that Peru could enter into a different historical progression from that characteristic of Europe, therefore making socialism possible. As Sanjinés notes, Mariátegui believed it was possible for the indigenous community to become one of the building blocks of a modern socialist Peru. Influenced by Sorel's rejection of historical progress, Mariátegui thus rediscovered independently one of Marx's most surprising insights proposed during his last years of life: the possibility of alternate routes to socialism.[64]

But, as Terán notes, the Peruvian's revaluation of the indigenous community as a potential building block for a distinct national and regional modernity, also owed much to what could be called the 'Marx' side of his thinking. Mariátegui thus writes: 'The defense of the "community" does not rest on abstract principles of justice or sentimental traditionalist considerations, but on concrete and practical reasons of a social and economic order'.[65] He follows this argument with a discussion of the reasons why, despite having stolen the best lands, the large agricultural holdings, that characterised the neocolonial Peruvian land tenancy system, had not been more productive than the indigenous communes. Of course, throughout his work, Mariátegui exhibits concern with what the 'Programmatic Principles of the Socialist Party' calls 'habits of cooperation and socialism',[66] that is the mindset or structures of feeling of indigenous culture and their most characteristic social institution, the commune. *Seven*

63   Sanjinés 2012, p. 420.

64   I am, of course, referring to the letter to Vera Zasulich, in which Marx states: 'The analysis in *Capital* therefore provides no reasons either for or against the vitality of the Russian commune. But the special study I have made of it, including a search for original source-material, has convinced me that the commune is the fulcrum for social regeneration in Russia. But in order that it might function as such, the harmful influences assailing it on all sides must first be eliminated, and it must then be assured the normal conditions for spontaneous development' (Marx 1975, pp. 71–2).

65   Mariátegui 1971, p. 58.

66   Socialist Party, p. 239.

Essays is much more emphatic about the cultural and psychological aspects of indigenous production and their implicit compatibility with Socialism:

> When expropriation and redistribution seem about to liquidate the 'community', indigenous socialism always finds a way to reject, resist, or evade this incursion. Communal work and property are replaced by the cooperation of individuals.[67]

Even if Mariátegui values the communities for their materially productive qualities, he also sees in their 'spiritual' and subjective dimension the core of their socialist and modern potential. However, it is also clear that as much as he celebrates these cultural values and habits of indigenous culture, in his mind they are not identical to radical or socialist values. Thus, Mariátegui argues:

> A revolutionary Indigenous consciousness will perhaps take time to form, but once Indians have made the socialist idea their own, they will serve it with a discipline, a tenacity, and strength that few other proletariats from other milieus will be able to surpass.[68]

Given that 'The Problem of Race in Latin America', the text from which this quotation comes, was presented at the First Latin American Communist Conference in Buenos Aires in 1929, a venue not favourable to the expression of ideas influenced by Sorel, Mariátegui may be here obfuscating his concern with the myth by calling it 'idea'. Be that as it may, he presents indigenous culture in a manner that emphasises the difference between its practical socialism, including the commune, and modern socialism. However, he also makes clear that indigenous values, while not identical, are still congruent with modern socialism. In his 'Preface to *The Amauta Atusparia*', his 1930 introduction to the historical chronicle of an 1885 indigenous uprising, Mariátegui notes that 'Socialism is the only doctrine that can give a modern, constructive orientation to the indigenous cause'.[69] Indigenous cultural values may be a necessary cause for Peruvian socialism and modernity, but they are not a sufficient one.

---

67   Mariátegui 1971, p. 58.
68   Mariátegui 2011, p. 325. One must note this quotation comes from the section of the text written by Mariátegui rather than the one ascribed to his close collaborator Hugo Pesce.
69   Mariátegui 2011, p. 330.

6   Conclusion

The originality of Mariátegui undoubtedly originates in the distance he felt from Europe and its culture. As he notes in an essay on his close friend the us writer Waldo Frank:

> I did not feel American except in Europe. On the roads of Europe, I found the American country I had left behind and in which I had lived almost as a foreigner as if I had been absent. Europe revealed to me the degree to which I belonged to a primitive and chaotic world; and, at the same time, made clear to me the obligation of an American task.[70]

The quotation above bears a strong resemblance to the oft-quoted passage in *Seven Essays*, 'The universal, ecumenical roads we have chosen to travel, and for which we are reproached, take us ever closer to ourselves'.[71] Read together, both passages imply a simultaneous sense of belonging and difference to Europe and (Latin) America. The notion of 'heroic creation' – that is 'to give life to Indo-American socialism with our own reality, in our own language' –[72] proposed in 'Anniversary and Balance Sheet', a politicised version of what later would be called transculturation, is his conceptual response to this sense of necessarily travelling through European roads to reach an American intellectual location.[73] Mariátegui's relation to Sorel can be seen as perfectly exemplifying the process of heroic creation. For Mariátegui, Sorel is the moderniser by means of whom 'Marxism assimilates the elements and achievements of philosophical currents after Marx'.[74] By transculturating Sorel into Peruvian terms and reality, Mariátegui is able to incorporate social psychology, even psychoanalytical concerns, into his own analysis. Sorel's concept of the myth permits Mariátegui to analyse the subjective elements in political action that had been neglected by the Marxism of his times; a concern with subjectivity that is also bolstered by Sorel's role as a mediator of the anarchist intellectual legacy. Moreover, Sorel's rejection of Europe's specific social history as constituting an iron law of histor-

---

70   Mariátegui 1981b, p. 192.
71   Mariátegui 1971, p. 287.
72   Mariátegui 2011, p. 130.
73   As Sara Castro-Klarén notes: 'Mariátegui's view of this perennial exchange is not unlike the transculturation theorized by Fernando Ortiz, and it does not imply a one way street with the colonized always assimilating forms and forces emitted by the center' (Castro-Klarén 2008, pp. 150–1).
74   Mariátegui 1981a, p. 21.

ical development helped Mariátegui find seeds of socialist modernity in Peru's indigenous cultures.

But Mariátegui changes Sorel as he makes use of him. Roland Forgues notes there is 'an essential difference between the Sorelian concept of the myth of the proletariat which identifies with the "general strike", and Mariátegui's conception which identifies it with "the social revolution". While for the former the myth deals with the means, for the latter the myth deals with the end.'[75] One can add to this perceptive comment that Sorel's goal with the 'general strike' was, as we have seen, the promotion of a heightened struggle between the bourgeoisie and the proletariat rather than the supersession of class struggle. Mariátegui, on the other hand, was, in addition to a social and historical analyst, an activist who worked for the instauration of socialism as a way of overcoming the social inequalities he rightly believed characterised Peruvian society. As we have seen, near the end of his life, he founded the Confederación General de Trabajadores del Perú, a labour union, and the (Peruvian) Socialist Party, not with the ultimate goal of radicalising the class struggle, but of ultimately, overcoming it through socialism. Although not without contradiction – Sorel, for instance, would celebrate the coming to power of the Bolsheviks in Russia –[76] the fact is that method and result are imbricated in the general strike, particularly given that the French syndicaliste saw a hardening of the class struggle as the desired social goal. Mariátegui, instead, worked for socialism, that is, for the attainment of an egalitarian and just social order, even if, as we have seen, he did not believe in the Marxian/Hegelian end of history. As Forgues again notes:

> Unlike what happens in Sorel, 'myth' and 'utopia' are not in Mariátegui incompatible but complementary concepts. 'Revolution' does not limit 'reform' and 'reform' can lead to 'revolution'.[77]

Or to phrase it differently, if Sorel's cult of violence leads ultimately to the total rejection of politics, Mariátegui, while sceptical about Peru's political institutions, believes in day to day political action – even if in immediate result

---

75   Forgues 1995, p. 212.
76   Sorel, however, praises Lenin more for the decisiveness of his leadership than for the specific measures he proposes: 'It could be said of Lenin that, like Peter the Great, he wants to force history. He intends, in effect, to introduce into his country the socialism which, according to the most authoritative representatives of social democracy, could only follow a highly developed capitalism' (Sorel 1972, p. 280). One must add that Mariátegui, who as a Peruvian also lived in a society that was seen by 'the most authoritative representatives of social democracy' as incapable of revolutionary change, must have found Sorel's description of Lenin appealing.
77   Forgues 1995, p. 214.

reformist – as long as it contributes in the long run towards the construction of a more egalitarian society. Despite the Peruvian's disdain for *criollo* and more generally electoral politics, Mariátegui's version of the myth makes everyday political activity possible. For Mariátegui, socialism was, as he famously put it, 'not an itinerary but a compass on the journey'.[78] Mariátegui's obsession with political organisation thus contradicts the anti-political bias that characterised his French forebear and the latter's anarchist forebears. If Sorel tries to push the European masses into violent action, Mariátegui ultimately believes in working with them, at their own pace, even if he does not a priori reject all possible uses of violence.[79] However, at the same time, he also feels the need to participate in the shaping of general opinion in order to create the necessary social and psychological synchronicity for radical political change to become possible. Organisation and education, not violence or unthinking action, became his modus operandi. Thus Sorel is transculturated as Mariátegui incorporates him into a different cultural milieu and rewrites him with a different set of political and ethical goals in mind.

---

78 Mariátegui 2011, p. 180. This passage comes from another fragment of *Defensa del marxismo* translated by Vanden and Becker.

79 As we will see, this is one of the many reasons why he so opposed the transformation of the APRA into the Partido Nacionalista Libertador, which he saw as an 'abortion' of what should have been a longer process (Mariátegui 1994, p. 373).

CHAPTER 4

José Carlos Mariátegui: From Race to Culture

Perhaps no aspect of Mariátegui's writings is more problematic for the contemporary reader than the presence of racial stereotypes in some of his writings. After all, for many, the struggle against racial oppression has been the paradigmatic social movement of the last sixty years. Whether in the US, South Africa, or, more recently, and, less successfully, Central America, the fight against racial discrimination, led by such charismatic and heroic leaders as Martin Luther King, Nelson Mandela, or Rigoberta Menchú, has justifiably inspired many to dream of a better world. Thus the racist comments in, for instance, *Seven Essays*, Mariátegui's emblematic work, contradict what is generally considered the sine qua non condition for one to be considered a progressive.

There is no denying the presence of demeaning racist stereotypes in Mariátegui's writings. For instance, when analysing the effects of racial mixture in Peru, he repeats all conceivable negative stereotypes ignorantly associated with Asians and blacks. He writes about the Chinese community in Peru that 'The Chinese, furthermore, appears to have inoculated his descendants with the fatalism, apathy, and defects of the decrepit Orient'.[1] His opinion on Afro-Peruvians is even more negative:

> The contribution of the Negro, who came as a slave, almost as merchandise, appears to be even more worthless and negative. The Negro brought his sensualism, his superstition, and his primitivism. His condition not only did not permit him to help create culture, but the crude, vivid example of his barbarism was more likely to hamper such creation.[2]

After these examples, can one come to any conclusion except that the Peruvian Marxist, regardless of his other insights and achievements, was a racist?

This view of Mariátegui as a racist has become commonplace among many Latin American and Latin Americanist academics. In fact, for some, this racism

---

1 Mariátegui 1971, p. 279. Underlying Mariátegui's misguided concern regarding the contributions, in his mind negative, of Asian immigrants to the construction of Peruvian nationality is the fact that about 90,000 Chinese peasants arrived to the country in the 19th century (Paerregard 2010, p. 41).

2 Mariátegui 1971, p. 279.

justifies the summary dismissal of his writings, actions, and person. Thus, according to literary critic Marcel Velázquez Castro, Mariátegui's *Seven Essays* presents 'a clear lesson in positivist racism, already obsolete at the time'.[3] For Norwegian scholar Birger Angvik, Mariátegui's 'racist postures' are indistinguishable from those of José de la Riva Agüero, his conservative predecessor and ideological opponent.[4] Even Neil Larsen, one of today's most important Marxist scholars and, otherwise, an admirer of Mariátegui, laments that the Peruvian 'maintained ridiculously archaic and racist views regarding Peru's blacks and Asian immigrants'.[5] As Roland Forgues has noted: '[Mariátegui's racist statements] have provoked intense and immediate reactions both among his critics, who haven't hesitated in calling him a "racist", and among his followers who have preferred to ignore and silence this aspect of his thought'.[6]

Furthermore, Gareth Williams, in an essay that actually values other aspects of Mariátegui's thought, notes that the *Seven Essays* 'reproduce many of the neocolonial racist categories of his day'.[7] Thus in addition to being racist, these descriptions repeat the racial views that had served to justify European colonial expansion and the maintenance of colonial institutions and racial hierarchies after independence. The description of Asians as fatalist, decrepit, and apathetic would seem to justify the presence of the supposedly forward-looking and energetic white coloniser. The putative sensual, superstitious, and primitive blacks would necessarily require supervision by hypothetically austere, rational, and modern whites. It would thus seem that not only are Velázquez and Angvik right, but, moreover, that Mariátegui would be a spokesperson for the colonialist ideology he supposedly criticises. But is this all one can say about Mariátegui's views on race?

1   The Peruvian and International Context

Any attempt at understanding Mariátegui's undeniably disturbing statements has to take into account the ideas about race prevalent in the Lima in which he grew up and in which he developed intellectually. As Forgues correctly notes, 'Mariátegui, like all human beings, is the product of his education, his cul-

---

3   Velázquez Castro 2004, p. 8.
4   Angvik 1999, p. 225.
5   Larsen 1995, p. 181.
6   Forgues 2009, p. 153.
7   Williams 2002, p. 50.

ture, and the social environment in which he lived during the early years of the formation of his conscience and personality'.[8] The Peru of the first years of the twentieth century was a society in which racial hierarchies served to justify the existence of social inequality and the unimpeded continuance of colonial structures. As Nelson Manrique notes:

> There was no substantial change after the rupture of the colonial links that connected us to Spain. Since there was no essential change in the colonial structures of domination, anti-indigenous racism went on to support the domination of the *criolla* elite and of the landowners in the countryside. In the oligarchic order that was imposed, racist discourse served to legitimize social domination, in the same manner that before it had served the Spanish colonizers, whose privileges were passed on to their *criollo* inheritors.[9]

For Manrique and many other commentators, including, as we will see, Mariátegui, there is a direct continuity not only between colonial and republican social structures, but also between the discourses on race that justified them. Manrique adds a vital point about the role played by racism in justifying human hierarchy:

> racism fulfills a decisive function in the legitimization of exclusions, since it 'naturalizes' social inequalities, consecrating an order in which each one has an immutable place, to the degree that this does not appear founded on a social origin but rather anchored in nature.[10]

According to racist ideas, rather than the product of the colonial or neocolonial system, inequality was the social manifestation of inherent human traits. Protest, reform, or revolution would all be by definition unnecessary, if not counterproductive. Nature could not be modified. Manrique's point about the ideological appeal to nature present in racist thought is exemplified by the writings on race of Clemente Palma, the son of the great writer Ricardo Palma. In addition to being the first Peruvian science fiction author, Clemente Palma was the country's main literary arbiter during the 1910s and 1920s.[11] In his B.A.

---

8   Forges 2009, p. 154.
9   Manrique 1999, p. 15.
10   Manrique 1999, p. 11.
11   Clemente Palma was also the main editor of *Variedades* one of the magazines that, after his

thesis, 'El porvenir de las razas en el Perú' (The Future of the Races in Peru), Palma writes:

> Human beings, like all animals, are divided into races or species, super-ior one to the other, be it in the amount or intensity of mental strength that it can bring into activity. Some are more intellectual, others more imaginative, others more gifted with character or will power. Others have greater physical strength. There are thus vigorous, muscular races that made people believe in dynasties of giants; just as there are those puny and weak, which made some believe in pygmy peoples.[12]

In addition to dividing the Peruvian population into inferior (Amerindians, blacks, and Chinese) and superior races (whites/Spaniards), Palma presents stereotypes commonly associated with these groups and that, one must add, were on occasion invoked by Mariátegui. Native Peruvians are described as an 'inferior race', as 'decrepit', and as 'the senility of the oriental race';[13] blacks are presented as 'savage' and 'unable to incorporate themselves to civiliza-tion';[14] and the Chinese are depicted as 'extremely worn down', 'vice-ridden', and 'decrepit'.[15] Palma also has a negative view of the 'mestizo race', despite finding in it 'superiority over the Indian and the black'.[16] Even the Spanish 'race', despite being classified as 'superior', is seen by Palma as 'impractical', 'nervous', 'turbulent and unstable'.[17] Given Peru's 'racial' composition, Palma argues in favour of promoting German immigration to the country with the goal for these to ultimately intermarry with the local population: 'Germans are physically strong: they will strengthen the muscles and blood of our race; they are intellectual, profoundly intellectual: they will solidify the mental life of our race'.[18] This 'whitening', as an answer to this imagined 'racial problem', contradicts the tenets of scientific racialism, which saw racial mixing as neces-sarily degrading whatever positive traits were seen as present in the original

---

      return from Europe in 1923, served as a venue for Mariátegui's articles. To his credit, after 1928, he resisted the pressures of the Leguía government to stop publishing Mariátegui's contributions.

12   Palma 1897 p. 4.
13   Palma 1897, p. 6.
14   Palma 1897, pp. 6–7.
15   Palma 1897, p. 7.
16   Palma 1897, p. 7.
17   Palma 1897, p. 6.
18   Palma 1897, p. 23.

races.[19] Nevertheless, the fact is that Palma and other Peruvian and Latin American racists repeat the racial hierarchy, as well as the stereotypes, proposed by 'positivist racism', which, in fact, was the science of the day.

As the example of Mariátegui proves, the presence – or traces – of racism and racial stereotypes was not limited to conservative intellectuals like Clemente Palma. They are also found, for instance, in the writings of Manuel González Prada, *fons et origo* of Peruvian progressive thought. Anarchist agitator, as well as poet and essayist, González Prada was in his 1904 essay 'Our Indians' among the first Latin Americans to debunk racism and to identify its function in justifying social inequality:

> Once we accept the division of humanity into superior and inferior races, once we acknowledge the superiority of whites and consequently their right to monopolize the running of the planet, what could be more natural than to suppress the Negro in Africa, the redskin in the United States, the Tagalo in the Philippines, the Indian in Peru.[20]

Yet despite this clear awareness of the function played by racist hierarchies in naturalising social inequality, both nationally and internationally, González Prada would, in his unpublished 'Memoranda', write about Chinese immigration to Peru: 'With the Chinese a vicious and decrepit germ was introduced into the national organism'.[21] Needless to say, González Prada shares in the stereotypes associated with Chinese immigrants that, despite political differences, are present in the writings of both Clemente Palma and Mariátegui.[22] Similar biased views of Asian immigrants and Afro-Peruvians were also found among Mariátegui's contemporaries. For instance, Abraham Valdelomar, Mariáte-

---

19   I have dealt with racial mixing, 'whitening', and their relationship to scientific racialism in *Mestizo Nations* (De Castro 2002, pp. 17–8, 60–1). One must add, that, as the son of Ricardo Palma, Clemente had black ancestry. The espousal of whitening, rather than the supposedly 'scientific' belief in the necessary degeneration of mixed individuals, thus responds not only to a national reality of *mestizaje*, but also to a problematic need to justify his family and personal history.

20   González Prada 2003a, p. 182. (González Prada's essay was, however, not published in book form until 1924). Mariátegui makes a similar comment in his *Seven Essays*: 'The concept of inferior races was useful to the white man's West for purposes of expansion and conquest' (Mariátegui 1971, p. 25).

21   González Prada 1975, p. 186.

22   In *Dragons in the Land of the Condor*, Ignacio López-Calvo provides a history of the Chinese immigration to Peru, their oppression and concomitant resistance, and, also, of the local, frequently racist, response to their presence (López-Calvo 2014, pp. 19–44).

gui's friend and original mentor in the *Colónida* literary group, partook of this clichéd view of the Chinese immigrant community as linked with vice, that is, with drugs such as opium, illegal gambling, etc. Several of his *Cuentos chinos* (1918), which imagine an orientalised and luxurious China, repeat a paradoxical and historically incorrect phrase, 'when Confucius smoked opium and gave lessons of morality at the University of Peking'.[23] One can add that Valdelomar's and Mariátegui's association of Chinese immigrants with vice probably reflected their own limited experience with this Asian community. According to José Vasconcelos, who visited the *Colónida* group during their heyday in 1916, Valdelomar, in his role of tourist guide, took the author of *The Cosmic Race* to an opium den. 'There, with ability, Valdelomar took a needle and wet it with the viscous liquid. Then, bringing the droplet to the flame, a shiny sphere formed, and a delicious aroma, penetrating and characteristic, disseminated'.[24] While there is no direct evidence of Mariátegui experimenting with drugs, except in his poetry,[25] as a member of *Colónida*, friend and disciple of Valdelomar, he must have been acquainted with opium dens.[26] What is surprising is that Mariátegui would repeat these stereotypes. After all, if Chinese immigrants participated in vice – that is, made a living satisfying illegal desires on the part of the population – it was surely a consequence of it being one of the few activities fully open to marginalised groups. Mariátegui was aware of the exploitative conditions underpinning Chinese immigration to Peru, since

---

23   Among these stories are: 'La historia del gran consejo de Siké', 'Las visceras del superior', 'El hediondo pozo siniestro', and 'Peligro sentimental' (see Valdelomar 1986). While there are records of the use of opium in Chinese medicine manuals for the treatment of diarrhea, 'the history of opium as an object of recreational consumption begins much later, not until the seventeenth century, when Dutch and English traders were extending their ever growing networks in Southwest Asia into China. They made the drug available by lacing tobacco, a drug substance coming around the globe from the other direction, with opium' (Brook and Wakabayashi 2000, pp. 5–6).

24   Vasconcelos 1955, p. 255.

25   Rouillón, in his unfortunately untrustworthy biography of the Peruvian Marxist, makes no reference to Mariátegui ever using drugs. However, one of Mariátegui's early poems is titled 'Morfina' and there are several references to drugs in his early writings.

26   In fact, Mariátegui, writing about the Chinese theatre's lack of impact on Peruvian culture, notes: 'The Chinese theater, almost exclusively reserved for the nocturnal amusement of people of that nationality, has made no impression on our literature except on the exotic and artificial tastes of the decadents. Valdelomar and the *colónidas* discovered it during their opium sessions, when they were infected by the orientalism of Loti and Farrere' (Mariátegui 1971, p. 279). One must add that Mariátegui was one of the *colónidas*.

he acknowledged that the Peruvian coast received 'contingents of Chinese immigrants who replaced the Negro slaves imported during the viceroyalty and emancipated partly as a result of the transformation from a feudal to a more or less bourgeois economy'.[27] But he never associated their participation in Lima's underworld with their position in the country's social and economic structures, nor did he attempt to gain a deeper knowledge of Chinese immigrants and their culture, which, obviously, was much richer and complex than he presented it.

Despite the fact that the history of Afro-Peruvians can be traced back to the conquest, they were also presented in stereotyped terms. In a fortunately little known early contribution to the 1917 essay on national identity, *Ensayos sobre la psicología del gallinazo* (Essays on the Psychology of the Buzzard), Valdelomar, who ironically had black ancestry, writes that 'The buzzard, in addition to its color, resembles blacks in its characteristic wheezing, in that coughing sound made by old, asthmatic blacks; in their wrinkled and creviced faces'.[28] Moreover, Valdelomar presents black people as not only opposed to white society, which could be interpreted as resistance, but rather as characterised by an anti-social inability for communal or civilised life: '[they] hate all things white; are fond of slaughterhouses where they play with coagulated blood and feed on innards; move in gangs; attack people in groups; lack aesthetic ideals'.[29] As is the case in Argentine writer Esteban Echeverría's short story 'The Slaughterhouse', arguably the founding text of his country's narrative tradition, Valdelomar presents black individuals as morally, socially and intellectually resembling animals more than humans – the whole purpose of the absurd comparison with the buzzard.[30] Moreover, he emphasises the incompatibility of Peru's black population with the national culture: they are presented as unable to live with people of other races. While there is no exact equivalence between Valdelomar's and Mariátegui's stereotypes – *Ensayos sobre la psicología del gallinazo* emphasises the 'rebelliousness' and 'aggressiveness' of black women and men rather than their putative sensuality – both describe Afro-Peruvians in terms that see them as lacking in the 'superior' virtues associated with whiteness, for Valdelomar, or modernity, in the case of Mariátegui.

---

27   Mariátegui 1971, p. 9.
28   Valdelomar 2003, p. 495.
29   Valdelomar 2003, p. 495.
30   In 'The Slaughterhouse', Esteban Echeverría describes Afro-Argentines in terms compatible with Valdelomar's essay. Echeverría thus writes: 'At his [the butcher's] back, following his every movement, romped a gang of children, Negro and mulatto women, offal collectors, whose ugliness matched that of harpies, and huge mastiffs, which sniffed, snarled, and snapped at one another as they darted after booty' (Echeverría 1999, p. 64).

One must, however, note that – without in the least justifying it – the racism of these writers is perfectly consistent with the ideas held throughout the Western world, including academia. Although González Prada is able to buttress his anti-racist arguments with quotations from Emile Durkheim and Jacques Novicow,[31] and, as we will see, Mariátegui finds similar authority in Bukharin and, less convincingly, in Vilfredo Pareto, racism was far from losing its imprimatur as science. Despite the anti-racist writings and, on occasion, activism from these and other thinkers, such as U.S. anthropologist Franz Boaz, the fact is that a hierarchical classification of races was among the cornerstones of the biological and social sciences of the time. In the 1920s, racist ideas were not 'obsolete'. Rather, they were clearly hegemonic throughout the Western world, including Peru, though not for this reason any truer.

2   The Discrediting of Racism

The discrediting of racial considerations within scientific discourse was not the consequence of intellectual debate, but rather of two central tragic historical events that marked the first half of the twentieth century. The first, the Great Depression, 'influenced thinking about social causality',[32] thus helping undermine the automatic ascription of behavioural traits and social results to race. However, the second event, the Nazis' coming to power in Germany and the resulting genocide of Europe's Jewish population, was undeniably the main cause for the loss of prestige of racial considerations in academia. If eugenics had been long deemed a reputable academic discipline, it fell into the dustbin of history as 'even last ditch defenders of eugenics began to recognize the enormity of the Nazi program as it escalated into the murderous horror of the Holocaust'.[33] Egged on by Boaz, in 1938, the American Anthropological Association passed a unanimous resolution denouncing discrimination against 'any people on the ground of racial inferiority, religious affiliation or linguistic heritage'.[34] As Carl Degler notes about this resolution,

> It was an early but not the last indication of the impact Nazi practices had on American scholarly thinking about race and biology in human

31   González Prada 2003a, p. 182.
32   Degler 1991, p. 202.
33   Degler 1991, p. 203.
34   Degler 1991, p. 203.

affairs. That impact can hardly be overestimated in explaining why during the 1930s and 1940s concepts and terms like 'heredity', 'biological influences', and instinct dropped below the horizon in social science.[35]

However, 'the [American Anthropological Association's] resolution recognised races as physical entities'.[36] In other words, while racism is denounced, the existence of races is not denied.

Needless to say, the writings of Mariátegui, who as we know died in April 1930, predate these two events – he only witnessed the very beginnings of the great depression – and thus are prior to the paradigm shift that took place in the social sciences after the horrors of Nazi racism and of the Holocaust became widely known.[37] Despite inconsistencies – exemplified in the racist stereotypes that creep into his arguments – he was primarily an early debunker of racism. Thus one can actually read his work as prefiguring the progressive intellectual consensus that was later exemplified in the United States by the resolution of the American Anthropological Association. Notwithstanding notorious contradictions, Mariátegui, refutes race as a factor determining human behaviour without fully denying its existence as a classificatory concept.

3   Mariátegui as Anti-racist

Mariátegui was a defender of Peru's indigenous populations. However, the manner in which the Peruvian Marxist solves the 'Indian problem' implies, if not quite a Copernican revolution, since González Prada had already sketched the same basic argument in 'Our Indians', at least the development of an approach to racial inequality in Peru that paradoxically leaves considerations

---

35   Degler 1991, p. 203.
36   Degler 1991, p. 203.
37   However, connected to the success of extreme rightwing politics, there has been a creeping return of 'race science', primarily, though not exclusively, in popular venues, during the last few years. As journalist Angela Saini states: 'Whenever ugly politics become dominant, you can be sure that there are intellectuals and pseudointellectuals ready to jump on board. Those with dangerous ideas about "human nature" and even more dangerous prescriptions for our problems are always content to bide their time, knowing that the pendulum will swing their way eventually. Intellectual racism has always existed, and indeed for a chunk of history, it thrived. I believe it is still the toxic little seed at the heart of academia. However dead you might think it is, it needs only a little water, and now it's raining' (Saini 2019, p. 205).

of race behind.[38] Thus for Mariátegui, 'The new approach locates the problem of the Indian in the land tenure system'.[39] He adds:

> We shall try to establish the basically economic character of the problem. First, we protest against the instinctive attempt of the *criollo* or mestizo to reduce it to an exclusively administrative, pedagogical, ethnic, or moral problem in order to avoid at all cost recognizing its economic aspect. Therefore, it would be absurd to accuse us of being romantic or literary. By identifying it as primarily a socio-economic problem, we are taking the least romantic and literary position possible. We are not satisfied to assert the Indian's right to education, culture, progress, love, and heaven. We begin by categorically asserting his right to land.[40]

Whether racial traits exist is, therefore, unimportant. Economic, educational, etc., inequality does not originate in racial essences, which, for instance, could hypothetically lead to behaviour that could hinder the economic success of indigenous populations. Instead, for Mariátegui it is the persistence, even strengthening, of colonial structures during the republic that explains the 'Indian problem'.

Despite this 'thoroughly materialistic claim', as Mariátegui calls it, one finds throughout his works occasional passages that express an essentialist vision of the Peruvian indigenous population. Thus he writes that

> In a race based on customs and an agricultural soul, as with the indigenous race, this dispossession [of land by the large landholders] has constituted a cause for their material and moral dispossession. Land has always been the joy of the Indians. Indians are wed to the land. They feel that life comes from the earth and returns to the earth. For this reason, Indians

---

38   After analysing, as we have seen, the role played by racism in the justification of colonialism and unequal social structures, González Prada notes that 'The Indian problem, more than pedagogical, is economic and social' (González Prada 2003a, p. 193). González Prada concludes the essay as follows: 'In short: the Indian will be saved by his own efforts, not by the humanization of his oppressors. Every white man is, more or less, a Pizarro, a Valverde, or an Areche' (Gónzalez Prada 2003a, p. 194). (Pizarro, as we all know, was the main conquistador of Peru, Valverde, the priest who aided him in the conquest, and Areche, the Spanish colonial functionary responsible for the brutal execution of Tupac Amaru in 1781).

39   Mariátegui 1971, p. 28.

40   Mariátegui 1971, p. 31.

can be indifferent to everything except the possession of the land which by their hand and through their encouragement is religiously fruitful.[41]

Ironically, the materialist argument that the measures needed to improve the standard of living of Peru's indigenous population are the destruction of the exploitative large estates and the redistribution of its land is presented in a language that smacks of essentialism. In this passage, there seems to be a slippage between a view of behaviour determined by culture – 'customs' – and a vitalist language – 'agricultural soul' – that hints at unchanging racial essences. However, Mariátegui's arguments – that positive changes in the material economic reality experienced by indigenous people will result in positive changes in the way they experience their lives and in how they contribute to the material well-being of society – are completely independent from this residual essentialism. That said, here he seems to present views and language that begin to move from the 'positivist racism' hegemonic during his lifetime towards the view represented, for instance, by US anthropologists in 1938 that, while admitting the existence of race as a scientific concept, paradoxically denies any relevance to it. In the slightly later 'The Problem of Races in Latin America' (1929), co-written with Hugo Pesce, Mariátegui presents his 'materialist demand' in a much more consistent manner.[42] Despite following conservative sociologist Vilfredo Pareto in still maintaining that race was 'just one of several factors that determine the shape of the development of a society',[43] Mariátegui stresses the role played by racism in the maintenance of neocolonial structures in Latin America:

Because of the servitude imposed on them since the Spanish conquest, the Indigenous races in Latin America are in a resounding state of backwardness and ignorance. The interests of the exploiting class, first the Spanish and later the *creole*, has invariable tended, under various guises, to explain the condition of Indigenous races on the basis of their inferiority or primitivism. By employing this, that class has not done anything but

---

41 Mariátegui 2011, p. 140.

42 Marc Becker, in a useful study that analyses the political and social contexts of the reception of 'The Problem of Race in Latin America', notes that 'the first part of the paper, "Considering the Issue", was written by Mariátegui, with some significant editorial contributions by Pesce in the rest of the essay' (Becker 2002, p. 203). One must note that the quotations in this chapter from 'The Problem of Race in Latin America' come from the sections written by Mariátegui.

43 Mariátegui 2011, p. 307.

reproduce the reasoning of the white race on the issue of the treatment and care of the colonial peoples in the national debate on this issue.[44]

Putative racial difference has no hold in this argumentation. If Spaniards or any other European group had been placed under servitude for centuries, they too would be backward and ignorant. Change in the material situation of the indigenous population is the necessary prerequisite for the elimination of a discrimination that ultimately underpins neocolonial social structures. Moreover, racism – 'the reasoning of the white race on the issue of the treatment and care of the colonial peoples' – plays a role in the continuance of indigenous 'servitude'.

Even his stereotyped view of Afro-Peruvians, though mistaken, was, perhaps contradictorily, associated with a materialist view of the history of this social group. Thus, in his *Seven Essays*, Mariátegui noted:

> The colonizer was not guilty of having brought an inferior race – this was the customary reproach of sociologists of fifty years ago – but of having brought slaves. Slavery was doomed to fail, both as a means of economic exploitation and organization of the colony and as a reinforcement of a regime based only on conquest and force.[45]

Afro-Peruvians' 'negative racial' traits would thus implicitly be the consequence of a history of exploitation and an economic system that brought them as slaves. Later, in the text, he expands on this putative affective affinity between Afro-Peruvians and the neocolonial culture that ideologically justified the country's neocolonial structures:

> The Spaniard imported the Negro when he realized that he could neither supplant nor assimilate the Indian. The slave came to Peru to serve the colonizing ambitions of Spain. The Negro race is one of the human alluvia deposited on the coast by Spain, one of the thin, weak strata of sediment that formed in the lowlands of Peru during the viceroyalty and the early period of the republic; and throughout this cycle, circumstances have conspired to maintain its solidarity with the colony.[46]

On the same page, he expounds on these vague 'circumstances':

---

44   Mariátegui 2011, p. 307.
45   Mariátegui 1971, p. 38.
46   Mariátegui 1971, p. 273.

> Colonial society made blacks into servants ... And thus is born a subordination, which has its first reason in the original importation of slaves and from which black individuals ... are only redeemed by economic and spiritual evolution that, transforming them into workers, progressively cancels and extirpates slavery's spiritual inheritance.[47]

Despite the presence of racist stereotypes in Mariátegui's description, he presents material reasons for his mistaken association of Peruvians of African descent with colonial values. In *Seven Essays* he concludes his discussion of Afro-Peruvians by arguing that 'Only socialism can awaken in him a class consciousness that will lead him to a definitive rupture with the last remnants of his colonial spirit'.[48] In his 'Problem of Races in Latin America', Mariátegui adds that 'Industry, factories, and unions redeem blacks from this domesticity'.[49] Instead of racial traits set in hereditary stone, there is a belief in the central influence of material reality on behaviour and psychological make-up. If Afro-Peruvians are incorrectly, given the history of slave rebellions, deemed by Mariátegui to be wedded to neocolonial mores, it is due to the experience of slavery and its imprint on their culture. Once new material realities – such as their participation in modern industry – become central to the experiences of Afro-Peruvian individuals and communities, their culture and behaviour will change in response.

Mariátegui's description of Asians, both in Peru and China, is also much more complex than what his critics generally acknowledge. Even the negative description of Chinese immigrants linked to vice (quoted above) ends on a somewhat surprising positive note:

> Only since the Nationalist movement, which has had wide repercussions among the expatriate Chinese of this continent, has the Chinese colony shown signs of an active interest in culture and progress.[50]

---

47   Mariátegui 2007, p. 208. I have provided my own translation. The English version renders the passage as: 'Colonial society turned the Negro into a domestic servant, very seldom into an artisan or worker ... Thus the very origin of slave importation created a subordination from which the Negro ... can be redeemed only through a social and economic revolution that will turn them into workers and thereby gradually extirpate their slave mentality' (Mariátegui 1971, p. 273). Mariátegui uses evolution ('evolución social y económica') not revolution in the Spanish original (Mariátegui 2007, p. 282).

48   Mariátegui 1971, p. 273.

49   Mariátegui 2011, p. 311.

50   Mariátegui 1971, p. 279.

Again, while one must object to Mariátegui's blindness to the myriad activities of the Chinese community in Peru, he now sees them as rapidly evolving in a progressive cultural and political direction.

The Peruvian Marxist identifies positive social developments not only in the Peruvian Chinese community, but also in that of Asia. The Nationalist movement originated in China, where it had its fullest practical manifestation. Thus the political ferment in early twentieth-century Asia, and, in particular, the rise of nationalist and progressive politics in Kuomintang China occupies a central, though frequently ignored, position in Mariátegui's thought. Current debunkers of Mariátegui would probably be surprised by the following passage (partly quoted above):

> The assumption that the Indian problem is ethnic is sustained by the most outmoded repertory of imperialist ideas. The concept of inferior races was useful to the white man's West for purposes of expansion and conquest. To expect that the Indian will be emancipated through a steady crossing of the aboriginal race with white immigrants is an anti-sociological naiveté that could only occur to the primitive mentality of an importer of merino sheep. The people of Asia, who are in no way superior to the Indians, have not needed any transfusion of European blood in order to assimilate the most dynamic and creative aspects of Western culture. The degeneration of the Peruvian Indian is a cheap invention of sophists who serve feudal interests.[51]

Thus Asia is the example that underlies Mariátegui's most characteristic political proposals. The nationalist awakening of Asia in the early twentieth century served as the basis for his belief in the revolutionary potential of the Peruvian indigenous population. Precisely because Mariátegui believed in the 'vicious' and 'decrepit' character of traditional Chinese culture, he could imagine a modernising potential for Peru's indigenous populations and their traditions. If China could evolve from a retrograde past to a vibrantly progressive present, so could Peru. In both cases, traditional cultures could become modern.

Not only does China serve as an example for Peru, so does Japan. In his 'Problem of Race in Latin America', he notes:

> Some time ago the Japanese showed the ease with which peoples of races and traditions distinct from that of Europe took to Western science and

---

51   Mariátegui 1971, p. 279.

adapted to the use of its productive techniques. In the mines and factories of the Peruvian highlands, the Indian peasant confirms this experience.[52]

Asian modernisation is presented as conclusive proof of the possibilities present in Indigenous population and culture.[53] As he notes in his *Seven Essays*:

> The experience of the Orient – in Japan, Turkey, and China itself – has proved to us that even after a long period of collapse, an autochthonous society can rapidly find its own way to modern civilization and translate into its own tongue the lessons of the West.[54]

The solution to the putative 'degeneration' of Asian and Peruvian populations and cultures is not 'whitening', as it was for the positivist generation of 1900, but, instead, the translation of modernity into local cultural terms. Despite the presence of racial clichés, there is an explicit rejection of racial hierarchies in *Seven Essays*. In fact, after the passage quoted above that presents stereotypes of Peru's Asian and black populations, Mariátegui concludes:

> The ethnic problem that has occupied the attention of untrained sociologists and ignorant analysts is altogether fictitious. It becomes disproportionately important to those who, abiding by the idea cherished by European civilization at its peak (and already discarded by that same civilization, which in its decline favors a relativist concept of history), attribute the achievements of Western society to the superiority of the white race.[55]

Additionally, a few lines below, the Peruvian Marxist refers derogatively to scientific racism as 'implausible zootechnical reasoning',[56] obviously parody-

---

52 Mariátegui 2011, p. 311.

53 However, the breakdown of the Kuomingtan nationalist front would lead Mariátegui, by 1929, to become sceptical regarding China as a political example: 'The full dimension of the betrayal of the Chinese bourgeoisie and the failure of the Kuomintang were not yet known. A knowledge of capitalism, and not just for reasons of social justice and doctrine, demonstrated how little one could trust, even in countries like China, the revolutionary nationalist sentiment of the bourgeoisie' (Mariátegui 2011, p. 267).

54 Mariátegui 1971, p. 284.

55 Mariátegui 1971, p. 281.

56 Mariátegui 2007, p. 290. The English-language version mistranslates 'inverosímiles razonamientos zootécnicos' as 'improbable zoological reasonings' (Mariátegui 1971, p. 281).

ing the scientific claims of racist ideas, which in reality were still hegemonic throughout Western culture. We are here faced with the main question raised by Mariátegui's writings on race. If on the one hand, in a very un-Marxist manner, the Peruvian thinker tends to accept the most absurd colonial racial stereotypes, on the other, in a manner much more congruent with the core of his analyses, he rejects race as an explanatory or causal factor for any social behaviour. (One could very well argue, moreover, that Karl Marx's occasional racist comments were, paradoxically, also un-Marxist. After all, the privileging of race as the central factor in the determination of actual social results contradicts the centrality of the economy and the mode of production, that is the main analytical innovation found in *The Communist Manifesto, Capital*, and Marx's other major works).

It would seem to be an insolvable contradiction, but one just has to read Mariátegui with some care to find an explanation that, without erasing the racist splotches in his work, helps us understand the main tendencies in his thought. Mariátegui concludes the previously cited passage by arguing: 'But all the relativism of the moment cannot abolish inferiority in culture'.[57] In other words, while he ultimately rejects race as a valid factor in the classification of human beings into inferior and superior groups, Mariátegui accepts culture as a valid criterion for establishing hierarchies among human societies. Thus, for the Peruvian Marxist, the putative flaws he had identified among Asian and black populations do not originate in hereditary racial traits, but rather in cultural characteristics acquired by these same groups through their material history. Rather than a collection of unchanging traits, culture is seen as subject to change and evolution, as evidenced in his remarks about China and Japan, in his belief in the modernising potential of indigenous populations and their institutions, as well as his view of Afro-Peruvians as evolving positively as they become integrated into factories, labour unions, and other modern institutions. What ultimately determines Mariátegui's evaluation of a specific human group is its culture's compatibility or not with modernity, and especially what for him seemed its culmination: socialism.

4   Conclusion

There is no question that Mariátegui's writings are marred by racist commonplaces that he, as an iconoclastic and revolutionary thinker, should have questioned. Nevertheless, there is, at the same time, a clear rejection of racial clas-

---

57   Mariátegui 1971, p. 289.

sifications, even as culture, seen as changing and changeable, is presented as a valid criterion for the punctual evaluation of human groups. However, there is a clear slippage between Mariátegui's use of race and the notion of culture. The late Aníbal Quijano, in his illuminating though problematic analysis of racial categories in Mariátegui's writings, 'Raza, etnia y nación en Mariátegui', notes:

> Race would be a bi-dimensional category. It refers at the same time to the physical characteristics and to the stage in civilizational development. And, though there is no indication regarding both dimensions of the category, the latter one, in particular, is linked to the relations of production.[58]

In a parallel manner, Marc Becker has argued that 'what Mariátegui understood as "race" in the 1920s, most people would see as "ethnicity" today'.[59] This is not the place to note the problematic nature of the concept of 'ethnicity', defined as 'of or relating to large groups of people classed according to common racial, national, tribal, religious, linguistic, or cultural origin or background' (m-w.com). Instead, what I find important in both Quijano's and Becker's comments is the in-between-ness of the concept of race in Mariátegui as being both linked to 'physical characteristics' and to culture. I would, however, add, that given Mariátegui's identification of race as a nominal marker for culture, the priority of culture over biology is the most plausible interpretation of the Peruvian Marxist's problematic comments on race. Moreover, cultural hierarchies in Mariátegui are not based on the automatic identification of one race or culture, be this regional or national, as an unquestioned or unquestionable model: not the United States, as the new imperial power, described as 'plutocratic, imperialist';[60] Europe, which in the 1920s experienced the growth of fascism; nor even Russia, despite the centrality of its Revolution for the Peruvian's thought and life. On the contrary, as he said in a famous passage: 'We certainly do not want Socialism in Latin America to be a copy or imitation. It should be a heroic creation. We have to give life to Indo American socialism with our own reality, in our own language'.[61] For Mariátegui, modernisation if it is to be successful, is ultimately the result of a translational process. And Asia, which has 'admirably assimilated Western culture' – assimilated, not reproduced, copied,

---

58   Quijano 1993, p. 184.
59   Becker 2006, p. 452.
60   Mariátegui 2011, p. 129. This quotation comes from 'Anniversary and Balance Sheet', his 1928 editorial for *Amauta*.
61   Mariátegui 2011, p. 130.

or mimicked – serves in his writings as example and proof of the historic viability of his translational view of cultural modernisation. While a radical cultural relativist or an anti-Western position – postures almost always more theoretical than practical among its proponents – would see in this centrality of modernisation the return of Hegelian Eurocentrism, the fact is that the prioritisation of modernity is implicit in any version of alternative modernisation. Even if Mariátegui clearly rejects the erasure of a Peruvian culture inclusive of (if not based on) its indigenous heritage, the fact is that indigenous and national traditions are seen as needing to assimilate and translate modernity.

Mariátegui's proposals are at their best not based on any notion of inherited racial traits. For instance, his analysis of land distribution and its relationship to the so-called Indian problem do not depend on racial stereotypes, in this case positive, that he occasionally repeats. However, Mariátegui's hesitations and contradictions manifest the transitional character of his writings on race. While Mariátegui, in a gesture more prophetic than descriptive, presents scientific racialism already as obsolete, in reality it would be fully discredited only after World War II. It is thus possible to see in his writings an incomplete, but still significant, attempt at leaving scientific racialism behind and replacing it with a vision of human behaviour as founded on a materialist version of culture. Without denying Mariátegui's contradictions, Marisol de la Cadena lucidly notes:

> In the 1920s, the period of high racial thought, the leftist thinker José Carlos Mariátegui joined the trend to define race in cultural terms and thus countered dominant European inclinations to racial pessimism.[62]

Even the 1938 declaration of the American Anthropological Association, one of the key moments in the debunking of racialism in the United States, does not fully abandon race as a classificatory concept. Nevertheless, Mariátegui still maintains ethno-cultural hierarchies, even if they are at their core delinked from hereditary racial considerations. One can easily imagine Mariátegui being amazed at a definition of racism separate from race, and at being accused of being a racist despite his explicit denunciations of racism. Nevertheless, contemporary discrimination, unlike that of the 1920s, often shies from explicit mention of race, substituting these with cultural considerations. For instance, Samuel Huntington's notorious attack on Latino and Latina immigrants stressed their inassimilability into the US cultural mainstream on cultural

---

62   De la Cadena 2000, p. 312.

rather than racial grounds.[63] This contemporary cultural racism, however, presents 'the implication that cultural differences are more or less immutable'.[64] A position that is the opposite of Mariátegui's ultimately materialist view on cultural malleability and translation.

Underlying the inability to understand Mariátegui's achievements, as well as to situate them and his flaws historically, is also the belief that racism is not only the main, but also the exclusive source of discrimination and inequality. The origin of this hypostatisation of race is to be found in US society and academia. Teresa Carrillo, who has been active in Mexicana/Chicana collaborations, has noted: 'Chicanas and Latinas in the United States have focused on questions of race and ethnicity while Mexicanas have focused on class issues and survival'.[65] Obviously, there is insight and blindness present in both privileging class over race and vice-versa. Moreover, the stress on race and ethnicity over class responds to the specific history of the United States, where traditionally racial discrimination has not only significantly overlapped with class exploitation – also a trait of Latin American racial stratifications – but, in fact, also frequently made it impossible for individuals to escape from discrimination regardless of their economic position or personal achievement.

This justified concern with cross-class racism has also geographically trickled down to Latin American thinkers, many of long presence in U.S. academia. The last works of Quijano, who, in addition to being an expert on the author of *Seven Essays*, was an important member of the Mariátegui tradition (to use Hosam Aboul-Ela's phrase), can serve as an example of this recent privileging of race over class among many Latin American intellectuals. His concept of the 'coloniality of power' originally developed in 'Raza, etnia y nación en Mariátegui', an analysis of his predecessor's ideas, notes the foundational role of the colonial experience, and the international economic divisions it created, on the development of both capitalism and racism:

The process of constitution of the structure of world power did not consist only in the establishment of new social material relations. It also implied, and at the same time, the formation of new social intersubjective

---

63 One among the many passages from Huntington's essay that presents his belief in Latinos and Latinas, in particular those of Mexican origin, as cultural threats: 'As their numbers increase, Mexican Americans feel increasingly comfortable with their own culture and often contemptuous of American culture. They demand recognition of their culture and the historic Mexican identity of the U.S. Southwest. They increasingly call attention to and celebrate their Hispanic and Mexican past' (Huntington 2004, pp. 254–5).

64 Marger 2015, p. 25.

65 Carrillo 2001, p. 394.

relations. Both dimensions of historical movement, in their correspondences and contradictions, were the basis of a new type of colonial power and, in the long run, of a new society and a new culture.[66]

Quijano here acknowledges the importance of 'social material relations', thus evidencing a (quasi-)Marxist concern with the economic and material underpinning of social evolution. However, by the end of the essay, the Peruvian sociologist is exclusively concerned with ideas about race:

> All of this points to the necessity of revisiting these questions [regarding racism], bringing to light the origin and character that still dominate the thought of peoples whose origin is in the violence of colonial domination and, because of this, have identity problems. In such questions still seem to reside the keys for Latin America.[67]

The point I am trying to make is not that racism should not be a central concern for scholars or citizens from Latin America or, for that matter, from anywhere else. Nowadays one cannot avoid coming face to face with the breakdown of what had once seemed a growing consensus, no matter how fragile or hypocritical, about the need for equal treatment, regardless of race or gender. Instead, I am noting the manner in which race is frequently reified to the exclusion of other considerations. It is symptomatic that Quijano concludes that the key questions faced by Latin America within the context of globalisation are not those of 'new social material relations' – that is, unequal economic exchanges, exploitation, etc. – but are rather primarily linked to the 'intersubjective' and even mental: the 'thought of peoples'.

As we have seen, underlying this privileging of race as the overriding political issue are concrete historical events that have marked the last thirty years. After the failure of existing socialism, the struggle against racial (and gender and sexual orientation) discrimination has replaced that against economic and social inequality as the goal of progressive politics. Mariátegui's priorities – equality, cultural and technological modernisation – are not those of most of the left today. However, there are signs, such as the rise of democratic socialist movements throughout the Western world, including, no matter how timidly, in Peru, that may indicate a growing awareness of the social need to focus again

---

66   Quijano 1993, p. 167.
67   Quijano 1993, p. 187.

on 'social material relations', such as an ever deepening economic inequality;[68] obviously without losing sight of the importance of resisting and eradicating the new rise in racist politics and politicians. But the sad reality is that as of the time of writing – 2019 – these tendencies are still emergent, at best. Be that as it may, the presence of ethno-cultural hierarchies in Mariátegui's work leads many to identify his views with those of his conservative positivist predecessors and antagonists.

However, this justified stress on the elimination of hierarchy based on prejudice frequently is often linked to a complete lack of interest in the change of social structures or the elimination of our growing economic stratification, which may, in part, underlie the current social fragmentation that has contributed to the return of virulent forms of racism. Mariátegui's materialist stress on the socio-economic dimension of the struggle against discrimination is as relevant today as it was in 1920s Peru. The presence of racist stereotypes in Mariátegui's work reminds us of the difficulty of going beyond shared cultural commonplaces, even in the case of a brilliant thinker. Many of the attacks on the author of *Seven Essays*, often written with the intention of debunking Mariátegui and through him any alternative to the current political and social consensus, serve as examples of the manner in which much of our contemporary thought is bound by the economic individualism that still constitutes the horizon of our time.

---

68   In the Peruvian elections of 2016, Verónika Mendoza, the candidate of the socialist *Frente Amplio*, ended third, with 18.8 percent of the votes. See Dosek and Paredes 2016.

CHAPTER 5

Mariátegui's Cosmopolitan Nationalism

In addition to his role as 'the first Latin American Marxist', it has become commonplace to identify José Carlos Mariátegui with regional or Peruvian nationalism. Mariátegui, as the title of Harry Vanden's study – *National Marxism in Latin America* – makes clear, would be a proponent of 'national Marxism': 'the first ... to successfully weave nationalism and Marxism into a cogent intellectual system'.[1] Alberto Flores Galindo also notes that the key contribution of Mariátegui to Latin American thought was 'the articulation between Marxism and nation, which, in other words, means the confluence between a phenomenon developed initially within the West and a cultural tradition many times different and perhaps incompatible with Europe'.[2] Similarly, Oscar Terán argues that 'especially' his 'fusion of his adherence to Marxism with the thematizing of the problem of the nation ... [marks] his difference and gives it specificity ... within the field of Marxism'.[3] Thus, in his work, Marxism would have been 'nationalised' and, therefore, made useful for anti-colonial and/or anti-imperial activity. Mariátegui's theoretical insistence on 'Peruvian reality', that is, on the need to take into account local cultural and social specificity as part of any attempt at interpretation, is implicit in the title of his best-known work, *Seven Interpretive Essays on Peruvian Reality*. But, in addition to correcting European Marxism's frequent disregard for local difference, Mariátegui also took into account the potential role of nationalism in political action. In his important 1925 essay 'Nacionalismo y vanguardismo' (Nationalism and Vanguardism), he writes:

> In no country of the world is socialism an anti-national movement. It may, perhaps, seem so in empires. In England, France, in the United States, etc., revolutionaries denounce and combat the imperialism of their own governments. But the idea of socialism plays a changed role in countries politically or economically colonial. Due to circumstance, in those countries, socialism acquires, without rejection of any of its principles, a nationalist attitude.[4]

1　Vanden 1986, p. 5.
2　Flores Galindo 1980, p. 11.
3　Terán 1985, p. 11.
4　Mariátegui 1981d, pp. 74–5.

Mariátegui's belief in this necessary taking into account of national difference at the level of theoretical analysis would probably have been seconded by Marx, whose work is buttressed by innumerable references to historical, legal, and social facts of Britain and elsewhere. However, the affective weaving of socialism and nationalism, particularly in colonial countries, would have surprised Marx and Engels, who famously claimed that the 'working men have no country'.[5]

In so doing, the Peruvian foreshadowed in the 1920s the uses to be made of Marxist ideas throughout Africa, Asia, and even Latin America during the anti-colonial struggles of the second half of the twentieth century. Mariátegui formulated the fusion of Marxism and anti-colonial agitation that would fuel independence movements throughout Asia and Africa during the following decades. He recognised the agglutinative power of nationalism even in – or perhaps more accurately especially in – colonial and neocolonial societies. He is arguably the first anti-colonial and anti-imperial Marxist theorist writing from the periphery. The author of *Seven Essays* is thus the first in the chain of 'Third World' and Latin American revolutionaries that would link socialism and anti-imperial struggle that stretches from Ho Chi Ming, Patrice Lumumba, Ernesto Che Guevara, Amilcar Cabral, and Salvador Allende to the Sandinistas and, perhaps, to the 'Pink Tide'.

But, in addition to these two presences of the 'nation' in his thought – as a lens that helps shape and reshape theoretical analysis – and as an affective buttress to radical, anti-colonial, and anti-imperial activity – Mariátegui found in 'national' local traditions possible sources for socialist modernisation. Following the lead of other Peruvian thinkers, such as Hildebrando Castro Pozo, Mariátegui identified in the indigenous community an institutional mediator for Peruvian socialism.[6] He noted 'the vitality of indigenous communism which invariably reacts by modifying its forms of cooperation and association'.[7] The 'Programmatic Principles of the Socialist Party', the political party he founded, argue that 'Socialism finds the same elements of a solution to the land problem in the livelihoods of communities'.[8] Rather than a hindrance, the nation –

---

5 Marx and Engels 2012, p. 58.

6 Mariátegui refers explicitly to Castro Pozo's *Nuestra comunidad indígena* (1924) – praising it for its socialist perspective and factual research – as a valuable source of information on the indigenous community (Mariátegui 1971, pp. 56–61).

7 Mariátegui 1971, p. 57. I have corrected Urquidi's translation. She mistranslates 'comunismo indígena' as 'indigenous community'. The Spanish original reads: 'la vitalidad del comunismo indígena que impulse invariablemente a los aborígenes a variadas formas de cooperación y asociación' (Mariátegui 2007, p. 67).

8 [Socialist Party] 2011, p. 239.

here national traditions, which, in the case of Peru, Mariátegui understood as primarily indigenous – make socialist modernisation possible.[9]

Undeniably, Mariátegui's blending of Marxism with Peruvian and Latin American traditions is what has made him such an important figure in the region's intellectual history. However, as Vanden, Flores Galindo, and Terán all note, Mariátegui's passion for local reality is noteworthy precisely because it is woven with a parallel preoccupation with European reality and culture.[10] Not only was the Peruvian thinker influenced by Marxism – an intellectual tradition not born in Peru or Latin America – but he freely borrowed from other currents of thoughts and thinkers of the time, including Nietzsche, Croce, Sorel, Bergson, Unamuno and Freud. He is thus always distant from any uncritical espousal or celebration of local cultural traits, as well as from the facile imitativeness that so often passes for cosmopolitanism. Nevertheless, clichéd readings of Mariátegui see in him a one-dimensional proponent of *indigenismo*, a nationalist opposed to any concern with the latest trends in world culture.[11]

---

9   As critics have noted, Mariátegui here is rediscovering on his own the then little known Marxist proposition that, in some cases, agricultural communes could become the basis for modern socialism. This was best expressed by Marx in his letter to the Russian Social Revolutionary Vera Zasulich: 'The analysis in *Capital* therefore provides no reasons either for or against the vitality of the Russian commune. But the special study I have made of it, including a search for original source material, has convinced me that the commune is the fulcrum for social regeneration in Russia. But in order that it might function as such, the harmful influences assailing it on all sides must first be eliminated, and it must then be assured the normal conditions for spontaneous development' (Marx 1975, pp. 71–2). On this aspect of Mariátegui's thought, see Quijano's introduction to *7 ensayos* (Quijano 2007a, pp. LXXXIV–LXXVI).

10 Flores Galindo, for instance, writes about a dichotomy in Mariátegui between the 'national and the international' (Flores Galindo 1980, p. 12). Vanden, for example, notes the importance of 'several individual Italians', such as Benedetto Croce, Antonio Gramsci, and Piero Gobetti, and, more generally, the Italian political and cultural context at the time Mariátegui stayed in the country (Vanden 1986, pp. 11–14). Terán makes the point that Mariátegui's European experience is processed through 'a specific gaze, a specific code' developed in Peru (Terán 1985, p. 53). Also see Terán 1985, pp. 55–64. I have dealt with some of these influences above in 'José Carlos Mariátegui: The Making of a Revolutionary in the Aristocratic Republic'.

11 While González may go too far in the direction of seeing in Mariátegui a post-national thinker, he is correct when he notes: 'For some writers, his detailed analysis of his own society, and in particular of the "Indian problem", makes him a "national Marxist". That seems to me to misunderstand his method and his Marxism, which is internationalist in its very essence. Throughout his writing he emphasizes the dialectics of the national and the international, whose specific dimensions are interdependent' (González 2019, p. 10).

Patricia D'Allemand makes an important point regarding this simplistic vision of Mariátegui as exclusively linked to national or other local realities and traditions:

> The selective treatment of Mariátegui's critical project can be understood to a certain extent in terms of the nationalist and anti-imperialist positions that have prevailed within intellectual production of the Latin American Left from the 1960s onwards. Within the region's cultural criticism, these positions have led to a privileging of literatures articulated to local traditional cultures, in opposition to and in preference to urban literatures which are a part of the internationalized circuits of culture. This bi-polarization of Latin American literature is actually a perspective more typical of contemporary criticism than of Mariátegui's proposals.[12]

Given the centrality of the anti-colonial and anti-imperialist push of the 1960s – represented by the Cuban Revolution and its (mostly) failed offshoots – in the intellectual configuration of the region's left, it is understandable that the revival of interest in Mariátegui during that decade and during the early 1970s foregrounded issues related to the nation, and, more generally, cultural identity, such as his revaluing of indigenous cultures and his promotion of *indigenista* and other literatures centered on local traditions.

Nevertheless, Mariátegui's dual interest in Peru and the world has frequently been simplified into a coarse nationalism or, at best, a unilateral defence of *indigenismo*, not only by those willing to disparage his critical legacy, but, on occasion, also by his admirers. The importance given by Mariátegui to his country's history and traditions has become caricaturised into a monolithic and unilateral concern with local Peruvian or Latin American issues. For instance, Timothy Brennan, precisely at the same moment he praises Mariátegui's notion of the nation as 'fiction', describes him as 'a publicist and organiser of Peru's Quechua-speaking minority in the 1920s'.[13] Doris Sommer, while presenting him as a positive ideological counterpoint to 'the increasingly conservative Mario Vargas Llosa', calls him 'chief ideologue ... for the indigenized Marxism that has ... marked left-wing Peruvian politics'.[14] This exclusive identification of Mariátegui with indigenous and local cultures, seen as the basis of national or regional identity and society, has also, on occasion, found its way into the

---

12   D'Allemand 2000, p. 81.
13   Brennan 1990, p. 49.
14   Sommer 1996, p. 93.

region's media. For instance, in Walter Salles's well-known film *The Motorcycle Diaries* (2004), the filmic Che Guevara is only able to make sense of his experiences with original peoples and cultures in Chile and Peru after being introduced to Mariátegui's work by Hugo Pesce.[15]

One must remember that Mariátegui's stress on the need to take into account local reality and his belief in the progressive potential of (some) local traditions, stood at the antipodes from Soviet Communism's attempt at imposing an 'only thought' applicable to all circumstances and locations. However, the cosmopolitan, global, and transnational aspects of Mariátegui are at least as central to an understanding of his ideas as those related to local or national reality. This chapter, therefore, attempts to redress the imbalance often found in studies of Mariátegui's writings.

1   **One World Not Three (or Two)**

In an article from 1924 titled 'Feminist Demands', Mariátegui wrote about the then relatively new, from a Peruvian perspective, issue of women's rights and feminism.[16] Women's suffrage had already been achieved in New Zealand (1893), Norway (1913), Canada (1918), United States (1919), and would soon be won in Uruguay (1927) and Brazil (1932), but in Peru women would only gain this right as late as 1955. Addressing the 'proponents of nationalism, of extremism' who, as with socialism, see 'feminism as another foreign idea ... injected into the Peruvian mind'. Mariátegui noted:

> We must not see feminism as an exotic idea, a foreign idea. We must see it simply as a human idea. It is an idea that is characteristic of a civilization and peculiar to an era. And thus it is an idea with citizen rights in Peru, as in any other segment of the civilized world.[17]

---

15   I deal with this encounter below in the chapter 'Mariátegui and Che: Reflections on and around Walter Salles's *The Motorcycle Diaries*'.

16   Although there had been an active women's cultural movement in nineteenth century Peru, suffrage had not been among its priorities. As historian Sara Beatriz Guardia notes about one of its most important members, novelist Mercedes Cabello de Carbonera, while she 'opposed in all her writings the passivity and inactivity to which she [woman] was condemned', 'nevertheless, she [Cabello de Carbonera] did not consider the conquest of her political rights necessary, because she did not assign to politics an ethical quality that privileged "moral force and the laws of justice and humanity" over "the brute force and power of weapons"' (Guardia 2017).

17   Mariátegui 2011, p. 367.

While the quotation includes the non-pc – as in politically correct and post-colonial – notion of 'civilized world', the point Mariátegui makes here is central to his writings: capitalist modernity has erased the distinction between what has been called 'civilisation' and 'non-civilisation', at least in the areas it has incorporated, such as Latin America. As important as they are, local differences do not eradicate a basic civilisational commonality rooted in the participation in global capitalism, nor should they be used as justification for the rejection of progressive cultural change. In his 'The World Crisis and the Peruvian Proletariat', given as a public lecture soon after his arrival to Lima from Europe in 1923, he had noted:

> capitalist civilization has internationalized the life of humanity; it has created the material connections among all people that establish an inevitable solidarity among them. Internationalism is not only an idea, it is a historical reality. Progress makes interests, ideas customs, the people's regimes unify and merge.[18]

Mariátegui can thus be seen as following in the footsteps of Marx and Engels as seeing the world as reshaped by what today we call globalisation. In the words of *The Communist Manifesto*: 'In place of the old local and national seclusion and self-sufficiency, we have intercourse in every direction, universal interdependence of nations'.[19] For Mariátegui in 1923, as for Marx and Engels in 1848, globalisation has created one world out of multiple cultures and societies. He fully shares in the positive interpretation of what today we call globalisation proposed by the founders of Marxism. However, as Marx and Engels do in other passages of the *Manifesto*, the Peruvian also looks at globalisation from below. He emphasises the connections between this process of internationalisation and the possibilities of an ever-growing solidarity among the oppressed. In 'Feminist Demands', he notes that 'progress' – the growth and development of capitalism – has led women, just as men, to have to enter the workplace both in factories and in other roles ancillary to production. Thus there is a need for women to have 'the same rights and obligations as men' since they perform 'new forms of intellectual and manual labor'.[20] For him, 'human ideas' are not rooted in romantic essentialism but in the material reality of economic and social evolution. Mariátegui thus sees in 'the human' – understood here not as necessarily European but instead as the result of a history of international

---

18   Mariátegui 2011, p. 296.
19   Marx and Engels 2012, p. 39.
20   Mariátegui 2011, p. 367.

economic, social, and cultural progress – as overriding any nationalist or local cultural argument against 'feminist demands'. The differing patriarchal character of Peruvian cultures – whether Hispanic or indigenous – is for the author of *Seven Essays* not a valid reason to object to equal rights for women. Local difference is trumped by global progress.

Thus Mariátegui, who identified local potential for socialist modernisation, is equally adamant at finding in globalised trends possibilities for human emancipation.

2   Making Peru Peruvian

'The World Crisis and the Peruvian Proletariat' has been seen as belonging to a first phase of Mariátegui's Marxist period that would predate a putative discovery of the vitality of Peru's Indigenous population and cultures. Quoting from 'Lo nacional y lo exótico' (What is National and What is Exotic). published on 28 November 1924, Terán argues about Mariátegui:

> If in ... 1924 he still claimed that the Spanish conquest had destroyed the Inca culture and, therefore, the 'only Peruvianness that had existed' ... when he discovers the buried Peru exhibited by indigenismo, he will propose a return, that is a jump into the future, a restoration that is actually a revolution.[21]

Mariátegui, who had just arrived from Italy, had not yet found in indigenous cultures the resources that made it possible to imagine a Peruvian socialism and modernization.

Until the publication of *Seven Essays*, Mariátegui had been best-known as a commentator on European art and politics. His first published book, *La escena contemporánea* (The Contemporary Scene, 1925), presents a textual book-long analogue to the ideas about globalisation analysed above. Thus, in addition to discussing European politics – fascism, liberal democracy, European social democracy, and the Russian Revolution – Mariátegui studies contemporary cultural trends: not only those from Europe, such as surrealism and futurism, but also the literary and political scene in Asia, including analyses of Mahatma Gandhi and Rabindranath Tagore.[22] In September 1925, Mariátegui began writ-

---

21   Terán 1996, p. 22.

22   According to Fernanda Beigel *La escena contemporánea* 'transcended within vast intellectual sectors of Latin America and gave life to Editorial Minerva' (Beigel 2006, p. 176). (Editorial Minerva was the publishing house founded by Mariátegui). However, as the

ing the column 'Peruanicemos al Perú' [Let's Peruvianise Peru]. According to Fernanda Beigel, 'This column in the magazine *Mundial* represents "the process of Peruvianization" of Mariátegui's project'.[23] Now not only was Mariátegui writing regularly on national topics, but phrases, passages, and ideas first expressed in 'Peruanicemos al Perú' would ultimately find their way into his *Seven Essays*. However, in an article significantly titled 'Peru's Principal Problem', published on 9 December 1924,[24] that is, only eleven days after 'Lo nacional y lo éxotico', and before he took over the column 'Peruanicemos al Perú', Mariátegui had already made clear the centrality that the 'Indian problem' had acquired in this thinking regarding Peruvian nationality. After noting that 'while the viceroyalty was a medieval and foreign regime, the republic is formally a Peruvian and liberal regime', the Peruvian Marxist went on to note that the exclusion and exploitation of the indigenous population continued despite the republic's 'responsibility to raise the status of the Indian'.[25] The republic was not only premised on the marginalisation of Peru's original people, but also actually built on their exploitation.[26] The consequence of this despoiling of Peru's indigenous population was not only an act of injustice but actually the dooming of the country's prospect as a nation:

> By postponing the solution of the Indian problem, the republic has postponed the realization of its dreams of progress. A policy that is truly national in scope cannot dispense with the Indian. The Indian is the foundation of our nationality in formation.[27]

    Argentine sociologist also notes, the critical success of Mariátegui's first work throughout Latin America helped consolidate him into 'the spokesperson of the "new Peruvian generation"' (Beigel 2006, p. 177).

23 Beigel 2006, p. 178. However, Mariátegui had almost from the start of his career as a journalist and progressively as a public intellectual emphasised his 'Peruvianness'. As we have seen in 'José Carlos Mariátegui: The Making of a Revolutionary in the Aristocratic Republic', when in 1917 he and César Falcón, with whom he published the radical newspaper *El Tiempo*, were accused by Luis Miró Quesada, the conservative mayor of Lima, of being 'Peruvian Bolsheviks', Mariátegui responded: 'Well, very Bolshevik and very Peruvian. But more Peruvian than Bolshevik' (quoted in Rouillón 1975, p. 202). This simultaneous claim to being both international – Bolshevik – and local/national – Peruvian – is one of the central characteristics of Mariátegui's writings.

24 I am following the information in the 1981 edition of *Peruanicemos al Perú*.

25 Mariátegui 2011, p. 140.

26 Needless to say, this is an early example of Mariátegui's awareness of the persistence of colonial social structures, institutions, and ideologies after Latin American independence.

27 Mariátegui 2011, p. 141.

Furthermore, 'When one speaks of Peruvianness, one should begin by invest-
igating whether this Peruvianness includes the Indian. Without the Indian
no Peruvianness is possible'.[28] Here Mariátegui introduces a key aspect of his
thinking about the Peruvian nation: it is in process of formation and this process will only conclude once the indigenous population are fully integrated and
have, precisely by having become part of a national project, transformed it. The
future, goal oriented, aspect of nationality present in the paradoxical aim of
'making Peru Peruvian', which, of course, also implies that presently Peru is not
Peruvian, is clarified in this essay. Peru will be Peruvian when it fully includes
its indigenous population and finds in them its guiding and defining element.

3   A Brief Pre-history of Mariátegui's *Indigenismo*

However, even if in an unarticulated manner, Mariátegui had always shown
passionate interest in indigenous cultures and topics even before he wrote
'Peru's Principal Problem' in 1924 or took over the column 'Peruanicemos al
Perú'. In a journalistic column of 1917, the 21-year-old journalist had responded
to an indigenous rebellion led by a mestizo ex-military under the name of Rumi
Maqui:

> National life is undoubtedly arriving at a very interesting moment. One
> can arguably claim that we are attending a Peruvian renaissance. We have
> Inca art; Inca theater; Inca music. And in order for it to be complete, we
> have an Inca revolution.[29]

With some exaggeration one could argue that some of his most characteristic
later ideas are to be found *in nuce* in this brief passage: the notion of indigenous cultures and population as central to Peruvian nationhood, the defense of
indigenismo, even the compatibility between indigenous traditions and revolution.

    Moreover, one finds a nascent concern with the role of indigenous popu-
lations and cultures in the constitution of Peruvian identity even in the essay
'Lo nacional y lo exótico', that, as we have seen, has been presented as a prime
example of Mariátegui's early disregard for indigenous traditions. In this supposedly Eurocentric essay, Mariátegui writes: 'Peru is still a nationality in form-

---

28   Mariátegui 2011, p. 141.
29   Mariátegui 1987a, p. 77.

ation. It is being built on the immobile indigenous strata by the alluviums of Western civilization'.[30] If agency is here assigned to Western civilisation, the population from which Peruvian nationality is to be constructed is the indigenous population. Therefore, rather than a clean break, a moment of intellectual turning, one must see the 'Peruvianisation of Mariátegui's thought' as an evolution that took place over years and that achieved a surprising crystallisation during the last months of 1924.

Mariátegui had from his return to Peru shown great interest in indigenous issues. For instance, he became friends with Pedro Zulen, the Sino-Peruvian philosopher and activist for indigenous rights.[31] In fact, in his obituary article for Zulen, from February 1925, 'Vidas paralelas: E.D. Morel-Pedro Zulen' ('Parallel Lives: E.D. Morel-Pedro Zulen'), Mariátegui notes with humor:

> I remember our meeting at the Third Indigenous Congress, a year ago. The stage and the first rows of seats were occupied by a colorfully dressed indigenous multitude. In the last rows, were seated the only two spectators: Zulen and I. No one else had shown interest in the debate.[32]

Moreover, in October 1924, Mariátegui and Zulen met Ezequiel Urviola, a mestizo activist, who, unbeknownst to most, passed as indigenous.[33] He would later write (in 1927) in his 'Prologue' to Luis Valcárcel's classic piece of *indigenista* agitprop *Tempestad en los Andes*:

> I remember the unexpected and impressive type of agitator I met in the Puno Indian Ezequiel Urviola. This encounter was the greatest surprise that Peru held in store for me after my return from Europe. Urviola represented the first spark of a fire to come. He was the revolutionary Indian, the socialist Indian. Tuberculous and a hunchback, he died two year later after untiring labor. It does not matter that Urviola is no longer alive. It is enough that he lived. As Valcárcel states, the highlands are pregnant with Spartacuses.[34]

---

30 Mariátegui 1981d, p. 26.
31 A lucid introduction to Zulen's writings and activism can be found in López-Calvo 2014, pp. 45–74.
32 Mariátegui 1981d, p. 39.
33 It may be worth noting that in Peru, the difference between mestizo and indigenous could very well be cultural, rather than exclusively racial.
34 Mariátegui 1976, p. 136.

Even if based on a misunderstanding, since Urviola was not of indigenous cultural provenance, to Mariátegui he seemed proof of the compatibility between Peru's indigenous population and revolutionary politics. But, in addition to the possible influence of Zulen and the obvious impact of Urviola, a third key event may help explain the differences found between 'Lo nacional y lo exótico' and 'Peru's Principal Problem'. Ricardo Portocarrero has argued that 'what mediates between the two articles is Mariátegui's attendance to the Cuarto Congreso Indígena [Fourth Indigenous Congress]' late November 1924.[35] In fact, Mariátegui highlights the importance of the Fourth Indigenous Congress in 'Peru's Principal Problem':

> In the Indian Congress, the Indian from the North has met the Indian from the Center and the Indian from the South. The Indian in Congress, moreover, have been in contact with vanguard leaders in the capital ... These emotions widen with this contact ... This is something that is still very vague, very confused, something outlined in this human nebula, which probably, surely, contains the seeds of the future Peruvian nationality.[36]

Not only is this congress the one specific event that can be pinpointed to have taken place during the eleven days that separate the two articles, but, as the quotation above evidences, it had a defining impact on the Peruvian thinker. However, without denying the effects of this congress on Mariátegui, the fact is that that his 'discovery' of the centrality of indigenous agency in any emancipatory process in Peru is the conclusion to at least a year-long process of thinking that began with his attendance to the Third Indigenous Congress, was nurtured by his friendship with Zulen, was furthered by the impact of Urviola's magnetic personality, and was catalysed by his attendance at the Fourth Indigenous Congress. Moreover, it brought to fruition experiences he had had and ideas that had begun to develop during his early years as a journalist. Be that as it may, in 'Peru's Principal Problem', Mariátegui's stress on the futurity of Peruvian nationality is clearly built on the indigenous population, while not excluding coastal *criollo* individuals free from colonial mentality. Moreover, the indigenous Congresses and the example of Urviola showed him that 'the solution of the problem of the Indian must be a social solution. It must be worked out by the Indians themselves'.[37] The construction of Peruvian nationality is,

---

35   Portocarrero 1996, p. 70.
36   Mariátegui 2011, p. 142.
37   Mariátegui 2011, p. 142.

therefore, not a process to be undertaken exclusively by the socially dominant *criollos* (Hispano-Peruvians) or mestizos (whether ethnically or culturally), but by the indigenous populations themselves. Agency is now primarily assigned to the numeral majority of Quechua and Aymara population.[38]

It would be a mistake, however, to see in 'Peru's Principal Problem' a rejection of the cosmopolitanism that had previously characterised Mariátegui's writings. The fact that 'Feminist Demands' was published in *Mundial* on 19 December 1924, that is, ten days after 'Peru's Principal Problem', makes clear how the 'Peruvianisation' of his thought did not lead to a rejection of internationalism.

4   Thinking Globally, Writing Locally

Mariátegui begins his classic *Seven Essays* by responding to those who accused him of being a Eurocentric thinker (ironically a frequent and obviously unfair attack made by some of his contemporaries):[39]

> There are many who think that I am tied to European culture and alien to the facts and issues of my country. Let my book defend me against this cheap and biased assumption. I have served my best apprenticeship in Europe and I believe the only salvation for Indo America lies in European and Western science and thought. Sarmiento, who is still one of the creators of argentinidad [Argentineness], at one time turned his eyes toward Europe. He found no better way to be an Argentine.[40]

Seven Essays is thus explicitly framed as his reply to that mistaken and misleading claim, though one arguably based on the centrality of European topics in his writings till then. Leaving aside for now a detailed analysis of the sur-

---

38   Ironically, given that Zulen had been one of the founders of the Asociación Pro-Indígena, a philanthropic institution that attempted to help and defend Peru's indigenous population, Mariátegui later in the essay rejects philanthropy, no matter how well-intentioned or how selfless the philanthropists: 'The problem of Indian, which is the problem of Peru, cannot find its solution in an abstract humanitarian formula. It cannot be the result of a philanthropic movement' (Mariátegui 2011, p. 141).

39   Beigel writes about the 'accusations of 'vanguardist' and 'exotic' leveled against the Amauta from reactionary and, in some case, virulently anti-Lima sectors' during the period previous to the publication of *Seven Essays* (Beigel 2006, p. 186). But, as we will see, similar attacks would be levelled against him by Haya de la Torre and members of the APRA, turned political party, after 1928.

40   Mariátegui 1971, p. xxxvi.

prising reference to Domingo Faustino Sarmiento,[41] Mariátegui here presents us with a set of paradoxical propositions. Rather than fully denying the Eurocentric slur, he embraces his European (self-)education, but claims it does not imply an ignorance of national reality. He also points out that local identity – Argentineness or Peruvianness – is not incompatible with European science, arts, and ideas. The national, perhaps, the local, is only understandable through the global. Argentine and other national identities can only be 'created' through Western thought. This reference to the interrelationship between Western knowledge and local identity is echoed precisely by a similar passage at the conclusion of 'Literature on Trial', the last chapter of *Seven Essays*. Mariátegui ends the book by stating that 'The universal, ecumenical roads we have chosen to travel, and for which we are reproached, take us ever closer to ourselves'.[42] The universal and the local are imbricated. Mariátegui seems to indicate that the way to understand the local is through the knowledge gained not only from Western, but, more generally, global sources. Universal knowledge, including that originating in Europe and North America, is the necessary route to a fuller understanding and belonging to local culture. However, in this second passage Mariátegui is describing a plural, collective experience rather than a personal one.

'Literature on Trial', the chapter from which this last quotation is taken, is his analysis of his country's literary history, not a statement about his own intellectual education. For Mariátegui:

> A modern literary, not sociological, theory divides the literature of a country into three periods: colonial, cosmopolitan, and national. In the first period, the country, in a literary sense, is a colony dependent on its metropolis. In the second period, it simultaneously assimilates elements of various foreign literatures. In the third period, it shapes and expresses its own personality and feelings.[43]

In this reading, literature is a collective creation that responds to specific social realities. Thus the colonial character of Peruvian literature – that 'Literature on Trial' notes continues long after independence – can be seen as linked to the country's colonial and neocolonial condition. Despite the presence of an ideal chronology in this passage – colonial literature giving way to cosmopolitan writing which, in turn, is superseded by national literature – Mariátegui's

---

41   I deal with the mention of Sarmiento and the apparent contradiction raised by this reference to an *anti-indigenista* by Mariátegui in the chapter 'Mariátegui and Argentina'.
42   Mariátegui 1971, p. 187.
43   Mariátegui 1971, p. 191.

essays on specific writers presents a more complicated model of literary development. For instance, figures such as Mariano Melgar, who died fighting for independence in 1815, and who adapted into Spanish the indigenous poetic genre of the *yaraví*,[44] or Ricardo Palma (1833–19), who in his *Tradiciones peruanas* collected anecdotes, phrases, and little-known historical events,[45] seem to present embryonic versions of a national literature. Nevertheless, both were active during periods in which, according to Mariátegui, colonial writing was hegemonic. Likewise, Manuel González Prada (1844–1918), the radical essayist, and the prime example in *Seven Essays* of a cosmopolitan writer, is followed chronologically by a reactionary restoration of colonial values on the part of the historian José de la Riva Agüero (1885–1944), writer and critic Ventura García Calderón (1885–1959) and other intellectuals. Even the optimistic bent of the conclusion of 'Literature on Trial' seems based in a perhaps naïvely positive evaluation of Mariátegui's generational cohorts, as the only fully national writer studied in *Seven Essays* is César Vallejo. Thus one can easily argue that 'Literature on Trial' presents the combined and uneven development of Peruvian literature, as the dominance of colonial literature in the country co-exists with individuals and even movements that are cosmopolitan or potentially national. Underlying what seems to be a linear narrative – colonial to cosmopolitan to national literature – is a mottled view of the mode of literary production in Peru that resembles Mariátegui's view of the country's economic structures as including modern, semi-feudal, and communal productive units. As Carlos García-Bedoya correctly notes, 'More than periods proper, Mariátegui distinguishes here among tendencies within the process of Peruvian literature'.[46]

'Literature on Trial' is thus primarily an attempt at tracing an ideal diachronic view of the country's literature, so that while there are colonial, national, and cosmopolitan writers during all stages, a chronology of its dominant tendencies is presented. Both cosmopolitanism and nationalist writers and traits are presented as simultaneously opposed to colonial literature. However, not only is cosmopolitanism presented as the necessary stage for the rise of a

---

44   In his *Seven Essays*, Mariátegui writes about Melgar: 'Indigenous sentiment was not totally unexpressed in this period of our literary history. Its first worthwhile exponent was Mariano Melgar'. He also says 'Melgar is very Indian in his primitive, peasant imagery' (Mariátegui 1971, p. 214, with corrections).

45   'But Ricardo Palma ... is also, despite his limitations, of this integral Peru that begins to take shape in us. Palma interprets the criollo, the mestizo, and the middle-class elite of a republican Lima which ... is no less the one that in our time criticizes its own tradition, rejects its colonial lineage, denounces its centralism, supports the claims of the Indian, and extends both hands to the rebels of the provinces' (Mariátegui 1971, p. 200).

46   García-Bedoya 2007, p. 18.

dominant national literature, but, as the example of Vallejo proves, national writing is itself as much based on cosmopolitan literary traits as on national traditions. After all, the writing of Vallejo, the major 'national' writer in Mariátegui's 'Literature on Trial', is also one of the pinnacles of the Latin American avant-garde.

5   The Nation as Myth

Despite the apparent essentialism found in this description of 'national' literature as 'expressing' the country's 'personality and feeling', Mariátegui can, overall, be seen as a precursor of contemporary views of the nation and national identity. As we have seen in his reference to Sarmiento as 'creator of *argentinidad*', national identity, instead of arising naturally from a specific set of essential differences – be they racial, linguistic, or cultural, is actually the result of individual and group agency. Rather than natural, the nation is artificial, a social creation.

These ideas are explicitly stated by Mariátegui in 'Literature on Trial': 'The nation itself is an abstraction, an allegory, a myth that does not correspond to a reality that can be scientifically defined'.[47] Like Benedict Anderson, for the Peruvian, the nation is an imagined community. Moreover, as the inclusion of his reflections on nation and nationalism in the chapter on literature indicate, his idea of nation, like Anderson's, is imagined to a great degree through literature. As Sara Castro-Klarén perceptively argues:

> Mariátegui notes, as postmodern theory later posits, that the nation is a construct. He calls it 'an illusion', 'a myth'. But he nevertheless understands it as a necessary construct for the achievement of other necessary human goals, goals which without a nation could, perhaps never be reached.[48]

Mariátegui writes about 'colonial nations' like Peru, 'In these peoples the idea of the nation has not yet run its trajectory nor exhausted its historical mission'.[49] The implication is that for the author of *Seven Essays*, the nation, even if a construct, is a necessary stage of human 'progress' and of the full achievement of modernity. Moreover, one that will be followed by what can only be

---

47   Mariátegui 1971, p. 47. This is the passage to which Brennan refers when he praises Mariátegui's view of the nation as 'fiction'.
48   Castro-Klarén 2008, p. 141.
49   Mariátegui 2011, p. 175.

understood as a new superior cosmopolitanism. Even though, understandably, Mariátegui, who was not given to facile utopianism, never speculated about this post-national future.

As we have seen, Mariátegui derived the concept of myth from Sorel.[50] While Sorel sees the myth as constructed, he also sees it as a necessary social mobilising agent.[51] Christianity, the revolution, and perhaps most significantly Giuseppe Mazzini's struggle for the unification of Italy, that is for the creation of a progressive Liberal Italian nation and identity, are seen by Sorel as being only made possible by the construction of a relevant myth. The myth is thus a necessary element in historical evolution. This is the view and use of myth that Mariátegui borrows from Sorel when writing about the nation.

6   Conclusion

It is tempting to see Mariátegui's view of Peruvian literature as evolving from colonial to cosmopolitan to national periods as a kind of Hegelian triad. The colonial stage as thesis, the cosmopolitan as anti-thesis, and the national stage as the dialectical synthesis of both. However, the manner in which Mariátegui sees the national stage as coming into being undermines the Hegelian progression. What is considered national is, even if socially determined, also to a degree an element of choice as much as of stages naturally superseding each other. Moreover, the local elements to be incorporated into the national are, by definition, those that are compatible with the progress of 'civilisation'. Thus, for Mariátegui, patriarchal traditions, even if found in the nation's Hispanic or indigenous sources, are to be eliminated. Rather than a simple historical progression, the attainment of the national is predicated on the precedence of cosmopolitanism and on its continuance. The national is both a consequence of cosmopolitanism, a superior stage that resolves earlier contradictions, as well as a supplement that depends on the attainment of cosmopolitanism as it denudes its lack. Mariátegui's concluding phrase to *Seven Essays* – 'the universal, ecumenical roads we have chosen to travel, and for which we are

---

50   See chapter 'Mariátegui, Sorel and Myth'.

51   'Men who are participating in a great social movement always picture their coming action as a battle in which their cause is certain to triumph. These constructions, knowledge of which is so important for historians, I propose to call myths; the syndicalist "general strike" and Marx's catastrophic revolution are such myths. As remarkable examples of such myths, I have given those which were constructed by primitive Christianity, by the Reformation, by the Revolution and by the followers of Mazzini' (Sorel 1972, p. 42).

reproached, take us ever closer to ourselves' – had earlier been used as the conclusion to his 1925 essay 'Nacionalismo y vanguardismo'.[52] In this essay, the phrase is used after a brief mention of Vallejo as the culmination of Peruvian literature's search to achieve a balance between nationalism and the international avant-garde, first represented by Mariátegui's older contemporary (and mentor), the short story writer, novelist, and poet, Abraham Valdelomar:

> In Valdelomar one finds the instance of a writer in whom one finds cosmopolitan and national feelings together and combined. The snobbish love for European things and fashions did not diminish Valdelomar's love for the rustic and humble things of his land and village. On the contrary, it perhaps provoked and intensified it.[53]

For Mariátegui, what is considered national – such as Valdelomar's childhood experiences in his home village – and what is considered cosmopolitan – for instance, European fashions – are compatible. True nationalism is necessarily linked to cosmopolitanism. It is its necessary consequence. In 'Nacionalismo y vanguardismo', Valdelomar – later in *Seven Essays* demoted to a precursor of national literature rather than its exemplar –[54] and Vallejo are national insofar as they continue being cosmopolitan. Even if Vallejo 'is truly ours, very Indian',[55] his work accentuates the phenomenon of the conjunction of the avant-garde and nationalism. The national writer is, therefore, also a cosmopolitan one.

It is tempting to compare Mariátegui's versions of cosmopolitan nationalism – or is it nationalist cosmopolitanism? – with the notion of 'partial cosmopolitanism' proposed recently by Kwame Anthony Appiah. For the Ghanaian philosopher, 'partial cosmopolitanism' implies 'that no local loyalty can ever justify forgetting that each human being has responsibilities to every other',[56] and can be defined as a sharing of 'local partialities and universal morality ... [of] being part of the place you were and part of a broader human com-

---

52   Mariátegui 1981d, p. 79.

53   Mariátegui 1981d. p. 79.

54   In *Seven Essays*, Mariátegui writes about Valdelomar: 'In tune with his times, Valdelomar was versatile and restless, "very modern, bold, and cosmopolitan". His humor and his lyricism occasionally foreshadow modern avant-garde literature' (Mariátegui 1971, p. 232). Nevertheless, Mariátegui concludes that 'Valdelomar does not herald a new era in our literature because too many decadent influences acted on him' (Mariátegui 1971, p. 233).

55   Mariátegui 1981d, p. 79.

56   Appiah 2006, p. xvii.

munity'.[57] For both Mariátegui and Appiah, a vivid sense of belonging to a worldwide human community and a heightened 'local loyalty' are fully compatible.

As in the case of Appiah, who describes his 'partial cosmopolitanism' as rooted in his personal experience in Ghana,[58] one can trace Mariátegui's imbrication of nationalism and cosmopolitanism back to his biography. He lived in Italy, where he met and married Anna Chiappe, and spoke Italian at home with his wife and children. One could, perhaps, also trace his cosmopolitanism further back to his childhood, when the ten-year-old Mariátegui began to teach himself French.[59] That said, Mariátegui's version of 'partial cosmopolitanism' has a political edge that is not explicit in Appiah's more individual and ethical version. For Mariátegui cosmopolitanism, by undermining colonial modes of thinking, permits the social realignment and reconceptualisation of what is understood as nationalism. In the case of Peru, cosmopolitanism permits the revaluation of the country's indigenous population and their culture. In 'Nacionalismo y vanguardismo', Mariátegui distinguishes between this nationalism open to the world and an alternative retrograde version, which, in Peru, he sees as an avatar of colonialism. He writes about this retrograde nationalism:

> Only by conceiving the nation as a static reality can one find a more national spirit and inspiration in the repeaters and rhapsodists of an old art than in the creators and inventors of a new one. The nation lives in the precursors of its future more than in the survivors of its past.[60]

For Mariátegui, true nationalism is ultimately another way of being cosmopolitan, just as true cosmopolitanism rescues what is of value in local elements.

Mariátegui's own literary and cultural activity, even after the 'Peruvianization of his project', exhibits this complementary nationalism and cosmopolitanism. He never stopped writing about world literary and cultural figures – George Bernard Shaw, James Joyce, Charles Chaplin, etc. He even completed a brief novel set in Italy: *La novela y la vida: Siegfried y el profesor Canella*, which was published in book form posthumously in 1955.

Furthermore, if one looks at the books published by Mariátegui's Editorial Minerva and Sociedad Editora Amauta, his two editorial endeavours, one does not necessarily see 'cosmopolitan' texts being replaced by 'nationalistic'

57   Appiah 2006, p. xviii.
58   Appiah 2006, pp. xix–xx.
59   Rouillón 1975, p. 55.
60   Mariátegui 1981d, p. 76.

ones, even if he understandably publishes mainly books written by Peruvian authors.[61] For instance, the two books published in 1930, the year of Mariátegui's death, are Ernesto Reyna's *El amauta Atusparia*, a chronicle of an indigenous uprising in 1885, and *9 poetas nuevos del Brasil*, Enrique Bustamante y Ballivián's translations of modernist Brazilian poets, including Mário de Andrade.

Mariátegui's nationalism is thus always in contact with the new, and given Peru's belonging to what today would be called the world system, this implied that nationalism could not supersede cosmopolitanism. Furthermore, by considering the asymmetrical elements present in the development of the Peruvian nation – the residuum of colonial exploitation, which would make orthodox Eurocentric Marxist analysis untenable – Mariátegui achieves a broader conception of both the nation and Marxism, even as he struggles to fit these new notions within the terms of his intellectual inheritance. For Mariátegui, cosmopolitanism and nationalism, what is international and what is local, are two sides of the same coin.

---

61   For practical purposes I am not distinguishing between Editorial Minerva, which served as both a publishing house and a print shop – i.e. publishing notebooks, school textbooks – and Sociedad Editora Amauta, an outgrowth of the first that, while using Minerva's print shop, included other members in its governing board. Both Minerva and Sociedad Editora Amauta were ultimately expressions of Mariátegui's editorial vision.

One can also add that Mariátegui's cosmopolitanism as an editor was reflected in the publishing contacts he establishes. Although his journal *Amauta* and the books he published are distributed throughout Peru, he also endeavoured to place them abroad. In fact, Minerva and Sociedad Editora Amauta also became distributors of what could loosely be called a network of progressive publishers from Europe including such still well-known corporations as: Macmillan, Larousse, and Mondadori. Additional information on Mariátegui's editorial network can be found in Beigel 2006, especially pp. 197–245.

José Carlos Mariátegui and the Politics of Literature

Despite the frequent – and justified – association of José Carlos Mariátegui with politics or the social sciences, more than 40 percent of his writings are on literary or cultural topics.[1] In fact, in *Seven Interpretive Essays on Peruvian Reality*, the foundational Marxist, perhaps even modern, study of Peruvian society, the longest essay is not the one on the economy, which is, in fact, the shortest, nor the ones on land tenancy or on the so-called 'Indian problem'. Instead the longest essay is 'Literature on Trial', Mariátegui's review of Peruvian literature. While Mariátegui's passion for literary and, more generally, cultural topics clearly originates in his personal background as litterateur – as a *Colónida* poet and playwright – it continued throughout his life.[2] In fact, one of his last texts was the genre bending short novel *La novela y la vida: Siegfried y el profesor Canella*, set in Italy.[3] But the bulk of his literary writings were critical rather than creative.

His literary essays are often considered to have played a central role in the development of modern literary criticism in his country and in Latin America as a whole. According to Vicky Unruh, given the centrality of book reviewing and literary commentary in Mariátegui's public activity, he can be considered 'one of Latin America's first practicing literary critics'.[4] Likewise, Argentine writer and journalist Damián Tabarovsky writes about Mariátegui: 'first and foremost, he was a literary critic; then a political theorist and social thinker'.[5] Be that as it may, what I want to focus on in this chapter are not the virtues, contradictions, or mistakes to be found in Mariátegui's qualitative evaluation of specific literary works or movements, but rather the political implications he identified in literature. I am concerned with the role Mariátegui believed literature played in the maintenance or subversion of social order. This chapter, therefore, deals with Mariátegui's view on the political valence and function of literature and, more generally, of culture.

---

1 One among many possible sources for this information is Beigel 2006, p. 20.

2 The *Colónida* group – named after the literary magazine they published – was post-*modernista*, that is, pre-modernist from an European perspective, and was led by the charismatic and brilliant novelist, short story writer and poet Abraham Valdelomar (1888–1919).

3 As proof of Mariátegui's true cosmopolitanism, shortly before his death in 1930, he planned to follow *La novela y la vida* with 'a Peruvian novel' (Mariátegui 1994, p. 730).

4 Unruh 1989, p. 45.

5 Tabarovsky 2007.

Despite his praise for Soviet novels, such as Feodor Gladkov's *Cement*, Mariátegui implicitly rejects the premises on which socialist realism would later be built; that is, the belief in a direct relationship between subject matter and style – clearly defined revolutionary topics expressed in what was believed to be a transparent manner – which would become the basic evaluative criterion for a work's political value.[6] Writing before 'Stalin's narrow aesthetic circumscribed it',[7] the Peruvian critic developed a view of the interrelationship among politics of art, literature and culture that is more inclusive and free-ranging than almost all other socialist critics of the late 1920s. If 'official' Communist critics would soon reject the avant-garde, Mariátegui became a defender of surrealism.[8] If Western Marxism found in the rigorous formalism of much modernism a rejection of literary and artistic populism, cheap politicisation, or nascent commercialism, Mariátegui promoted not only what he called proletarian realism, exemplified precisely by *Cement*, but also imagined an *indigenista* literature that, in its combination of cultural representation, political advocacy, and technical mastery, would only be fully exemplified years later by the novels of Ciro Alegría and José María Arguedas.[9]

---

6   In one of the founding documents of socialist realism, Karl Radek stated: 'It is this activity [of the construction of socialism], with all its contradictions that the artists of the USSR and the revolutionary artists of capitalist countries are rightly desirous of reflecting in art. Realism means the portrayal of this reality in all its basic connections. Realism means giving a picture not only of the decay of capitalism and the withering away of its culture, but also of the birth of that class, of that force which is capable of creating a new society and a new culture. Realism does not mean the embellishment or arbitrary selection of revolutionary phenomena; it means reflecting reality as it is, in all its complexity, in all its contrariety, and not only capitalist reality, but also that other, new reality – the reality of socialism' (Radek 2004, p. 156).

7   Vanden and Becker 2011b, p. 408.

8   While the First Soviet Writer's Congress of 1934 marked the official adoption of socialist realism as the only revolutionary literary style, the growing tensions between the avant-garde and official communism throughout the 1930s are evidenced by the expulsion of André Bretón from the French Communist party in 1933. (Breton had joined the party in 1927).

9   The locus classicus of Western Marxism's rejection of literary realism is Theodor Adorno: 'The more total society becomes, the more completely it contracts to a unanimous system, and all the more do artworks in which this experience is sedimented become the other of this society. If one applies the concept of abstraction in the vaguest possible sense, it signals the retreat from a world of which nothing remains except its caput mortuum. New art is as abstract as social relations have in truth become. In like manner, the concepts of the realistic and the symbolic are put out of service. Because the spell of external reality over its subjects and their reactions has become absolute, the artwork can only oppose this spell by assimilating itself to it' (Adorno 2013, p. 42).

1   Art, Revolution and Decadence

Mariátegui deals explicitly with the political value of the avant-garde movements of his time in his 1926 essay 'Art, Revolution and Decadence'. In this text,
the Peruvian Marxist attempts to separate the political wheat from the rhetorical chaff, that is, revolution from decadence, in surrealism and futurism.[10]
Writing about artists who innovate only in technique and those whose formal
innovations 'correspond to a new spirit', Mariátegui notes:

> Distinguishing between these two contemporaneous categories of artists
> is not easy. Decadence and revolution, as they coexist in the same world,
> also coexist within the same individuals. The artist's consciousness is the
> agonistic circus of struggle between these two spirits. The understand-
> ing of this struggle almost always escapes the artists themselves. But in
> the end, one of the two spirits prevails. The other is left strangled in the
> arena.[11]

From the above passage one notes that Mariátegui's writings on literature, as
on other topics, make use of a vitalistic language – i.e. 'spirit' – which, again,
may seem unexpected in a Marxist, but was very much of his time. However,
even more so than in the case of his writings on economic or social topics, the
juxtaposition of radical politics and non-Marxist language formally reflects the
point of the essay, which is that radicality in politics and form are not necessarily synonymous. Mariátegui's 'conservative', even decadent, language – from
a dogmatic Communist perspective – contains a radically innovatory view of
literature. Furthermore, there is the clear implication in the passage that while
in politics it might be possible to clearly separate revolution and decadence –

---

10   The reference to decadence may also have had a personal connotation for Mariátegui. As
      we saw, the young poet who wrote a love poem titled 'Morphine' – it begins 'Your love
      is my morphine' and ends 'I don't want to know if it poisons me/ this morphine which
      when I sleep/will nirvanarize my melancholy' – surely could be described as decadent
      ('Tu amor es mi morfina'/ ... / Y no quiero saber si me envenena/ esta morfina que al
      dormir mi pena/nirvanizara mi melancolía/) (Mariátegui 1987b, p. 84). One could also
      categorise as such the often celebrated happening in the cemetery in 1917, in which the
      then twenty-two-year-old journalist and his friends helped convince visiting Swiss dan-
      cer Norka Rouskaya to perform Chopin's Funeral March, in the Lima cemetery, only to be
      interrupted by the police. (Needless to say, this event was a major scandal in 1917). The
      'dance' is analysed in the first chapter of this study 'José Carlos Mariátegui: The Making of
      a Revolutionary in the Aristocratic Republic'.
11   Mariátegui 2011, p. 423.

perhaps, even reaction – it is not as easy when it comes to works of art. The clear linkage between, to use flawed terms, politics and style, as was the case in the somewhat later socialist realism, the ease in identification of explicit ideology, characteristic of so much politically based criticism, as well as the modernist association of artistic innovation with progressiveness – Ezra Pound's injunction to 'make it new'[12] – are all rejected by Mariátegui. Furthermore, by presenting works of art as necessarily mottled, as uncomfortable combinations of politically progressive and regressive aspects, Mariátegui denies any relevance to authorial intention or biographical data. Political meaning is thus independent of the author's explicit ideology or aesthetic credo. Here, Mariátegui unwittingly reminds one of Marx's passion for the novels of Balzac, which, in their lucid description of the workings of nineteenth-century French society, did not necessarily support the novelist's personal monarchist tendencies.[13] However, Mariátegui actually goes further than his illustrious predecessor by noting that the delinking of author and work originates not only in the non-unanimity of individual intention – no one fully knows what she is aiming for – but also in the heterogeneity of the psyche. As Mariátegui puts it, the psyche is an 'agonistic circus' in which revolution and decadence, and progressive and regressive, elements and goals perform. Given the plurality of the self, it is impossible to trace a linear relationship between individuals and their works.

Implicit in Mariátegui's ideas is the centrality of the critic for the understanding of a work of art. If the artist is unable to understand her creation – intention, as we have seen, is irrelevant – it behooves someone who stands outside the creative process to analyse and evaluate the artistic work. An implied equivalence between the critic and the psychologist or psychoanalyst is proposed in the quotation above. It is not only artists who are torn psychologically; it is individuals, in general, who do not know who they truly are. Individuals and works of art require analysis in order to be able to figure out 'who' is the real winner in the Roman coliseums of the mind and of the text. Not surprisingly, Mariátegui helped introduce Freud in Peru.[14]

---

12   Ironically, the origin of Pound's modernist motto is to be found in Chinese antiquity. (Pound was an amateur sinologist). 'The source is a historical anecdote concerning Ch'eng T'ang (Tching-thang, Tching Tang), first king of the Shang dynasty (1766–53 BC), who was said to have had a washbasin inscribed with this inspirational slogan' (North 2013).

13   According to Alex Callinicos, 'Marx also greatly admired Balzac, for his realistic portrayal of class relations in post-revolutionary France. One of his many unrealized projects was a study of Balzac' (Callinicos 2013, p. 35).

14   Mariátegui published 'Resistence to Psychoanalysis', a text by Sigmund Freud in the first issue of *Amauta*, the cultural journal he founded in 1926. According to Krauze, this was the first translation of Freud into Spanish (Krauze 2011, p. 110). It had been believed that Mari-

Later in the same essay, Mariátegui explains what he means by revolutionary art: 'The revolutionary aspect of these contemporary schools or tendencies
does not lie in their creation of a new technique. Nor is it the destruction of
the old technique. It is in the repudiation, the removal, the mockery of the
bourgeois absolute. Consciously or not, art is always nourished by the absolute
of an epoch'.[15] Thus the revolutionary character of a work is not necessarily
deducible from the technique used. He will often present Marinetti and the
Italian futurists as examples of a reactionary modernity.[16] For Mariátegui the
key to evaluating a work of art's political value resides in identifying its relation
with the 'bourgeois absolute'. For the Peruvian, only works that undermine this
'absolute' can be considered 'revolutionary'.

But what does the Peruvian Marxist mean by absolute?

2   The Absolute in Bergson, Ibérico, and Mariátegui

As the reader has probably realised, Mariátegui borrowed the notion of the
absolute from an unexpected source: Henri Bergson. While Bergson was extremely influential during the 1920s, his stress on intuition as a source of knowledge contradicted the rationalism that characterised the writings of Marx.
However, Mariátegui thought extremely highly of Bergson. In 'Veinticinco años
de sucesos extranjeros' (Twenty five Years of Foreign Events), written in 1929,
that is, after Mariátegui had established connections with the Soviet-led
Comintern, he goes as far as describing Bergson's best-known philosophical
work, *Creative Evolution*, as 'a more important event than the creation of ...
Yugoslavia'.[17] He, however, added:

> Bergsonism has influenced such different, even contradictory, events of
> varied importance, as the literature of Bernard Shaw, the Dada insur-
> rection, the theory of revolutionary syndicalism, Fascist squadrismo, the

---

átegui, who read German, had translated this text (Beigel 2003, p. 101), However, according
to Claudio Lomnitz Adler, his gradfather Miguel Adler was the transator (Lomnitz 2018,
p. 100).

15   Mariátegui 2011, p. 424.
16   In his 'Marinetti y el futurismo', Mariátegui argues that 'Unlike cubism, expressionism
and dadaism, futurism is not only a school or tendency of the art of the avant-garde. It
is primarily a peculiar aspect of Italian life' (Mariátegui 1980c, p. 185). After noting that
futurism has become fascist, Mariátegui concludes 'Futurism has, therefore, paradoxically become outdated' (Mariátegui 1980c, p. 189).
17   Mariátegui 1980b, p. 198.

novels of Marcel Proust, the dissemination of Christian Science's neo-Thomism, Theosophy, and the mental confusion of Latin American college students.[18]

That said, in Bergson, 'the absolute' is never completely explained. As the French philosopher notes: 'In the absolute we live and move and have our being'.[19] 'The knowledge we possess of it is incomplete, no doubt, but not external or relative. It is reality itself, in the profoundest meaning of the word that we reach by the combined and progressive development of science and of philosophy'.[20] The ground for being, Bergson's absolute, is in its totality unknowable, except partly by science and philosophy. In a characteristic paradox, philosophy is seen as having in intuition one of its principal tools.

In Mariátegui, Bergson's 'reality itself' is reinterpreted as something akin to *weltanschauung* or, perhaps, structure of feeling:

> Historically, Bergson's philosophy has contributed, to a greater degree than any other intellectual element, to the ruin of Bourgeois idealism and rationalism, and to the death of the older absolute.[21]

This reinterpretation of Bergson is influenced by the work of Peruvian philosopher Mariano Ibérico, whose *El nuevo absoluto* was published by Mariátegui's Editorial Minerva in 1926, the same year that Mariátegui wrote 'Art, Revolution, and Decadence'. In *El nuevo absoluto*, Ibérico notes:

> Loneliness in time, religious will, the new absolute are expressions that we use to designate the principal aspects of contemporary ferment. These aspects summarize the negative elements and the possibility of affirmation. They reveal the discomfort, the interior contradiction, the relative incoherence characteristic of every period of transition.[22]

Mariátegui's stress on the contradictory traits of his time and its characteristic works of literature and art is already present in Ibérico's description of the 'new absolute'. In fact, Ibérico also sees in socialism 'a liberation, an attempt to vin-

---

18   Mariátegui 1980b p. 199.
19   Here Bergson is paraphrasing a sentence from *Acts* 17:28: 'For in him we live, and move, and have our being; as certain also of your own poets have said, for we are also his offspring'.
20   Bergson 1911, p. 199.
21   Mariátegui 1980b, p. 199.
22   Ibérico 1926, pp. 213–14.

dicate humanity as an end and not as a means'[23] However, Mariátegui gives a much clearer political spin to Ibérico's resemantisation of 'the absolute'. For him the 'bourgeois absolute' is composed by a constellation of ideas and emotional elements that help justify the existing political and social status quo in Europe and beyond.

3   Revolutionary Literature and Reality

Despite Mariátegui's enthusiasm for *Cement*, he is overall sceptical of the value of an explicitly revolutionary literature (perhaps as a consequence of his denial of the links between intention and the resulting text). In an article on Miguel de Unamuno's *Agony of Christianity*, also of 1926, when the Spanish writer was long past any flirtation with socialism, Mariátegui notes that it 'contains more revolutionary spirit than several tons of socialist literature'.[24] Writing about the 'literary populism' of some French writers of the 1920s, which at least in Mariátegui's description bears some similarity to the socialist realism being codified at the time, he surprisingly concludes that 'on the desk of a revolutionary critic, independently of any hierarchical consideration, a book by Joyce will be a more valuable document than one by any neo-Zola'.[25] One must note here that, four years after Mariátegui wrote these words, during the Soviet Writer's Congress in 1934 which helped institutionalise socialist realism in the international Communist movement, Karl Radek described Joyce's *Ulysses* as 'A heap

---

23   Ibérico 1926, p. 223. One must also note that Mariátegui's frequent vindication of religion and, particularly, of socialism as religion is also to be found in Ibérico: 'In its deepest meaning [socialism] is a religious will. This is the reason why ultimately its efficacy will depend in its mysticism and its capacity to illuminate with one final hope all human desires' (Ibérico 1926, p. 223).

24   Mariátegui 1980g, p. 120.

25   Mariátegui 1980, p. 35. Of course, other Marxist critics rejected Zola. For instance, according to Georg Lukács, when reading a text by Zola, despite, or, better said, because of the thoroughness of data and information presented in the text, 'the characters are merely spectators more or less interested in the event. As a result the events themselves become only a tableau for the reader or, at best, a series of tableaux. We are merely observers' (Lukács 2005, p. 116). For Lukacs, unlike the epic realist narrative of a Balzac and Dickens which portrayed society organically and, therefore, implied the possibility of human intervention, Zola presents a society as detached from readers and, therefore, as a fact beyond change. Mariátegui's criticism is different. He sees Zola as the epitome of a failed traditional realism. For Mariátegui, he is the writer whose obsession with physical detail was not supplemented with a similar interest in the psychological and spiritual human dimension.

of dung, crawling with worms, photographed by a cinema apparatus through a microscope such is Joyce's work'.[26] It therefore makes perfect sense that Mariátegui would reject *avant la lettre* both the new literary dogma and the condemnation of Joyce, which was in fact the founding gesture of socialist realism.

Despite Mariátegui's support of the avant-garde, Unruh is correct in noting that: 'Unlike Marinetti, Breton, or Huidobro, Mariátegui was neither a "believer" in vanguardism nor a promoter of a specific aesthetic creed. Rather, he viewed the avant-gardes as the most important aesthetic development of the postwar era'.[27] But, as we will see, Mariátegui's eclecticism is, however, not the result of a lack of conviction or theoretical consideration of the different artistic movements.

Even if not a card carrying member of the surrealist international, Mariátegui singled out the work of Breton and his confreres as the central literary innovation of the 1920s. For instance, in his 'A Balance Sheet of Surrealism', published in 1930, Mariátegui notes: 'None of the vanguard literary and artistic movements of Western Europe had ... the significance or historical content of Surrealism'.[28] Undeniably, the fragile alliance between the political left and artistic avant-garde during the 1920s – represented in Breton's explicit alignment with Soviet-led communism – played a role in Mariátegui's evaluation.[29] In 'Art, Revolution, and Decadence', Mariátegui emphasises the need for artists to embrace what following Sorel he calls myth, extolling the surrealists for having accepted that of communism.[30] However, the explicit political radicalism of the movement is not the primary reason for Mariátegui's celebration of surrealism. In 'La realidad y la ficción' (Reality and Fiction), also written in 1926, he presents Waldo Frank, who was close to the US Left, and Luigi Pirandello, already aligned with fascism, as surrealists, despite their not explicitly belonging to the movement. In this essay, he describes this avant-garde movement as including artists 'far and wide from the surrealist handful in Paris'.[31] He then

---

26　Radek 2004, p. 153.
27　Unruh 1989, p. 50.
28　Mariátegui 2011a, p. 415.
29　In 'A Balance Sheet on Surrealism', Mariátegui includes the movement's actual political evolution among his reasons for his positive evaluation: 'It [surrealism] accepts and supports the specific program of the concrete, current revolution: the Marxist program of proletarian revolution. It does not occur to Surrealism to subordinate politics to artistic rules and taste. Just as in the field of physics, there is no objection to the data of science; in the realms of politics and economics it is deemed puerile and absurd to attempt original speculation based on artistic data' (Mariátegui 2011, p. 416).
30　On Sorel's myth, see 'Mariátegui, Sorel, and Myth' in this study.
31　Mariátegui 1980a, p. 23.

adds: 'more than discovering the marvelous, it [surrealism] seems destined to reveal the real to us. Fantasy, when it does not bring us closer to reality, is of little use'.[32] Mariátegui is here partially echoing the view the surrealists had of themselves. Unruh notes: 'futurists, dadaists, and surrealists alike affirmed that in rejecting representation, they were turning toward reality, not away from it. 'I love nature but not its substitute', wrote dada artist Hans Arp in opposing the artistic practices of naturalism'.[33] But the quotation from 'La realidad y la ficción' differs from the surrealist celebration of reality, which is potentially compatible with the complete delinking of sign and signifier and the conversion of literature into a non-referential discourse. For Mariátegui, the value of surrealism and implicitly all literature would be its ability to bring hitherto marginalised aspects of reality – the real, as he also calls it – to the reader's attention. Fantasy, sexuality, the unconscious, all marginalised by traditional realism and, one can add, also absent from the future socialist realism, but undeniable and central aspects of reality as experienced by individuals, are brought into literature and, therefore, placed before the reader by the best new writers. Thus, nineteenth-century realism and its early twentieth-century epigones are seen as having failed miserably at this nominal task: 'The death of old realism hasn't hindered in the least our knowledge of reality ... It has freed us from the dogmas and prejudices that limited it'.[34] One can add that these dogmas and prejudices are but another version of the 'bourgeois absolute', and that it is by breaking free from these, not necessarily through their stylistic innovations, or explicit ideology, that surrealism or Joyce are able to present a fuller portrait of the real, thus becoming of use for the revolutionary critic. Furthermore, as we saw in 'Art Revolution and Decadence', Mariátegui argues that 'consciously or not, art is always nourished by the absolute of an epoch'.[35] The Peruvian critic values works that at some level are able to put into

---

32 Mariátegui 1980a, p. 23.

33 Unruh 1989, p. 51. Of course, surrealism also presented itself as sublating the distance between art and life. As Unruh states: 'On the one hand, in rejecting mimetic conventions, avant-garde artists sought a more 'authentic; apprehension of life and a return to primary experience unmediated by censors of reason. On the other hand, they attacked the artist's autonomy and distance from everyday life, a privileged status originating with romanticism and culminating in late nineteenth-century aestheticism. Although it can be argued that the vanguardists created their own brand of elitism by producing highly inaccessible works, they also promoted the model of a critically engaged artist as an alternative to the self-involved poète maudit of the art-for-art's-sake mode' (Unruh 1989, pp. 46–7).

34 Mariátegui 1980a, pp. 23–4.

35 Mariátegui 2011, pp. 423–6.

question this 'absolute'. Moreover, this questioning is not necessarily present, as we have seen, at a conscious level, at the level of authorial intention or explicit ideology.[36] Unamuno's ambiguous politics – characterised by a left to right zigzag – or Pirandello's ultimate espousal of fascism, are not relevant for Mariátegui. Instead, it is the distance that he finds between the texts – regardless of their contradictions – and this bourgeois absolute that Mariátegui celebrates. It is the political unconscious of the text that determines the subversive potential of literature.

4   On Chaplin

Mariátegui further expands his discussion of this subversive potential in art in his 1928 essay 'On Explaining Chaplin', even if he does not explicitly use the phrase bourgeois absolute. This article is notable, not only for dealing with a major filmmaker, actor, and historical celebrity, but also for being the longest essay the Peruvian Marxist ever dedicated to film. Moreover, for once in his writings, Mariátegui expands his analysis from literature to a popular art. However, as was the wont of the time, Chaplin is analysed as a major cultural figure, rather than specifically as a filmmaker. Again, what interests me is not his evaluation of the individual films he writes on – *The Gold Rush* and *The Circus* – but rather what he says of the social function of film, literature and, more generally, art.[37]

---

36   While Mariátegui's rejection of authorial control over texts predicted the ideas associated in the United States with the so-called 'New Critics', hegemonic from the 1940s to the 1970s, there are significant differences. The 'New Critics' attempted to delink texts from their immediate historical and political contexts. This delinking was formalised in William K. Wimsatt and Monroe Beardsley's essays 'The Intentional Fallacy' (1946) and 'The Affective Fallacy' (1949). Both essays are included in their *The Verbal Icon: Studies in the Meaning of Poetry* (1954). Wimsatt and Beardley argued in 'The Intentional Fallacy' that authorial intention should not be taken into account when interpreting a text, and in the 'Affective Fallacy', denied relevance to the emotional impact of a text. Both 'fallacies' serve to isolate literature from the social contexts in which it is produced and consumed. Mariátegui, on the other hand, delinks textuality from authorial intention in order to situate a text within a society's specific ideological and political tendencies.

37   In this essay, Mariátegui assimilates film to literature by quoting, with at least partial approval, Henri Poullaile's comment that '*The Gold Rush* is the best contemporary novel'; and arguing himself that this film 'surpasses Mr. H.G. Wells's *The Outline of History* and Bernard Shaw's theater' (Mariátegui 2011, p. 433). One must note that he admired both writers, in particular Shaw, whom he considered 'a brilliant man, whom glory has not domesticated', 'a revolutionary, a heterodox' (Mariátegui 1981b, p. 168).

After a lucid description of Chaplin as a clown and of his career's links with the contemporary historical 'moment when the axis of capitalism was silently shifting from Great Britain to North America',[38] Mariátegui writes:

> But the United States has not spiritually assimilated Chaplin. Chaplin's tragedy and humor receive their intensity from an intimate conflict between the artist and North America. The prosperity, the energy, the élan of North America hold and excite the artist, but its bourgeois puerility, its prosaic social climbing, are repugnant to the bohemian, who is a romantic at heart. North America, in turn, does not love Chaplin. As is well known, Hollywood bosses consider him subversive, antagonistic. North America feels there is something in Chaplin that escapes them. Among the neo-Quakers of Yankee finance and industry, Chaplin will always be linked to Bolshevism.[39]

Perhaps predicting the travails Chaplin would face twenty years later, Mariátegui here stresses the resistance from sectors of US society to the great comedian's art. He also describes the tensions faced by a popular artist who is both fascinated by the United States' expanding modernity – its 'prosperity, energy, élan' – but repulsed by its base materialism – 'puerility, social climbing'. Borrowing from the language used by Mariátegui in 'Art, Revolution, and Decadence', one can argue that Chaplin, in his films and as a cultural figure, represents a view of life that contradicts, at least in part, the bourgeois absolute of the US. But in the last sentence, Mariátegui mentions an additional trait of this national 'absolute': its repressive puritanism – which is how I interpret the unexpected reference to 'neo-Quakers'. (Obviously, Mariátegui was not particularly cognisant of the history and beliefs of the Society of Friends). Furthermore, the moral freedom exhibited by Chaplin is presented as linked, at least in the mind of the narrow minders financiers of the US, with Bolshevism.

Be that as it may, it is clear that the Little Tramp's moral freedom is one of the reasons why the Peruvian values Chaplin. He concludes the essay by noting:

> The cinema allows Chaplin to assist humanity in its struggle against sorrow with a breath and simultaneity that no artist has ever achieved. The image of this tragically comic bohemian provides a daily ration of joy

---

38 Mariátegui 2011, p. 438.

39 Mariátegui 2011, p. 438. I have corrected Vanden's And Becker's translation by changing their translation of the original Spanish phrase 'prosaísmo arribista' as 'upstart prosiness' into 'prosaic social climbing': see Mariátegui 1981b, p. 73.

across five continents. In Chaplin, art achieves the maximum of its hedonistic and liberating function. He alleviates the sadness of the world with
his pained smile and hurt expression. And he contributes more to the
miserable felicity of humanity than any of its statesmen, philosophers,
industrialists, or artists.[40]

This paragraph is a surprising celebration of art as entertainment – even if the
totality of the essay presents Chaplin as dealing with politically relevant topics, such as gold, which Mariátegui sees as linked to the origin of capitalism –
and, even more so, of the cinema's then unmatched universality and ease of
dissemination.

However, the passage also clarifies and stresses the point implicit in the
earlier reference to US capitalism's puritanism, erroneously ascribed to the
Quakers. Art, or, better said, true art, is characterised by 'its hedonistic and liberating function'. In fact, one cannot help but feel that Mariátegui is arguing
that it is liberating because it is hedonistic. The fake morality that Mariátegui
sees as characteristic of the culture of the elites of US capitalism in the 1920s
is undermined by Chaplin and the film medium's uninhibited production of
pleasure. This celebration of pleasure and sensuality is somewhat surprising
for the author of 'El alma matinal' (The Morning Soul), the titular essay of the
collection that includes his essay on Chaplin. In the former, the Peruvian compares unfavourably the decadent bourgeois sybarite who enjoys long, exhaust-
ing, and materially unproductive nights – what he significantly calls 'the night
of decadence' – to the 'new man [who] is the man of the morning',[41] implicitly a worker or anyone participating in an organised productive activity.[42]
However, in the contemporaneous 'Explanation of Chaplin' – both were published in 1928 – hedonism is free from any association with decadence. Instead
it is presented as life-affirming. Here, perhaps, one can find another connection
between Mariátegui and Freudian notions of repression. This fake and repressive morality is, at least in this essay, the key complaint against US capitalism. For
once in Mariátegui's work, bolshevism and hedonism, revolution and pleasure,
are intertwined.

---

40   Mariátegui 2011, pp. 438–9.
41   Mariátegui 1981b, p. 13.
42   Some have seen in this reference to the 'new man' a precedent for, perhaps an influence
      on, Ernesto Che Guevara's concept of the 'new man'. I deal with the possible relationship
      between both authors and their respective versions of the 'new man' in the chapter 'Mari-
      átegui and Che'.

Chaplin's celebration of sensuality and his bohemian rejection of social climbing and the obsession with material possessions are seen as contradicting, perhaps even undermining, North America's bourgeois absolute and thus as politically and personally liberating. Mariátegui sees film, literature and, more generally, art as both mapping the ideological borders of a specific social formation – thus its use for the revolutionary critic – and as playing a role in the enforcement or subversion of these limits.

5   Literature on Trial

One can see in 'Literature on Trial', the last chapter in *Seven Essays*, the application of these ideas to his country's literature. However, unlike Europe or the US, Peru is seen by Mariátegui as a heterogeneous combination of the modern and the premodern. For the Peruvian Marxist, capitalism, rather than destroying earlier modes of production, and the social groups associated with these, has incorporated them into an unequal and incomplete modernity based on earlier social injustices and inequalities. As he notes about the rise of a Peruvian bourgeoisie:

> The bourgeoisie that developed in Peru was related in its origin and structure to the [landed] aristocracy, which, though composed chiefly of the descendants of colonial landholders, had been obliged by its role to adopt the basic principles of liberal economics and politics.[43]

Writing about the Peru of the 1920s, he adds:

> the elements of three different economies coexist in Peru today. Underneath the feudal economy inherited from the colonial period, vestiges of the indigenous communal economy can still be found in the sierra. On the coast, a bourgeois economy is growing in feudal soil; it gives every indication of being backward, at least in its mental outlook.[44]

Given this survival of colonial institutions and mores, it is not the bourgeois absolute that informs Peru's literature, but one that instead could be called neo-colonial.

---

43   Mariátegui 1971, p. 11.
44   Mariátegui 1971, p. 16.

It is thus not surprising that Mariátegui's view of Peruvian literature is over-all negative, despite the presence of writers such as Mariano Melgar, Ricardo Palma, Manuel González Prada, and José María Eguren, who in their articulation of popular and/or modern perspectives contradict the country's coloniality of culture. The title of the essay 'Literature on Trial' implies this negative and critical view. As Mariátegui states:

> The word 'trial' in this case is used in its legal sense. I do not propose to present a discourse on Peruvian literature, but only to testify in what I consider to be an open trial. It seems to me that so far in this trial the witnesses have been almost entirely for the defence and that it is time to call some witnesses for the prosecution.[45]

He would be one of these witnesses.

As we have seen, Mariátegui singles out for criticism the Generation of 1900, also known as Futurists, who were a group of conservative intellectuals culturally hegemonic during the beginning of the twentieth century in Peru.[46] (Since the Peruvian Futurists were generally aesthetically conservative, their only connection to the Italian avant-garde movement is in the name). Given that, despite the notable exceptions mentioned above, Mariátegui sees the country's literature as either colonial or neocolonial, one could question the reason for this specific animosity. In fact, the members of the Generation of 1900 were among the modernisers of Peruvian culture during the first two decades of the twentieth century. Marcel Velázquez Castro notes that

> The Generation of 1900 was our first group of modern intellectuals, but they had to fulfill traditional tasks that ought to have been faced by the positivist scholars of the nineteenth century: the creation of a cultural and historical past, and the establishment of the basis of our literary history; in other words, the first organic reflection on identity and the search for a national state.[47]

As we have seen earlier in this study, José de la Riva Agüero founded the study of Peruvian history as an academic discipline and Francisco García Calderón produced the first comprehensive socio-historical analysis of Peru, *Le Perou*

---

45   Mariátegui 1971, p. 182.
46   On the Generation of 900 also see 'José Carlos Mariátegui: The Making of a Revolutionary in the Aristocratic Republic'.
47   Velázquez Castro 2004, p. 8.

Contemporain. One is, therefore, tempted to see in Mariátegui's criticism of the Generation of 1900 an example of ideology run amuck;[48] or, perhaps more charitably, another example of the anxiety of influence which often dictates the devaluation of one's predecessors as the road to one's critical acceptance. If during the 1960s, when the Boom[49] was elbowing its way to critical acceptance in Latin America and abroad, Mario Vargas Llosa pooh-poohed the region's earlier novel as 'primitive',[50] Mariátegui described his intellectual predecessors, in particular Riva Agüero, whom he singled out as the most influential of the group, as expressing neocolonial points of view. Thus the author of *Seven Essays* presents Riva Agüero's influential *Carácter de la literatura del Perú independiente* (The Character of the Literature of Independent Peru [1905]) as 'colored, not only by his political beliefs, but also by the sentiments of a class system'; adding later, 'It is at the same time a piece of literary historiography and a political apologia'.[51]

---

48   Raúl Tola's novel, *La noche sin ventanas* ('*The Night Without Windows*'), depicts Mariátegui's reaction to the Generation of 1900 in similar terms to those expressed by Velázquez in his 'Mariátegui Unplugged'. This novel, which fictionalises the experiences under the Nazi occupation of Francisco García Calderón, then ambassador of Peru to France, and Madeleine Truel, a martyred French resistance fighter born in Peru, presents Mariátegui as consumed by an inexplicable hatred towards the 'Generation of 1900'. According to the novel, Mariátegui in *Seven Essays* attempts 'a reckoning with the "Generation of 1900"'. In order to achieve this goal, Mariátegui used all possible weapons, including referring to private conversations he had held with the purpose of buttressing his infamies' (Tola 2017, p. 310). The novel concludes, 'More than the attacks, what hurt him [Francisco] was his evil'. 'What future is there for my country in the hands of young people like him [Mariátegui]' (Tola 2017, p. 310).

49   The Boom is the name often used to describe the Latin American novels and novelists of the 1960s who became world famous; in particular, Gabriel García Márquez, Carlos Fuentes, Julio Cortázar, and Mario Vargas Llosa.

50   According to Vargas Llosa, 'The failure of the primitive novel is to a great extent the result of the disdain which its authors demonstrated toward the strictly technical problems of artistic creation' (Vargs Llosa 1989, p. 266) (Vargas Llosa's includes among these 'primitive' novelists: Clorinda Matto de Turner, Mariano Azuela, Alcides Arguedas, Eustasio Rivera, Ricardo Guiraldes, Romulo Gallegos, and Ciro Alegria). By contrast, for the 2010 Nobel Prize winner: 'The creative novel is thus a relatively recent phenomenon' (266). Among these, he includes Borges, Onetti, Fuentes, Carpentier, Guimaraes Rosa, Cortázar, and Garcia Márquez, who 'have not only put our novel, bluntly speaking, on an equal footing with even the best of other countries; they have in addition made the narration of the twenties and thirties appear in comparison to be as anachronistic as that of the nineteenth century' (Vargas Llosa 1989, p. 267).

51   Mariátegui 1971, p. 184. One must note that what is being criticised on 'Literature on Trial' is not the fact that Riva Agüero has a political position. What is criticised are the colonial values, what we could call the 'neocolonial absolute', present in the Generation of 1900's

However, if the Generation of 1900 helped modernise academia and, more generally, thinking about Peru, the key question is regarding the kind of modernisation they proposed. Perhaps a brief and necessarily superficial perusal of Riva Agüero's works can answer the question and clarify the reasons for Mariátegui's criticisms. For instance, if one looks at his *Carácter de la literatura del Perú independiente* one finds a full dependence on race as determining the value of the literature produced in a specific society. In fact, Riva Agüero believed that racial declension held the key to understanding his country's literature: 'The Spanish race transplanted to Peru, degenerated in its character as *criollismo*'.[52] He even repeats the canard that the American climate led to a weakening of European traits.[53]

An even greater flaw from Mariátegui's perspective is that the text is characterised by what could be called a celebration of literary dependence. Although Riva Agüero considers that Peruvian and Latin American literature is capable of true excellence, even of developing a limited originality, he ultimately concludes:

> We must recognize our subordination to the European or Anglo-American ideal. A forced subordination that is not only past or present, but future. Therefore, one must recognize that in Latin America's literature, over the original element, covering and even asphyxiating it, will continuously rise the element of foreign imitation.[54]

Despite the acknowledgment of the artistic potential of the nation's literature, in Riva Agüero, colonialism and neocolonialism, past and present subordinations become, for all practical purposes, indistinguishable.[55] Peru must not

---

writings, and the fact that Riva Agüero and his generational cohorts hide this under a pseudo-scientific veneer.

52   Riva Agüero 1905, p. 8.
53   Riva Agüero 1905, p. 8.
54   Riva Agüero 1905, p. 230.
55   Perhaps the essay where Riva Agüero's ultimate celebration of colonialism – the 'sentiments of his class' – becomes most clearly evidenced is his '[Elogio del] Inca Garcilaso' (1916), where he writes about the common-law relationship between Garcilaso's parents – conquistador Sebastián Garcilaso de la Vega y Vargas and the Inca princess Chimpu Ocllo: 'In the intervals of his [Sebastián Garcilaso de la Vega] [military] campaigns, he had an affair with a young Inca princess, the nusta Isabel Chimpu Ocllo, grand daughter of the earlier monarch Túpac Yupanqui, one of the timid Indian flowers with which the fierce Castillians found pleasurable relief' (Riva Agüero 1962, p. 9). Despite the celebration of *mestizaje*, that is, racial and cultural mixture, expressed by Riva Agüero in the essay, this is clearly a Hispanist and politically conservative version, in which the author identifies

merely participate in world or even Western culture – a position with which Mariátegui agreed – but has to come to grips with the fact that this participation can only take place in a necessarily permanent subordinate and subaltern position, something the author of *Seven Essays* rejected.

Thus, even if one accepts the description of Riva Agüero as a moderniser, the fact is that the Peruvian historian is a proponent of modernisation within dependence. This 'Futurist' modernisation is thus consistent with Mariátegui's description of the country's failed or incomplete capitalist modernisation. Despite its potential modernising slant, Futurism would be the cultural logic of Peru's dependent and neocolonial capitalism.[56] An additional cause for Mariátegui's animosity towards the Generation of 1900 is that he believed they helped revitalise neocolonial ideologies that had been undermined by Peru's military defeat at the hands of Chile during the War of the Pacific (1879). Impacted by that defeat, González Prada and other radicals had presented a left-liberal interpretation of the country's history and society that implied the possibility of significant political changes. As Mariátegui notes in 'Literature on Trial':

> The emotional and ideological authority of the heirs to colonialism had been undermined by fifteen years of Radical teachings. After a period of military caudillos similar to the one that followed the wars of independence, the latifundium class had reestablished its political control but not its intellectual dominion. Radicalism had been strengthened by the moral reaction to defeat, for which the people blamed the plutocracy, and had found a favorable climate for spreading its revolutionary gospel. Its propaganda had especially stirred the provinces and a wave of progressive ideas had swept the republic.[57]

---

with the conquistadors; thus transforming racial oppression, gender inequality, and the most despicable violence into 'relief'.

56 Given Riva Agüero's belief in the centrality of race and his defence of subordination it may not surprise that he became a fascist in the 1930s. As José Ignacio López Soria notes: 'in Riva Agüero, fascism, confessed without euphemism and professed with fervor, coincided with his return to the Catholic faith ... For Riva Agüero ... fascism, turned Christian at the baptismal font of an ultramontane Catholicism, [was] the only ideology capable of stopping atheistic socialism and protestant liberalism' (López Soria 1981, pp. 19–20). Riva Agüero was not the only member of the Generation of 1900 who embraced fascism in the 1930s: Víctor Andrés Belaúnde, the author of *La realidad nacional* (1931), a conservative Catholic riposte to *Seven Essays*, wrote articles supportive of fascism under the pseudonym of Ayax in *La Prensa*, the journal in which Mariátegui had begun his public career (López Soria 1981, p. 32).

57 Mariátegui 1971, p. 223.

As *Seven Essays* makes clear it, this return of the neocolonial 'absolute' to hegemony is only possible by the modernising tendencies also present among these so-called Futurists: 'It made use of modernism only for the elements it needed to condemn the unrest of romanticism'.[58] What could be paradoxically called the Futurist restoration – that is the conservative cultural modernisation proposed by Riva Agüero and his cohorts – thwarted, according to Mariátegui, the possibility of a true and full cultural modernisation, the development of a 'modern absolute' – be it fully bourgeois or socialist – and the concomit-ant structural and political modernisation of Peru. Mariátegui's analysis of the Generation of 1900 and its relation to González Prada and the Radicals high-lights the Futurists' reactionary character precisely in the terms posited by Corey Robin as characteristic of conservatism since its rise in the aftermath of the French Revolution. Robin writes:

> Far from yielding a knee-jerk defense of an unchanging old regime or a thoughtful traditionalism, the reactionary imperative presses conservat-ism in two rather different directions: first, to a critique and reconfigur-ation of the old regime; and second, to an absorption of the ideas and tactics of the very revolution or reform it opposes.[59]

One could, in fact, argue that their role in modernising Peruvian academia and, more generally, culture is interwoven with their conservatism.[60] Their mod-ernising tendencies, including their incorporation of *modernismo* – it is not fully clear if Mariátegui is here referring to the Latin American poetic move-ment of the late nineteenth and early twentieth centuries or to modernity itself, though both were present in the writings of González Prada, who was a both precursor of *modernista* poetry and a proponent of significant social changes – is an example of the reactive character of their conservative proposals and, according to Robin, of conservatism tout court. When, in an alternate version of 'Mariátegui unplugged', Velázquez argues that 'Riva Agüero is not a defender of the colony, but, rather, a severe critic of colonial literary forms',[61] he is unwit-tingly describing the way in which conservative thought works according to Robin. By being a moderniser, by criticising the past, Riva Agüero manages to rearticulate the ideological elements that make the defence of neocolonial-

---

58   Mariátegui 1971, p. 223.
59   Robin 2011, p. 42.
60   With some exceptions, such as sociologist Joaquín Capelo, the radicals exercised their influence outside the university.
61   Velázquez Castro 2002, p. 127.

ism possible in the twentieth century. As we have seen, the cultural and racial hierarchies that comprised the cornerstone on which the Peruvian neocolonial system was built were reaffirmed by the writings of Riva Agüero. The Generation of 1900 expressed in their literature what could be called the 'neocolonial absolute'.

Writing about the celebration of the colonial past, in particular, though not exclusively, in the works of the chronicler and poet José Gálvez, Mariátegui notes:

> The 'futurist' generation follows the ideas of Riva Agüero ... the 'futurist' generation makes use of his [José Gálvez's] nostalgia and romanticism in the serenade under the balconies of the vice-royalty, which is intended politically to revive a legend indispensable to the supremacy of the heirs to the colony.[62]

And:

> The feudal caste has no titles other than those of colonial tradition, nothing that advances its interests more than a traditionalist literary current. At the core of colonialist literature are found only the urgent requirements for the life force of a class, a 'caste'.[63]

Even without using the concept of 'absolute', Mariátegui describes the writings of the Generation of 1900 as presenting and popularising the narratives, values, and the structure of feeling that he feels are necessary for the maintenance and reproduction of the country's neocolonial modernity. However, because Riva Agüero's writings were mainly historical, it is the literary writings of the Generation of 1900 that ultimately fulfil the central political role. It is as if the 'neocolonial absolute' could only be disseminated in a manner capable of convincing readers indirectly and unconsciously through literature rather than scholarship. Nevertheless, given literature's necessarily agonistic character, the 'neocolonial absolute' is more clearly expressed in Riva Agüero's essays rather than in the necessarily more complex and contradictory literature of José Gálvez.

---

62   Mariátegui 1971, pp. 226–7.
63   Mariátegui 1971, p. 227.

6   César Vallejo

As we have seen, the one writer singled out by Mariátegui as ushering in a new
period in Peruvian literature is the great poet César Vallejo.[64] As is noted in
'Literature on Trial', 'Cesar Vallejo's first book, *Los heraldos negros*, ushers in the
dawn of a new poetry in Peru'.[65] The section of the essay dealing with Vallejo
is noteworthy as an example of Mariátegui's perceptiveness (he was perhaps
the first critic to acknowledge the poet's genius); and occasional lapses, by celebrating him as a poet marked by essentialised indigenous traits: nostalgia,
pessimism, collectivism. Thus, according to 'Literature on Trial', 'Vallejo is a
poet of race. In Vallejo for the first time in our history indigenous sentiment
is given pristine expression'.[66] However, Mariátegui's own text permits a less
problematic reading that is not dependent on the (for us) hoary concept of
race. As the essay notes:

> Vallejo, moreover, is not entirely symbolist. Especially his early poetry
> contains elements of symbolism, together with elements of expression-
> ism, dadaism, and surrealism. Vallejo is essentially a creator, always in the
> process of developing his technique, a process which in his art reflects a
> mood. In the beginning, when Vallejo borrows his method from Herrera
> Reissig, he adapts it to his personal lyricism.[67]

Rather than racial determinism, Mariátegui here notes Vallejo's ability to adapt
avant-garde methods and technique with a personal sensibility, which he argues is rooted in indigenous, which is to say local, values, discourse and culture.
To repeat the phrase Mariátegui used to describe his dreamed-of fusion of Peruvian traditions and socialism, Vallejo's poetry would also be a 'heroic creation':
that is, a successful transcultural hybrid of cosmopolitan innovations and local
cultural traditions that founds a new national literature. For Mariátegui:

> This art announces the birth of a new sensitivity. It is a new, rebellious
> art that breaks with the courtly tradition of a literature of buffoons and

---

64   As previously mentioned, in his 1925 'Nacionalismo y vanguardismo', Valdelomar had also
      been seen as a full-blown modern Peruvian writer, but by the time he reworked his earlier
      essays into 'Literature on Trial', his mentor had been demoted to the role of precursor. See
      'Mariátegui's Cosmopolitan Nationalism'.
65   Mariátegui 1971, p. 252.
66   Mariátegui 1971, p. 252.
67   Mariátegui 1971, p. 252.

lackeys. The great poet of *Los heraldos negros* and of *Trilce* ... appears in his art as a precursor of the new spirit, the new conscience.[68]

If one were to read this essay together with 'Art, Revolution, and Decadence', one can identify the 'new sensitivity' as compatible with revolution. Vallejo's poetry would thus imply the definite break with the neocolonial absolute. But Vallejo's ability to incorporate the avant-garde without falling into Riva Agüero's subordinate imitation also helps reconcile the tripartite division into colonial, cosmopolitan and national periods that characterises Mariátegui's survey of his country's literature. As Mariátegui notes:

> In the first period, the country, in a literary sense, is a colony depend-ent on its metropolis. In the second period, it simultaneously assimilates elements of various foreign literatures. In the third period, it shapes and expresses its own personality and feelings.[69]

Despite the obvious problems with assuming any kind of 'personality' to het-erogeneous human and textual groupings, Mariátegui's periodisation helps un-derstand the importance he ascribes to Vallejo.[70] However, it is also necessary to keep in mind that if the colonial period is described as something that must necessarily be superseded, the cosmopolitan and national are instead imbric-ated.[71] Vallejo is able to break with the Generation of 1900's neocolonialism,

---

68   Mariátegui 1971, p. 257.

69   Mariátegui 1971, p. 191.

70   Mariátegui acknowledges the limitations of this division when he notes: 'this theory of literature does not go any further, it is broad enough four our purposes' (Mariátegui 1971, p. 191). However, it is arguably applicable to Latin America and perhaps other postcolonial regions and subaltern groups. For instance, Grinor Rojo has praised the relevance of Mari-átegui's periodization comparing it, with perspicacity, to that proposed by Frantz Fanon regarding the evolution of both the intellectual and literature from colonized to revolu-tionary, and Elaine Showalter's parallel classification of women's writing from imitation, to protest, to self-discovery (Rojo 2009, p. 201). Rojo writes about Mariátegui's periodisa-tion and, in particular, to the positing of cosmopolitanism as precedent to the discovery of the national: 'This means that after the dependence on a single center and before the writer having reached the goal of identitary self-determination, a preliminary delinking regarding the first and exclusive center, and an exploratory opening to all other [centers], would have taken place' (Rojo 2009, p. 202). In other words, for Mariátegui, cosmopolitan-ism implies a break in the colonial culture of dependence and, therefore, a move towards the possibility of a national culture participating in a heterogeneous world culture com-posed of many compatible and diverse local ones.

71   On the relationship between nationalism and cosmopolitanism see 'José Carlos Mariáteg-ui's Cosmopolitan Nationalism'.

and the underlying neocolonial absolute, because he incorporates both cosmopolitan, i.e. avant-garde, and indigenous local traits. Moreover, if the Generation of 1900 assimilates *modernismo* in what could be called a homeopathic manner in order to reproduce and update the neocolonial absolute, Vallejo fully incorporates modern literature in order to achieve the heroic creation of a new national avant-garde literature. Traditional traits have long existed but can become national only when they have become modern or made compatible with modernity. Vallejo's poetry is, in a sense, an example of modernisation that ought to be followed politically, socially and economically by Peru. As Vallejo assimilates the avant-garde he goes beyond any type of literary dependence.

7   Conclusion

Despite its undertheorisation – a problem that must be faced by any reading of his often journalistic works addressed to a general audience – Mariátegui's notion of the 'bourgeois absolute' prefigures many of the terms that would later be developed by Marxist theorists to understand the political valence of cultural and literary products, as my use of phrases such as 'cultural logic', 'structure of feeling', or 'political unconscious' implies. Instead of seeing in literary and cultural products the passive superstructural reflection of an economic base, Mariátegui sees these as playing a role in the maintenance and reproduction of social and economic structures. It is, therefore, not surprising that the Peruvian's political activity is deeply interrelated with what could be called his cultural praxis: not only, as we have seen, in his personal investment in criticism – from his perspective necessary to an understanding of the political valences of literary works – but also in the creation of Editorial Minerva, a book and magazine publishing firm in 1925.

His rejection of the Generation of 1900 and the neocolonial absolute underlying their work is evidenced not only in his groundbreaking political and artistic journal *Amauta*, but also in the historical and analytical works he published in Editorial Minerva. These were books dealing with Andean topics – Luis E. Valcárcel's classic indigenista manifesto *Tempestad en los Andes* (1927), Abelardo Solis's *Historia de Jauja* (1928) – or working class history – Ricardo Martínez de la Torre's *El movimiento obrero en 1919*. Needless to say, these Andean and working-class topics present the history of Peru from a different perspective from that of the upper class, Hispano and Lima centric works of the Generation of 1900.

But, his more literary publications express his belief in the political value of literary works and styles. His sympathy for the avant-garde as potentially undermining bourgeois and neocolonial absolutes is exemplified in his publication of poetry collections, such as Carlos Oquendo de Amat's *5 metros de poemas* (5 Meters of Poems 1927), printed in one large 5 metre fold-out page; Enrique Bustamante y Ballivian's *9 poetas nuevos del Brasil* (9 New Poets from Brazil 1930), which included translations of poems by Mario de Andrade and Manuel Bandeira; of Serafín Delmar's *Radioprogramas del Pacífico* (Radio Programs from the Pacific 1927), one of the first poets to exhibit Vallejo's influence. Moreover, he published the work of women avant-gardists, such as Magda Portal's *Una esperanza i el mar* (One Hope and the Sea 1927) and the Uruguayan Blanca Luz Brum's *Levante* (Levant 1926). He even published the 'pure poet' José María Eguren's *Poesías* (Poems 1928). These and other works that represented modern, marginal, Andean, female views, undermined the neocolonial absolute by presenting perspectives and ideas that contradicted and mocked hegemonic views. Mariátegui's work as an editor and publisher reflected his belief in the necessity of a modernisation that would incorporate silenced and marginalised Peruvian voices and traditions, while at the same time participating in the more radical Western artistic movements.

The centrality of his cultural work should not lead one to forget that unlike later Western Marxists, whose work was shaped by the knowledge that the revolution had failed, Mariátegui was a tireless union organiser and the founder of the (Peruvian) Socialist Party.[72] Nevertheless, the importance of the cultural struggle was such that towards the end of his life, when facing governmental censorship and harassment, and criticism from the Comintern and from his former APRA comrades, Mariátegui decided to emigrate to Buenos Aires to continue publishing a version of *Amauta* and his editorial work.

For Mariátegui, political change was impossible without a cultural revolution.

---

72   Western Marxism must be differentiated from Soviet communism, Trotskyism, as well as the Marxism of the sympathisers of these two movements. As Perry Anderson notes: 'The hidden hallmark of Western Marxism as a whole is thus that it is a product of defeat. The failure of the socialist revolution to spread outside Russia, cause and consequence of its corruption inside Russia, is the common background to the entire theoretical tradition of this period' (Anderson 1989, p. 42).

José Carlos Mariátegui and the Culture of Politics

In January 1928, news reached José Carlos Mariátegui that the exiled Víctor Raúl Haya de la Torre, with whom he had often cooperated in political and editorial projects, had decided to transform the Alianza Popular Revolucionaria Americana (The American Popular Revolutionary Alliance), better known as APRA, into a political party: the Partido Nacionalista Libertador del Perú (National Liberating Party of Peru) or Partido Nacionalista Peruano (Peruvian Nationalist Party). (Both names were used in the Party's founding documents). In Mexico, Haya, together with other collaborators and till-then friends of Mariátegui, such as the poets Magda Portal and Serafín Delmar,[1] redacted a platform for the new party titled 'Esquema del plan de México' (Outline of the Mexico Plan), which also proclaimed Haya's candidacy for Peru's presidency in the scheduled 1929 elections. It was distributed primarily among the Peruvian members of the APRA.[2] The APRA, which had been founded by Haya in 1924, soon after his forced exile from Peru, had been, till then, a loose, international, anti-imperialist coalition, with members throughout Latin America and Europe. Such diverse figures as Eudocio Ravines, soon to be 'man from Moscow' in Lima (and, even more in the future, 'man from Washington'),[3] poet César Vallejo, and future leaders of the APRA party, Manuel Cox and Manuel Seoane, were all members. The attraction of the alliance among the region's progressive intelligentsia is evidenced by the fact that the three intellectuals proclaimed

---

1 The personal and professional closeness of Portal and Delmar with Mariátegui is evidenced by the fact that Editorial Minerva published the former's *Una esperanza i el mar: varios poemas a la misma distancia* (1927) and Delmar's *Radiogramas del Pacífico* (1927). Moreover, Mariátegui included a section on Portal in 'Literature on Trial', his chapter on Peruvian literature in *Seven Essays*.

2 While Portal and Delmar signed the 'Esquema del plan de México' and continued defending Haya vehemently even after Mariátegui's death, Portal later claimed: 'Personally I thought the whole idea premature and didn't care for it. We made criticisms and argued so strenuously that Haya threatened to resign as leader, which didn't happen' (quoted in Weaver 2009, p. 99). The next elections were held in 1931, after colonel Luis Miguel Sánchez Cerro deposed Augusto Leguía. Sánchez Cerro, representing the new (semi) fascist party Unión Revolucionaria in results that have been contested. For many, Haya had won the 1931 elections but they were stolen (see Chang-Rodríguez 2012, p. 292). Masterson has, however, argued that these were 'the most honest in Peruvian history to that time' (Masterson 1991, p. 47).

3 I deal briefly with Ravines's sinuous political career in 'José Carlos Mariátegui: The Making of a Revolutionary'.

Maestros de la Juventud ('Teachers of the Youth') during different congresses of Latin American students – the Argentines, José Ingenieros, perhaps that country's best-known essayist and thinker, and Alfredo Palacios, radical legislator and legal scholar; and the Mexican José Vasconcelos, former Secretary of Public Education and the theorist of the 'Cosmic Race' – all aligned themselves with the APRA.[4]

The APRA was characterised by a radical pan-Latin Americanism and an overt anti-imperialism. These traits were clearly expressed in the movement's platform first published by Haya in the British Communist magazine *Labour Monthly* in 1926:

> 1. Action of the countries of Latin America against Yankee imperialism. 2. The Political unity of Latin America. 3. The nationalization of land and industry. 4. The internationalization of the Panama Canal. 5. The solidarity of all oppressed people and classes of the world.[5]

The structure of the APRA was, in Haya's words, 'a united front' that 'works to include in its ranks all those who in one way or another have struggled and are still struggling against the North American danger in Latin America'.[6] As Mariátegui's early support for the APRA exemplifies, he was fully aware of the oppressive effects of US and other imperialisms. In addition to his important 'Anti-Imperialist Point of View', written a year after his break with Haya, Mariátegui's acknowledgment of the reach of imperialism is evidenced by the stress made by the Confederación General de Trabajadores del Perú (General Federation of Workers of Peru) – the labour union he helped found in 1929 – in organising workers in the mostly foreign-owned mining corporations. That same year his working-class journal, *Labor*, was closed by the Leguía regime over its coverage of the walkout of the 15,000 miners working for the US-owned Cerro de Pasco Corporation. *Amauta* had also published articles detailing and criticising the presence of US corporations in Peru before the break with Haya, such as Jorge Basadre's 'Mientras ellos se extienden' (While They Grow), which were among the reasons that led to the temporary closing of the journal in

---

4 Ingenieros, Palacios and Vasconcelos were named 'maestros de la juventud' (teachers of the youth) during El primer congreso iberoamericano de estudiantes (Mexico, 1925) (Graciano 2008, p. 109). One must note that during a visit to Lima in 1919, in response to Alfredo Palacios's expressed support for the reform of the pedagogical and administrative structures of the universities in Peru, the students of San Marcos had already named him 'maestro de la juventud' (see Biagini 1999, p. 208).

5 Haya 1926, p. 756.

6 Haya 1926, p. 756.

1927. However, unlike Haya, for Mariátegui anti-imperialism was never the primary concern. The author of *Seven Essays* always saw political change as a holistic process that included anti-imperialist agitation and action, but, perhaps primarily, also a relentless struggle to eradicate neocolonial institutions, legislation, and ways of thinking.

Portal's comments about the intellectual and personal differences between the two leaders of the Peruvian left, precisely at the time of their personal break, are illuminating:

> With J.C. Mariátegui, at the get togethers in his home, the conversations were always open-ended, free-wheeling, always having to do with socialist thought but not geared towards ideological definition, political education, or proselytizing. Haya, however, put forward a specific goal. His intention was to lay the groundwork for a new sociopolitical movement in Latin America.[7]

Mariátegui's open-ended discussion was contrasted with Haya's political and institutional purposiveness. It is, therefore, not surprising that Portal should date her full embrace of anti-imperialism to her becoming Haya's disciple in Mexico. As her biographer notes: 'Haya's anti-imperialist emphasis now struck her with revelatory force'.[8]

Despite these personal differences, the growing distance between their ideas, and even the obviously diverging views of what political actions should be taken in Peru, Mariátegui expressed admiration for Haya in his *Seven Essays*.[9]

---

7   Quoted in Weaver 2009, p. 42. Jorge Basadre, who in his youth was a friend of Mariátegui and, as we have seen, a collaborator of *Amauta*, describes the ambiance during the regular get-togethers in his home: 'There was no vanity in his conversation, nor autobiographical references, nor any histrionic rhetoric, nor platitudes. On the contrary, he was objective in judgement, ready to hear and ask, avoiding any allusion to himself, immune to any cliché ... One did not find in the get-togethers anything planned, mandatory, or that implied any kind of obligation ... The conversations had no doctrinaire purpose. One spoke about current affairs, especially in relation to books, paintings or music. There was no place for gossip or any other pettiness' (Basadre 2014, pp. 273–4).

8   Weaver 2009, p. 52.

9   Rouillón, in his biography of Mariátegui, presents him and Haya as becoming aware of having different political beliefs from their very first meeting in 1923, and, from that moment, 'leading indirectly to a battle in the field of ideas' (Rouillón 1984, p. 207). On the other hand, those close to Haya, like Portal in the 1930s, have always argued that Mariátegui was a follower of Haya: 'Mariátegui was an aprista until 1927' (Portal 1930, p. 4). That said, while the statement is true in the sense that Mariátegui supported the APRA before it became a political party, it did not imply a personal fealty to Haya, as Portal attempts to portray.

When making his seminal proposal that 'The problem of land is obviously ... bound up with the Indian problem',[10] Mariátegui took time to note:

> After writing this essay, I find ideas in Haya de la Torre's book *Por la eman-cipacion de la America Latina* that fully coincide with mine on the agrarian question in general and the Indian community in particular. Since we share the same points of view, we necessarily reach the same conclusions.[11]

Later, in the same book, when discussing Haya's re-evaluation of Ricardo Palma's writings as critical of colonialism, he praises the APRA founder's 'political acumen and historical perspective'.[12]

Nevertheless, the result of Haya's candidacy was the complete breakdown of the camaraderie and collaboration that had till then characterised not only the relations between the two political leaders, but also the interactions among the different factions of the Peruvian left.[13]

1   Mariátegui's Anti-politics

In a letter written to Samuel Glusberg, his main Argentine interlocutor, Mariátegui noted:

---

10   Mariátegui 1971, p. 31.
11   Mariátegui 1971, pp. 58–9.
12   Mariátegui 1971, p. 197.
13   While Mariátegui limited the discussion to politics and the ethics of politics, Portal and Haya made use of virulent ad hominem attacks in their dismissal of the Peruvian Marxist's arguments. (For an example of Haya's vituperative dismissal of Mariátegui, see the appendix to Flores Galindo's 'Un viejo debate: el poder', which consists of the letters sent by Haya to Eudocio Ravines [Flores Galindo 1988, pp. 73–106]). Also see Haya's letter to Mariátegui from 20 May 1928 (Mariátegui 1994, pp. 378–9). Portal even made use of an obituary article for the journal APRA to accuse Mariátegui of having made a pact with the conservative Civilista Party, in which, in exchange for unspecified support, he would have been named Minister of Education (Portal 1930, p. 4). (No evidence was presented for this charge and the accusation was rapidly dropped from the anti-Mariátegui argumentation). Kathleen Weaver, Portal's biographer, asks 'what accounts for Magda's participation in the verbal assault on Mariátegui, her friend and mentor, the champion and publisher of her poetry?' and then she replies: 'she was probably acting under the influence of Haya de la Torre' (Weaver 2009, p. 62). Portal resigned in 1948, after 20 years in the APRA, of which she was the most important female leader, in protest against Haya's decision to no longer accept women as members of the party.

From 1928, nauseated by *criollo* politics – as a journalist and for some time as political and parliamentary editor I knew the political parties inside out and saw statesmen in informal situations – I started moving in the direction of socialism.[14]

The importance of this quotation is that it clearly shows that Mariátegui's political evolution in the 'direction of socialism' was linked to his disillusionment with Peru's mainstream politicians – who showed themselves less than statesmen in private – and with the way in which politics was practised in Peru, that is, the often corrupt give and take characteristic of the aristocratic republic.

Perhaps it would not be too far-fetched to see in this quotation Mariátegui's embrace of socialism as predicated in the dismissal of electoral politics *tout court*. Jesús Chavarría has argued that Mariátegui's rejection of representative politics was linked to the influence of Georges Sorel, who had helped unmask 'all the illusions associated with universal suffrage and electoral politics'.[15] One can add, however, that in the case of the aristocratic republic in Peru, elections helped cover a whole substratum of neocolonial sins perhaps not known in Europe. As James Higgins notes, 'Democracy was limited, since the electoral law of 1895 had excluded illiterates, and as a result *civilista* governments were voted in by a small minority of literate male electors who made up only about four percent of the total population'.[16] This law, of course, excluded the vast majority of the rural indigenous population. It would have taken a great degree of self-delusion – or a complete identification with its neocolonial mentality – to see in the aristocratic republic anything but a sham version of democracy. While Augusto B. Leguía's coming to power had been characterised by growing North American political and economic influence, it had not signalled a full upturning of neocolonial hierarchies or of the traditional elites' hold on the country's putatively democratic institutions. Even though elections were held twice during his regime – in 1921 and 1929 – the results were manipulated and used to justify a de facto dictatorship. In fact, the 1929 'election', which Haya planned to enter, 'was largely understood to be rigged by Leguía'.[17] Mariátegui didn't need to read Sorel to see Peruvian democracy and, concretely, the 1929 elections as 'a most vulgar electoral agitation'.[18] Be that as it may, according to

---

14   Mariátegui 1994, p. 331.
15   Chavarría 1979, p. 134.
16   Higgins 2005, p. 146.
17   Jansen [2008], p. 20.
18   Mariátegui 1994, p. 373.

Mariátegui, by becoming a candidate, Haya had become part of the corrupt *criollo* politics he saw as opposed to even the possibility of radical change.

2   Haya's Impossible Candidacy

Haya's candidacy was announced in a communiqué from a 'National Directing Committee of the Partido Nacionalista Peruano' (Comité Directivo Nacional del Partido Nacionalista Peruano) located in the Andean town of Abancay, though in reality all of the leaders of the new party were exiled in Mexico.[19] (This document, unlike the 'Esquema del plan de México', was meant to be widely distributed among the Peruvian population). The communiqué echoed the language of *indigenista* texts, such as Luis Valcárcel's *Tempestad en los Andes*, in its criticism of Lima as 'sensual and colonised' and its claim that the 'new Peru, like the Peru of the Incas, arises from the southern Andes'.[20] It was clear that Haya and his circle, despite most not having been born in Andean regions nor being of indigenous ancestry, were making a claim for *indigenista* credentials. Mariátegui understandably charged that this was 'basing a movement ... on a bluff and a lie'.[21]

But Haya's candidacy raised additional reasons for scepticism. He was legally ineligible given that the Peruvian constitution required candidates to be 35 years or older and he was only 33. Therefore, even if the elections had been free, he would not have been allowed to register as a candidate and, if, by chance,

---

19   As mentioned above, one of the many unusual aspects of this first candidacy by Haya de la Torre is that two names are used for the new party. Thus, in the 'Esquema del plan de México', the party is named as 'Partido Nacionalista Libertador del Perú', while in the communiqué produced in Abancay, it was now named 'Partido Nacionalista Peruano'. Eugenio Chang-Rodríguez notes that 'Víctor Velázquez, a student from the Southern Andes, returned surreptitiously to Abancay and there began to organize the first militants of the Partido Nacionalista' (Chang-Rodríguez 2012, p. 327).

20   Partido Nacionalista Peruano 1979, p. 352. According to the communiqué, 'Our Party proclaims from the depth of the southern Andes this call. The new Peru, like the Peru of the Incas, arises from the southern Andes. Lima, sensual and colonized, cursed by Bolívar, will not continue to dominate and exploit the country willy-nilly ... But the 'Partido Nacionalista Peruano' is not an imposition by Lima: it is a cry from the provinces, it is imposed by the Nation. That is why ... it is a provincial man of Andean background who leads us' (Partido Nacionalista Peruano 1979, p. 352). In reality, Haya de la Torre had been born in the coastal city of Trujillo, in the department of La Libertad, and was culturally and phenotypically white, at least as such is defined in Peru. On Luis Valcárcel, see 'José Carlos Mariátegui: The Making of a Revolutionary in the Aristocratic Republic'.

21   Mariátegui 1994, p. 372.

he had registered and won, he could not have been sworn in as president. Not surprisingly then, Haya's candidacy ultimately floundered and Leguía ran unopposed.

Given Haya's disdain for any action that did not fulfil a specific political goal, it makes sense to look for possible reasons behind this bluff. It is, for instance, not far-fetched to speculate that Haya probably saw the 1929 campaign as a trial run for the real elections that would take place after the overthrow of Leguía that, given the weakening of the regime, he probably suspected would not be too far off in the future. By means of this fake candidacy, Haya, known primarily to students and Lima working-class organisations, would gain national notoriety and, perhaps, create a cadre of militants and supporters that could later be mobilised in his support. Moreover, as the Abancay communiqué states, one could see in Haya's impossible run for the presidency a means to unmask the electoral charade put in place by Leguía:

> We know that the bayonets paid with Yankee gold will impose over the blood of our compatriots the reelection of the agent of the foreign imperialists. We know that the farce of 1924 will be repeated, but we want to make the effort to show the country that we are ready to use legal means before we embark in the name of the supreme interests of the country to claim using all means what is being denied violating laws and principles.[22]

By presenting a candidate – even if one who was ultimately symbolical – and thus not allowing Leguía to run unopposed, the new party would force the president to show his true colours and repress democracy publicly.

One could thus find in Haya's candidacy an echo of Francisco Madero's campaign against Porfirio Díaz, which served to unmask the falsity of the Mexican dictator's call for elections and helped start the Mexican Revolution. Haya had become cognisant of the history of the Mexican Revolution during his stay in Mexico as the secretary of José Vasconcelos between 1923 and 1924. Moreover, for Haya, the Mexican revolution was the measuring stick against which all Latin American political movements were to be measured.[23] The 'Esquema del

---

22   Partido Nacionalista Peruano 1979, p. 350.
23   Partido Nacionalista Libertador 1948, p. 292. In his later (1936) *El antiimperialismo y el apra*, Haya writes 'No historical experience … is closer or more useful for Indo-Americans that that which Mexico presents. In my opinion, the Mexican Revolution is our Revolution' (Haya 1936, pp. 144–5).

Plan de México' – concluded by stating that 'The motto of the movement will be that of Land and Freedom that Emiliano Zapata gave to the Mexican Revolution'.[24]

However, according to some historians, the true goal of the Partido Nacionalista Libertador and of Haya's would-be presidential campaign was something different from an impossible – for the reasons given above – electoral victory. As Eugenio Chang-Rodríguez argues, 'in reality, Haya's candidacy was part of a program of distraction ... This trick hid the true purpose of a projected armed rebellion'.[25] Thus, simultaneously with the electoral campaign, Felipe Iparraguirre, reputed to be a former captain in the Peruvian Army living in El Salvador, arrived surreptitiously in Talara, a city in northern Peru, to organise a military insurrection under Haya's instructions. The uprising failed. Haya notes, in a private letter dated 1929,[26] 'in his last letter he [Iparraguirre] advised me of the formation of an army based on 2,500 workers in Talara. I would have received an agreed telegram to travel to Peru immediately'.[27] Although Haya assumed that Iparraguirre had been tortured, and, perhaps, executed, in reality he had simply been deported after being captured.[28]

---

24   However, in the Abancay communiqué, it is stated that: '"Peru for Peruvians and not for Yankees!" is the motto of our Party' (Partido Nacionalista Peruano 1979, p. 349).

25   Chang-Rodríguez 2012, p. 327.

26   While much of the correspondence that was generated by this debate can be seen as public documents – for instance, the letter from Mariátegui from which I have been quoting is addressed to the 'Mexico group' rather than to a specific individual – others must be seen as private; whether they were means of achieving support from specific individuals – such as Haya's letters to Ravines between 1926 and 1929 – or Haya's letter to César Mendoza quoted above.

27   Quoted in Manrique 2009, p. 79. Manrique casts doubt on the existence of Iparraguirrre's army, given the traditional lack of support for Haya in Talara and Piura and the fact that the totality of the Peruvian army consisted of 10,000 men, see Manrique 2009, pp. 79–80.

28   Manrique 2009, p. 81. Iparraguirre was a rocambolesque character. According to Manrique, who follows historian Víctor Villanueva, he was not an active captain of the Peruvian Army, but only an officer in the reserve, who taught fencing at the Lima garrison, moved to Mexico and married a rich landowner's daughter and got divorced. Then, he moved to El Salvador, where he married the daughter of that country's War Minister, who named him an instructor of the Salvadoran army. After participating in the failed Partido Nacionalista Libertador rebellion, he went to Chile, from where he returned to Peru as fencing master of General Pablo Martínez, who tried to challenge then President Sánchez Cerro to a duel. After this, he seems to fade from historical writings. Regarding Martínez, the animosity between him and Sánchez Cerro originated when Martínez led a failed coup attempt in 1931. Sánchez Cerro mistreated Martínez while he was in prison. However, rather than accepting the duel, Sánchez Cerro managed to have the question handled by an 'honour tribunal' (Chocano 2011, p. 172).

Mariátegui had no knowledge of this would-be uprising. However, one doubts that he would have approved. He probably would have seen it as but another example of *criollo* politics, which, moreover, had not been exempt from uprisings and putsches. Instead he argued for an ethical politics devoid of the byzantine manoeuvring that he had observed up-close as a journalist. In his letter to the Mexico group, he note: 'I believe our movement must not base its success in trickery or decoys. Our strength, our only strength, our best strength, is the truth'.[29] But as will be seen, Mariátegui's opposition to Haya's candidacy went beyond ethical considerations or, for that matter, a distrust of 'bourgeois' democracy.

Mariátegui's vociferous criticisms, as well as the intemperate rejoinders of Haya de la Torre and his followers, led not only to the personal distancing of this debate's two main protagonists, but also to the disaggregation of the Peruvian left. However, and this is what is relevant for this study, the breakup with Haya can serve to shine a light on Mariátegui's specific approach to radical political change.

3   The New Spirit

The Peruvian left in the 1920s had been constituted by the agglutination of groups with diverse interests and, ultimately, agendas, brought together by their opposition to the core values of the aristocratic republic of the early twentieth century. Fernanda Beigel has argued that the main consistent thread around which this progressive coalition had been weaved was the awareness of the centrality of the indigenous issue.[30] While there is no doubt that most – if not all – of these 'progressive' groups felt the need to eliminate indigenous servitude, the exploitation of this population, and the incredibly unequal tenure of land, this was a period of crisis for both the neocolonial Peruvian aristocratic republic, and, more generally, Western culture and its constitutive values and institutions: liberalism, democracy, and capitalism.

Not only national events – such as the beginning of industrial modernisation, the growing presence of US capital, especially in mining, the improvement in transportation and communication within the country, the rekindling of unsolved territorial issues with Chile – but also international ones – the Mexican and Russian Revolutions, the student Córdoba Reform that helped mod-

29   Mariátegui 1994, p. 372.
30   Beigel 2003, p. 20.

ernise Argentine universities, as well as the negative economic effects of World War I and its aftermath – led to a crisis of legitimacy of the aristocratic republic. If the dictatorial Augusto B. Leguía regime, in its opening to and defence of the newly hegemonic US capital that had replaced that of Britain, was one response to this crisis, another was the rise of a diverse, heterogeneous, somewhat inchoate, opposition not only to the government, but also to the neocolonial aristocratic republic that it was attempting to bring up to date.

The oppositional groups included the mostly working-class anarchists (the most significant of these groups until the mid-1920s); nationalists (whose patriotism had been rekindled by the issue of the reincorporation of the 'lost provinces' of Tacna and Arica, as well as the growing presence of US capital in the country);[31] *indigenistas* (both defenders of indigenous rights and artists interested in indigenous cultures); budding socialists (in particular the activists associated with Mariátegui and left-leaning workers, such as Julio Portocarrero); students (such as the young Haya), who inspired by the 1918 Córdoba Reform wanted to participate in the solution of social problems; and avantgarde artists (who rejected the country's colonial culture). (There was obviously some overlap among these groups and individuals). These divergent factions had found ways to work together in such significant causes as the struggle for the eight-hour workday, protests against rise in prices, and the popular mobilisation of 23 May 1923, rejecting President Augusto Leguía's bizarre and demagogic attempt at dedicating Peru to the Sacred Heart of Jesus. (Tellingly, given his characteristic sympathy for religious expression, Mariátegui did not participate in the last demonstrations).[32] As Beigel notes, this was 'a universe that was born in a period of crisis and was constructed in the praxis of collective subjects who looked for an alternative to that imposed by the *criollo*-oligarchic

---

31   As mentioned earlier in this study, Peru had lost in the War of the Pacific (1879–83) the territory of Tarapacá to Chile. However, the peace signed in 1883 (Peace Treaty of Ancón) stipulated that the provinces of Arica and Tacna, would remain under Chilean control for ten years, after which a plebiscite would determine whether they would stay in Chile or return to Peru. The plebiscite was never held. Instead in 1929, the Treaty of Lima determined that Arica would remain in Chile, while Tacna would return to Peru.

32   As Chavarría notes, 'Mariátegui chose to remain on the sidelines, saying the protest lacked concrete revolutionary ends' (Chavarría 1979, p. 74). According to Chang-Rodríguez, Mariátegui's refusal to participate in the anti-clerical protests was one of the first instances of disagreement between both leaders of the Peruvian left (Chang-Rodríguez 2012, p. 193). Chang-Rodríguez also insinuates that persisting loyalty to Leguía, who had sent him on 'paid exile' to Europe, explains Mariátegui's opposition to the anti-clerical demonstrations. I would argue, however, that it was Mariátegui's opposition to any anti-clerical or anti-religious policies, perhaps itself expression of a residual religiosity, that best explains his absence from the demonstrations. Also see Chang-Rodríguez 2012, p. 177.

perspective'.[33] This 'intersubjective universe', as well as the 'praxis of collect-ive subjects' that it could have made possible, was blown to pieces by Haya's decision to transform the APRA into a political party and by the acrid debate it generated.

Of course, the reason it was so easy to destroy the loose unity of the Peruvian progressive forces resided precisely in their heterogeneity. The terms Mari-átegui used to describe them in 'Anniversary and Balance Sheet', his response to the transformation of the APRA into a party, imply this fragility:

> 'New generation', 'new spirit', and 'new sensibility' are all terms that have grown old. The same must be said of other labels: 'vanguard', 'left', 'renov-ation'. They were new and good in their moment.[34]

For Mariátegui, the solution to this breakdown was a new aggregation around socialism understood as 'a heroic creation',[35] that is, as we have seen, one adap-ted to Peruvian reality and capable of incorporating the indigenous population, their needs and demands.

4   The Platform of the Partido Nacionalista Libertador del Peru

In many respects, the 'Esquema del Plan de México', the platform of the Partido Nacionalista Libertador, is a faithful reflection of the 'new spirit' that had char-acterised the inchoate Peruvian left. If as Beigel noted, the indigenous question was central to the 'new generation', the document responds to this concern by highlighting the need for a radical redistribution of land. This is, of course, already implicit in their borrowing of the phrase 'land and freedom', by iconic Mexican revolutionary Emiliano Zapata, as the new party's motto. But, in addi-tion to this rhetorical nod to the issue of land reform, the party's platform explicitly refers to the land tenancy problem several times.[36]

---

33   Beigel 2003, p. 29.
34   Mariátegui 2011, p. 128.
35   Mariátegui 2011, p. 130.
36   The preamble notes that Peru is 'subjugated today by the tyranny of the national landown-ers and foreign imperialism represented by the regime of don Augusto B. Leguía' (Partido Nacionalista Libertador 1948, p. 290). The sixth point stresses 'the return of the land to the Peruvian people, giving it to those who work it, destroying latinfundism and procur-ing to reestablish, on the basis of the indigenous communities ... the new agrarian and agricultural organism' (Partido Nacionalista Libertador 1948, p. 291). The seventh point reaffirms the centrality of the indigenous community and adds the need to bring 'all the

But agrarian reform is not the only topic central to the new generation present in the Partido Nacionalista Libertador's platform. In fact, most of the five points that constituted the platform of the APRA proposed in 1926 were included in the 'Esquema del Plan de México'. As one would expect from any text associated with the Haya of the 1920s, anti-imperialism is also highlighted throughout the 'Esquema del Plan de México', even if not one specific point in the party platform is dedicated to the topic.[37] Haya's pan-Latin Americanism also appears in point 2 – which promises to pursue the union of Latin American countries – and point 14, which promises citizenship to all Latin Americans who align with the party.[38] Its fifth point argues for the 'nationalisation of land and industry'.[39] (This point is also relevant to the issue of land tenancy). The topic of solidarity with other liberation movements is explicitly mentioned in point two. In fact, only the call for the internationalisation of the Panama Canal is absent from 'Esquema del Plan de México'.

5   Party Structure

Given that Mariátegui's objected primarily to the transformation of the APRA into a political party, it is necessary to look at what kind of party the Partido Nacionalista Libertador was meant to be. The PNL saw itself as exclusive vehicle for political renovation: 'for the realization and efficacy of the liberating revolution of Peru, it is established that the only organization that will achieve it ... will be the Partido Nacionalista Libertador del Peru'.[40] But not only is the new party presented as the only vehicle for radical change, but the 'Esquema del plan de México' also stresses the PNL's strict hierarchical organization. Haya is presented as the 'supreme leader' and the members of the Mexico 'committee',

---

help of modern technology to the admirable Inca system' (Partido Nacionalista Libertador 1948, p. 291). The eight point restates the importance of incorporating 'scientific bases' in this 'renovation of the system of production in land' (Partido Nacionalista Libertador 1948, p. 291). The twelfth, thirteen and fourteenth points all refer, in different ways, to the need to 'abolish the power of the land holding class' (Partido Nacionalista Libertador 1948, p. 292). And, as we have seen, the fifteenth and final point takes up Zapata's motto – 'land and freedom' – as that of the new political party.

37   Anti-imperialism is, however, central to the appeal made to public opinion in the Abancay communiqué (Partido Nacionalista Peruano 1979).

38   Partido Nacionalista Libertador 1948, pp. 290, 292.

39   Partido Nacionalista Libertador 1948, p. 291.

40   Partido Nacionalista Libertador 1948, p. 290.

that is, Delmar, Portal and others, as next in line.[41] Furthermore, rigid discipline – the party is described as a 'revolutionary political military organism' –[42] in other words, unblinking obedience to the dictates of the leadership – were to be the hallmarks of this new party.[43]

The references to hierarchical organisational structures and rigid military-style discipline as necessary to the constitution of any radical political party are already present in the letters Haya wrote to – of all people – Eudocio Ravines, who, unbeknownst to the APRA leader, was in the process of becoming a Soviet agent.[44] In 1926, two years before the split between the APRA leader and Mariátegui took place, Haya had written to Ravines: 'What is essential in this moment is to form proletarian cadres, constitute the red army, in a word';[45] and: 'Not the multitude, nor the guerrilla, but cadres, unit, Army. These are what win revolutions'.[46] Two years later, now during the time of his break up with Mariátegui, Haya reaffirmed the importance of military-like discipline and hierarchy:

> We would waste time in explanations, all because of a lack of revolutionary faith, preparation, organization, in our lines. What we need now is discipline, military discipline ... These words about controlling the leaders, can they be uttered in an army? No.[47]

Given this stress on a hierarchical party led by an absolute leader, it is, perhaps, not surprising that the Abancay communiqué builds up Haya into a heroic figure, worthy of the exalted position of being the exclusive representative of Peru's youth. Referring to a 1922 encounter between Leguía and the young Haya, the communiqué notes:

---

41 Partido Nacionalista Libertador 1948, p. 290.
42 Partido Nacionalista Libertador 1948, p. 290.
43 The Abancay Communiqué calls for 'making our [party] an army of civil soldiers for the true cause of national regeneration' (Partido Nacionalista Peruano 1979, p. 348).
44 While much of the correspondence that was generated by this debate can be seen as a kind of public document – for instance, the letter from Mariátegui from which I have been quoting is addressed to the 'Mexico group' rather than to a specific individual – others must be seen as means of achieving support from specific individuals. This is the case of Haya's letters to Ravines between 1926 and 1929. They are included in full as a supplement to 'Un viejo debate: el poder' (Flores Galindo 1988, pp. 72–106).
45 Flores Galindo 1988, p. 73.
46 Flores Galindo 1988, p. 78.
47 Flores Galindo 1988, p. 83.

Leguía, representing the old generation, burdened with crimes and mistakes, embodying all the vices of the oligarchies that have betrayed the fatherland, found himself face to face with Haya de la Torre, who represented the new national generation, pristine, honest and sincere to the point of sacrifice, and capable as no previous one.[48]

While one could easily see the language used to describe Haya de la Torre as nothing but an exaggerated example of typical electoral discourse that builds candidates into champions of vaguely described social struggles, it also seems coherent with the personalist nature and the hierarchical structure of the new party presented in the 'Esquema del plan de México'.[49]

6   *Caudillismo* or/and Fascism

Mariátegui will simultaneously propose two interpretations for the evolution of the Mexico group into the Partido Nacionalista Libertador. The first could be described as backward-looking. We have already seen how he interpreted the new party as indulging in *criollo* politics. He therefore easily assimilated the celebration of the 'absolute leader' in the 'Esquema del plan de México' and the exaggerated celebration of Haya found in the communiqué as representing the caudillo tradition in Latin America. The Abancay communiqué, in particular, would be an example of *criollo* methods characterised by 'the caudillesque declamation, the empty and boastful rhetoric'.[50] In a slightly later letter to Ravines, Mariátegui elaborates on this criticism of Haya: 'Haya suffers too deeply the demon of *caudillismo* and personalism'.[51] And:

---

48   Partido Nacionalista Peruano 1979, pp. 341–2.
49   There is also a clear echo of González Prada's 'Speech at the Politeama Theater' in the Abancay communiqué, for instance, when González Prada declared: 'Old men ought to tremble before children because the rising generation always accuses and judges the declining generation' (González Prada 2003b, p. 46). And: 'Old men to the grave, and young men to the task at hand!' (González Prada 2003b, p. 50). As Chang-Rodríguez notes, 'From its inception, the APRA recognized in González Prada one of its precursors and in its program for action stressed the recommendations of the Master: morality, federalism, the redemption of the Indian, democratization of literature, separation of Church and State, but rejected its anti-Catholicism' (Chang Rodríguez 2012, p. 163).
50   Mariátegui 1994, p. 373.
51   Mariátegui 1994, p. 490.

I know *caudillismo* can still be useful, but only in condition that it be totally subordinated to a doctrine and a group. If one has to adapt to the environment, we have nothing to criticize the old politics ... Haya does not care about language; I do. And not due to a literary consideration but because of ideology and morals. If we do not, at least, distinguish ourselves from the past, I fear that in the end, for the same reasons of adaptation and mimicry, we will end but differing ourselves on in the individuals, in the personalities.[52]

Despite the surprising acceptance of a possible progressive *caudillismo*, perhaps unique in his writings, Mariátegui's stress is on the subordination of individuals to the political movement and to the doctrine. Instead of the party being a vehicle for the caudillo coming to power, he saw in the charismatic candidate a means for a movement's ideas to be disseminated. This stress on the means, rather than the ends, is also characteristic of his consistent emphasis on the importance of the language used in politics. For Mariátegui, rather than the hyperventilated prose of early twentieth-century Latin American – and other – politics, clarity and analysis were to be at the core not only of political discourse but of the possibility of it interpellating individuals towards new ways of seeing reality.

Simultaneously to tracing the structures and discourse of the Partido Nacionalista Libertador back to its Peruvian sources (*caudillismo*), Mariátegui would also interpret it as repeating, in a Peruvian key, the developments that had led to fascism:

Who constituted the first fascists? Almost all these elements had a deeper revolutionary background and history than we do. They were extreme radical leftists, like Mussolini, a protagonist of the red week in Bologna; heroic revolutionary unionists, like Carridoni, a formidable worker organizer; anarchists who were great intellectuals and philosophers, like Massimo Rocca ... All these people were or felt revolutionary, anticlerical, republican, 'beyond communism', according to Marinetti's phrase ... Tactics forced them to attack the revolutionary bureaucracy, break with the socialist party, destroy the workers' organization ... Socialism, the

---

52   Mariátegui 1994, p. 491. One must note that if Mariátegui here considers the possibility of progressive personalist politics, it is in a private, not a public letter. In his public texts, this possibility is not considered.

proletariat, were, despite all its bureaucratic deadweight, the revolution. Fascism had necessarily to be a reactionary force.[53]

In addition to the rejection of 'personalism' and of the heated political discourse of the day – not intrinsically different from ours, one may add – Mariátegui criticised the new party because, in its two founding documents, 'the word socialism is not mentioned once'.[54] Perhaps, simplistically, Mariátegui felt that any claim to social change that did not present socialism as an inspiration and/or goal necessarily would end up in fascism, that is, in an anti-democratic cult and practice of violence, and in the repression of individual and class rights in favour of those of property. Mariátegui seems unaware that, as Haya stated in a letter to Ravines, the latter's conception of what a political party should be, and of the importance of hierarchical discipline in its structure and functioning, originated in his study of Lenin and the Russian Revolution: 'what is essential in this moment is to form a proletarian cadre, to constitute the red army'.[55] As Manrique and others have argued, for Haya, the party was conceived as 'the revolutionary vanguard that would be the subject of the forthcoming revolution'.[56] Moreover, for Haya in the mid-1920s, radical discourse and action are necessarily rooted in Lenin's ideas: 'We must understand and make reality that maxim of Lenin: "The essential question in a revolution is the question of power"'.[57] But, by 1928, the references to Lenin had faded from Haya's correspondence and writings.[58]

---

53   Mariátegui 1994, pp. 372–3.
54   Mariátegui 1994, p. 372. Haya would also link Mariátegui to fascism when trying to convince other members of the 'new generation' to support the Partido Nacionalista Libertador. Thus, in one of his letters to Ravines, he argued: 'I know that military fascism similar to that in Chile is being developed for Peru. Mariátegui, like the Italian communists in 1921 is opening the doors for them. The Mussolini with epaulets of Peru (helped by the imperialists) will build Mariátegui a monument with one leg' (Flores Galindo 1988, pp. 98–9). Haya's mention of the hypothetical monument having one leg is a reference to the fact that Mariátegui had one leg amputated.
55   Flores Galindo 1988, p. 73.
56   Manrique 2009, p. 87.
57   Flores Galindo 1988, p. 79.
58   Flores Galindo argued that, despite Haya's reference to Lenin, the true roots of his belief in hierarchy and obedience as the key to politics, understood primarily as the acquisition of governmental power, were to be found in Peruvian society. In 'Un viejo debate: el poder', the great historian argues: 'This authoritarian view of revolution is not his [Haya's] invention, nor is it a consequence of his European experience, or [derives] from some text by Lenin. On the contrary, in Peru there is a long tradition that could go back to the colonial hierarchies or to the antiquity of the State in the Andean space' (Flores Galindo 1988, p. 67). Haya would then reproduce in his thought and in his attitudes and emotions

Despite his awareness of the authoritarian tendencies at work in the Soviet Union, in his letters of this period, Mariátegui presents dogmatism and repression as the exclusive domain of fascism. The fact that by 1928, Leninism was in an advanced stage of its morphing into Stalinism was something that Mariátegui seems incapable of accepting.[59]

7   Partido Socialista

Mariátegui will respond to the short-lived Partido Nacionalista Libertador by helping found the Partido Socialista (Socialist Party) in October of 1928. A brief perusal of its 'Programmatic Principles' is necessary in order to grasp the politics supported and proposed by the author of *Seven Essays*. One must, however, keep in mind that the conditions in which the party was founded, as a reaction to what he felt was a distortion of the political potential found in the 'new generation', and the fact that it was developed in conversation with other founding members, should lead one to see the 'Programmatic Principles' as a political compromise rather than as a full expression of the kind of politics in which Mariátegui actually believed.

Already in the name of the party one can see how Mariátegui thought about politics. The explicit reference to socialism contradicts the Partido Nacionalista Libertador's refusal to name its politics in both the 'Esquema del plan de México' and the Abancay Communiqué, despite the references made in both documents to revolution as the new party's political goal. (Haya countered in a letter to Mariátegui that 'we will make the revolution distributing lands and

precisely the structure of feeling that had served as foundation for Peruvian neocolonial society. However, both views – regarding the Leninist or the Peruvian origins of Haya's obsession with hierarchy and discipline – are not necessarily incompatible. Perhaps the appeal of Leninist party structures for Haya originates in their consonance with Peruvian historical tradition and social structures. In fact, Lenin himself may have been echoing the hierarchical social traditions of Russia. Even the greatest innovators innovate within specific cultural and social contexts and, therefore, are not immune from the influence of the society in which they work and think and even aim to change.

59   One can, however, find in Mariátegui's writings an acute analysis of the growing authoritarian tendencies in the Soviet Union, even if marred by a misguided optimism when prognosticating the ultimate results of the country's political evolution. Already in his 'El partido bolchevique y Trotsky', published in 1925, Mariátegui portrayed sympathetically Trotsky's calls for a 'true worker's democracy' (Mariátegui 1979, p. 150), noted the antidemocratic evolution of the regime, but concluded that, regardless of personal tensions, the party would adapt and incorporate Trotsky's demands (Mariátegui 1979, pp. 154–5).

fighting against imperialism without mentioning socialism').[60] But the name of the party raises additional questions. In 1919, during the second congress of the Communist International, Lenin proposed – and the delegates passed – twenty-one conditions for the participation of any political party in the Communist movement. Condition 17 clearly stated:

> In this connection all those parties that wish to belong to the Communist International must change their names. Every party that wishes to belong to the Communist International must bear the name Communist Party of this or that country (Section of the Communist International). The question of the name is not formal, but a highly political question of great importance. The Communist International has declared war on the whole bourgeois world and on all yellow social-democratic parties. The difference between the communist parties and the old official 'social democratic' or 'socialist' parties that have betrayed the banner of the working class must be clear to every simple toiler.[61]

By calling the new party socialist, Mariátegui violated one of the conditions that is explicitly described by the Lenin-led International as 'not formal, but ... of great importance'. It is, therefore, not surprising, that only towards the end of Mariátegui's life, in March 1930, would the Socialist Party request its formal affiliation with the Communist International. The most probable conclusion is that, despite Mariátegui having established communication with the International in 1927, despite his stress on the international dimension of all radical activity, he did not consider the Soviet-led communist movement as capable of directing Peruvian political practice. He could call the party socialist simply because he did not plan for its full affiliation with the Comintern.

However, for many, including members of the later Communist Party, the name of the party is not an issue. For instance, Jorge del Prado, in his 'Mariátegui-Marxista Leninista' simply disregards the actual name Mariátegui gave to the party by stating that '[he] understood the need to found the Peruvian Communist Party'.[62] Del Prado provides what will become the standard explanation for Mariátegui's actual use of socialist in the name:

> due to tactical considerations (that later Mariátegui was to recognize as a mistake and then make corrections), it was given at first the name of

---

60   Mariátegui 1994, p. 378.
61   [Communist International] [1977/1919].
62   Del Prado 1980, p. 80.

Socialist Party … José Carlos thought that by doing so it was more feasible to attract all revolutionaries to the party and [thus] to make it into a great and true mass party.[63]

Del Prado, therefore, argues, that since Mariátegui wanted to call the party Communist and made a mistake by calling it Socialist – even if he gives a valid reason for the use of the alternate name – the issue is moot. Needless to say, del Prado's argument disregards the fact that, since the twenty-one conditions were public knowledge, Mariátegui must have known that by naming the party Socialist he was contradicting the Comintern's (and, one must add, Lenin's) directives to all parties applying for membership in the governing body of international communism.

Nevertheless, the fourth 'principle' of the Socialist Party seems to place it clearly within the gravitational field of the Comintern:

Capitalism is in its imperialist stage. It is the capitalism of monopolies, of finance capital, of imperialist wars for the plundering of markets and providing sources of raw materials. The practice of Marxist socialism in this period is that of Marxism-Leninism. Marxism-Leninism is the revolutionary method in the stage of imperialism and monopoly. The Peruvian Socialist Party takes it as its method of struggle.[64]

Despite the implicit reference to Lenin's *Imperialism*, what is actually meant by 'Marxism-Leninism' is never stated in the Programmatic Principles.

Roland Forgues has argued that:

one can read in the 'Programmatic Principles of the Peruvian Socialist Party' that it takes 'Marxism-Leninism' as its 'method of struggle', but we don't find even one mention of what constitutes its specific basis: 'the dictatorship of the proletariat'. It is thus clearly discarded as an element of its own political practice, and therefore, 'Marxism-Leninism' has been reduced to a concept emptied of its real content.[65]

In fact, as Forgues notes:

---

63   Del Prado 1980, p. 84.
64   [Socialist Party] 2011, p. 238.
65   Forgues 1995, p. 223.

the concept of the 'dictatorship of the proletariat', present in the ... conferences from 1923–1924 and in his first book [*La escena contemporánea*] is, after that first period, practically banished from Mariátegui's vocabulary.[66]

This banishment is, perhaps, best exemplified by the fact that in *Defensa del marxismo*, a book often read as a criticism of social democracy, neither the phrase 'dictatorship of the proletariat' nor that of 'Marxism-Leninism' are ever used.[67]

The deviations of the 'Programmatic Principles' from Comintern orthodoxy show how Mariátegui strove to rethink leftist politics within a Peruvian context. Even those who like del Prado accept the idea that Mariátegui wanted to name the party Communist but for practical reasons felt obliged to call it Socialist are unwittingly noting the way the Peruvian Marxist always privileged local reality over international dogma. Again, he was fully knowledgeable of the conditions posited by the International and, therefore, was willing to risk criticism, even censure, in order to adapt political practice to Peruvian conditions. It is difficult, therefore, not to see in 'Programmatic Principles' a response not only to Haya and the Mexico group but also to the Comintern.

The 'Immediate Vindications' included in the Programmatic Principles clearly mark a distance from the APRA in the concrete nature of their demands – they propose that the party fight for a minimum wage, the redistribution of haciendas to indigenous communities, the establishment of social security and social assistance, etc. But they also establish the new Party's divergence from the Comintern's cookie-cutter communist parties in their implicit description of the party as pluriclassist – they explicitly call for the support of these 'vindications' by 'the proletariat and by the conscious elements of the middle class'[68] Despite the Programmatic Principles' reference to the Socialist

---

66   Forgues 1995, p. 69.
67   However, the phrase 'Marxist-Leninist' appears in a peculiarly ironic context when writing about intellectuals who despair when they are disregarded by the masses: 'A Writer, more or less absent from history, more or less foreign to the Revolution taking place, imagines herself sufficiently inspired to present the masses with a new conception of society and of politics. Since the masses do not give her enough credit and, without waiting for her magical discoveries, prefer to continue with the Marxist-Leninist method, the writer becomes disgusted with socialism and the working class, [becomes disgusted] with a doctrine and class she barely knows and which she approaches with all her academic, group, or café prejudices' (Mariátegui 1981a, p. 123).
68   [Socialist Party] 2011, p. 242.

Party as the 'vanguard of the proletariat', the party was actually proposed as being made up by members of diverse class origins.[69]

But, if the class composition of the new party is at odds with the explicit demands of the Comintern, the lack of mention of the structure of leadership – this would be hammered out in meetings that Mariátegui, due to his health, did not attend – can be seen as contradicting Haya's concern with hierarchical party discipline.[70] As Flores Galindo notes:

> distrust towards any [type] of elite is a frequent [trait] in Mariátegui. During the time of the discussion with Haya, [he] writes about Charles Chaplin to remind us that, in any case, 'elite means elected', always subordinated to the majority.[71]

Needless to say, this stress on the subordination of political elites also implied a rejection of the Leninist view of the necessarily hierarchical centralisation of the party.[72]

---

69   [Socialist Party] 2011, p. 240.
70   According to Martínez de la Torre, during the Herradura Meeting that discussed the foundation of the Partido Socialista Peruano, it was decided that there would be a secret cell running the party. This 'secret cell' was to constitute a radical Marxist core within the Socialist party. However, Mariátegui never mentions it in any of his texts – whether public or private. As Flores Galindo notes: 'The main problem with the model of a two-faced party is that it puts in question [its] internal democracy, because, if the majority ignores the existence of the cell, it means the majority ignores the direction the party is taking ... depending on the perspective taken, it is, therefore, a refined or crass manipulation, that evidently contradicts the notion of politics as truth held by Mariátegui' (Flores Galindo 1980, p. 34). There is no record of this proposal in any of Mariátegui's extant texts, whether public or private.
71   Flores Galindo 1980, pp. 68–9.
72   The statutes for the Communist Parties approved during the Third Congress of the Comintern, in 1921, that is during Lenin's watch, clearly state: 'Formal or mechanical centralisation would mean the centralisation of "power" in the hands of the Party bureaucracy, allowing it to dominate the other members of the Party or the revolutionary proletarian masses which are outside the Party. Only enemies of Communism can argue that the Communist Party wants to use its leadership of the proletarian class struggle and its centralisation of Communist leadership to dominate the revolutionary proletariat. Such assertions are false. Equally incompatible with the principles of democratic centralism adopted by the Communist International are antagonisms or power struggles within the Party' ([Communist International] [1980/ 1921]).

8   Popular Fronts

The founding of the Partido Socialista was at its core Mariátegui's compromise with politics, both local and international. Of course, this was unavoidable given, on the one hand, the Comintern's rigidity, and, on the other, Mariátegui's simultaneous belief in the necessarily international dimension of radical political change – even if he did not immediately seek the Socialist Party's affiliation with the International – and the need to adapt politics – as well as analysis – to local conditions and history. However, where Mariátegui's non-Leninist (if not anti-Leninist) politics is fully manifested is in the founding of the Confederación General de Trabajadores del Perú (General Confederation of Peruvian Workers; CGTP) in 1929, that is after the creation of the Socialist Party. By stressing the need for worker unity and participation across ideological and political lines, Mariátegui will again contradict the Comintern's and Lenin's requirements for Communist Parties. The second condition states that every organisation that wishes to affiliate to the Communist International must regularly and methodically remove reformists and centrists from every responsible post in the labour movement (party organisations, editorial boards, trades unions, parliamentary factions, co-operatives, local government).[73] Mariátegui instead proposes a kind of popular workers' front that would incorporate members of all political stripes as long as they held on to the goals and methods of the new labour union. The 'Manifesto of the General Confederation of Peruvian Workers' declares as its first goal the 'fight for the creation of a united labor front without any distinction as to political tendencies in a United Proletariat Central'.[74] Although now clearly focused on the development of a class identity, Mariátegui can be seen as attempting to radicalise united front policies within a Peruvian political reality fractured by the constitution of the Partido Nacionalista Libertador, and against the Comintern's hierarchical democratic centralism and policy of subordination to party and, more generally, Soviet dictates. Mariátegui is here continuing the kind of labour politics he had promoted from his return to Peru in 1923. That very same year, he presented his lecture 'The World Crisis and the Peruvian Proletariat' before a hall filled with workers. In this presentation, his first after his return from Europe, he uses the ur-Leninist term 'vanguard' in a very non-Leninist manner when discussing the need for workers to pay attention to the political and revolutionary goings on in Europe and elsewhere:

73   [Communist International] [1977/1919].

74   General Confederation of Workers 2011, p. 346.

This need is even greater in that the socialist, laborite, syndicalist, or anarchist[75] part of the proletariat constitutes the vanguard. That part of the proletariat is most combative, conscious, and more prone to struggle and is prepared. That part of the proletariat is charged with the direction of the great proletariat actions. That part of the proletariat whose historic role is to represent the Peruvian proletariat in the present instance [world revolution]. In that part of the proletariat, whatever its particular creed, in a word, that has class conscience, has revolutionary conscience.[76]

In *What is to be Done*, Lenin consistently links the notion of vanguard to the (then) Social-Democratic party:

We must take upon ourselves the task of organising an all-round political struggle under the leadership of our Party in such a manner as to make it possible for all oppositional strata to render their fullest support to the struggle and to our Party.[77]

For the Russian leader, political and ideological homogeneity were the necessary means to achieve political change. For Mariátegui, on the other hand, unity in goals, not ideology, was the requisite for radical political action. Marxists (though it is unclear whether communists or Social Democrats); syndicalists, influenced by Sorel; labourites, unexpected Peruvian disciples of Sydney and Beatrice Webb; anarchists, followers of Bakunin and Malatesta: all can be part of the vanguard despite differences in ideology and politics. As he noted in his later 1927 'Message to the Workers' Congress', 'In the work for today, nothing divides us. Everything unites us'.[78] Even if the Socialist Party claimed Marxism-Leninism as the necessary method, no matter how vague as a concept, Mariátegui as a labour organiser rejected imposing any explicit ideological restrictions. Revolutionary consciousness was possible among workers of any political stripe.

It is true that the Comintern had from the period of 1922 to 1928 supported a policy of united fronts, whereby Marxists could collaborate with non-Communists in promoting the basic interests of the working class – for

---

75   I have corrected Vanden and Becker's translation. They use libertarian for Mariátegui's original *libertaria*. The main meaning of *libertario* is anarchist if used as a noun, anarchistic if used as an adjective.

76   Mariátegui 2011, pp. 297–8.

77   Lenin 1999, p. 52.

78   Mariátegui 2011, p. 183.

instance, fighting for an eight-hour workday, etc. – though without losing their organisational separation. If one were to disregard the already detailed evidence of his distance from international Communism, one could argue that Mariátegui's collaboration with Haya – from 1923 to 1928 – responded in principle to the Comintern's united front policy. Moreover, Mariátegui broke with Haya precisely as the united front was substituted by a 'class against class' policy that saw in the non-Marxist left but another bourgeois movement, in its own way, not different from fascism.

Mariátegui's union organising, however, tells another story. He clearly disregarded Lenin's twenty-one conditions in order to work across ideological and political boundaries. In fact, he never abandoned united front politics. In 1929, after the break-up with Haya and the bitter, on occasion, scurrilous mutual accusations, Mariátegui wrote to Bolivian union leader Mario Nerval, who sympathised with Haya's politics:

> If your party [APRA], hypothetically at the moment, becomes a mass party, we will not have any inconvenience in eventually collaborating with it on clearly established objectives.[79]

Mariátegui held on to united front policies, despite the personal tenor of the polemic with Haya and the directives of the Comintern.

9   Conclusion

One can see Mariátegui's view of politics as homologous to his view of culture. This homology is evident if one briefly looks at *Amauta*, the centrepiece of what Fernanda Beigel has called the Peruvian Marxist's 'aesthetic political project'. For her, the magazine's well-known opening to numerous and occasionally discrepant positions exemplified the 'aesthetic-political fusion [that] inaugurated a new instance, that cannot be identified with either the aesthetic or the political vanguard in their traditional and divergent meanings'.[80] While, in a parallel gesture to the founding of the Socialist Party, after 1928, *Amauta* no longer received collaborations supporting Haya or his politics, and will now insist on the socialist character of the publication,[81] it continued publishing

---

79   Mariátegui 1994, p. 597.
80   Beigel 2003, p. 53.
81   Despite the demonisation of Mariátegui on the part of the Mexico (APRA) group, Antenor

politically and culturally heterogeneous texts. For instance, *Amauta* put out an issue celebrating the symbolist Peruvian poet José María Eguren in 1929.

Mariátegui's inclusionary editorial policy represents a cultural and intellectually political version of the united front policies he so favoured. As Beigel also notes, Mariátegui's 'collective project and praxis' is the 'result of the editorial networks, get-togethers, polemics, the party'.[82] The differences that Portal pointed out between Mariátegui's free-ranging, though meaningful, conversations and Haya's disciplined and hierarchical political activity, reappear in a different context.

Despite superficial similarity, Mariátegui's agglutinative policies and politics have a different goal from those present in other attempts at left-wing coalition building in Latin America and elsewhere. During the Fourth Congress of the Comintern (1922), the delegates saw the united front policy as alternatively a way to 'pull members out of Social-Democratic organizations'[83] or as a way to build a militant and united worker-led movement against capitalist and fascist attacks, to counter growing inter-imperialist conflicts with heightened working-class internationalism, and to promote an effective, united movement for colonial freedom.[84] While Mariátegui, obviously, sympathised with these goals, for him, the united front in both politics and culture fulfilled another objective. If the Comintern, before the change in policy in 1928, had sought to both undermine social-democracy and resist fascism, Mariátegui's praxis aimed to interpellate individuals and direct them towards radically different social and individual goals. As he puts it in, of all places, *Defensa del marxismo*, 'If socialism should not be realized as a social order, it would be enough as a work of education and elevation to be justified in history'.[85] Mariátegui aimed at nothing less than to change the way Peruvians thought individually and collectively.

It is thus tempting to connect Mariátegui with political thinkers like John Holloway, who, inspired by the Zapatistas in Chiapas during the 1990s, attempt to delink revolutionary attitudes, if not strictly politics, from the takeover of the state:

Orrego, a supporter of Haya, contributed an article – '¿Qué es una filosofía?' – to the November/December 1929 issue of *Amauta*.

82   Beigel 2003, p. 51.
83   Riddell 2012, p. 11.
84   Riddell 2012, p. 2.
85   Mariátegui 2011, pp. 204–5.

The scream, the No, the refusal that is an integral part of living in a capitalist society: that is the source of revolutionary movement. The weaving of friendship, of love, of comradeship, of communality in the face of the reduction of social relations to commodity exchange: that is the material movement of communism. The non-subordinate are the anti-heroes of the revolution.[86]

For Mariátegui, like Holloway and other contemporary theorists, radical politics is not immediately political in an electoral, Jacobin, Leninist or, for that matter, *Hayista* sense. Needless to say, both Holloway and Mariátegui are responding to the anarchist and, in the case of the Peruvian Marxist, the Sorelian heritage that sees political change as starting at the level of the individual.

But even if the author of *Seven Essays* was wary of politics defined as primarily the taking over of the state, or as the artificial suturing of diverse interest that Ernesto Laclau defines as politics itself,[87] Mariátegui clearly believed in the struggle for specific political goals, such as land reform, the minimum wage, or the establishment of social security. He sees this struggle as an educational process that leads to the development of class awareness, to the elimination of colonialist modes of thinking and ultimately to socialism. Workers of all racial and cultural backgrounds, indigenous peasants, students, who do not find jobs or activities in which their knowledge can be put to uses that benefit society, and nominally middle-class individuals who see that their interests are better served by a profound democratisation of society, would constitute a new even more radicalised 'inter-subjective universe'. For Mariátegui, the struggle for concrete goals creates real sutures, linking different groups that discover they have more in common than originally believed. Thus also contradicting Ernesto 'Che' Guevara, who believed that the goal of the revolution was to create new women and men, Mariátegui sees only new subjectivities and identities as capable of making a true revolution and not repeating bourgeois or fascist nationalist structures. Even if the conquest of power is not the immediate goal, Mariátegui still believes in the need for revolutionary change, but only new subjects formed through ethical struggle will be capable of creating a new society. As mentioned above, Forgues has noted that although Mariátegui borrows the concept of the myth from Sorel, he adapts it in ways that, to a great

---

86   Holloway 2010, p. 211.

87   'The unity of the social agent is the result of a plurality of social demands coming together through equivalential (metonymic) relations of contiguity, the contingent moment of naming has an absolutely central and constitutive role' (Laclau 2005, p. 227).

degree, modify its political meaning.[88] For Mariátegui, revolution – understood as the construction of new social structures built on new subjectivities – is a goal that, as Forgues again argues, 'leaves, therefore, to the means a vast gamut of possibilities', not, as in the case of Sorel, limited to violent strikes.[89] Social reform, a 'new spirit', even a new modern literature, are all valuable in and of themselves, yet they also contribute to the possibility of achieving the ultimate goal of systemic social change, of the creation of a new more equal and more just Peru and world. Thus Mariátegui can be seen as reconciling reform and revolution, anarchism and Marxism, individual evolution and social revolution and, as Forgues proposes, the democratic radicalism of Jean Jaurès and Georges Sorel's violent disregard for elections.[90]

But, had he lived, would he have been able to hold on to his unusual view and practice of politics? The 1920s had been a time when the breakdown of the aristocratic republic in Peru seemed to open the doors to utopia – or, at least, to dreaming of it. We have already seen how he felt forced to found a political party; that is, to take a measure that was bound to weaken, though not necessarily forestall, his united front politics. Haya's founding of the Partido Nacionalista Libertador, that is, a proto-populist party, heralded the changes that would take place as the 1920s turned into the dark 1930s. This latter decade would be a time when the rise of Nazism, the entrenchment of Stalinism, the impact of the great depression, the coming to power in Peru of a cycle of right-wing dictatorships, and the failure of populism, as represented by Haya's APRA party, foreclosed political change.

---

88   See, 'Mariátegui, Sorel, and Myth'.
89   Forgues 1995, p. 213.
90   'Everything happens [in Mariátegui's writings], in effect, as if consciously Mariátegui felt the need to opt for the revolutionary and violent way of Sorel, but from an attitude that unconsciously makes him privilege the democratic and reformist way of Jaurès' (Forgues 1995, pp. 208–9).

Mariátegui and Argentina: Celebrating Buenos Aires, Criticising Communism

By late 1929 and early 1930, Mariátegui's fragile health had taken a turn for the worse. Though already wheelchair bound after the amputation of his right leg in 1924, the chronic osteomyelitis he suffered now put his life in danger. Furthermore, the therapies prescribed by his Peruvian doctors – which included regular visits to the beach – had shown itself to be ineffectual. Mariátegui came to the conclusion that he needed the advanced treatment only available in more modern cities.

But his political projects were also hanging by a thread. In 1927, under the pretense of a Communist coup, Mariátegui had been placed under arrest in the Hospital Militar San Bartolomé. Ironically, this purported Communist coup predated Mariátegui's first contacts with the Comintern in 1928. Furthermore, in November 1929, his house was raided, his visitors jailed, and he was placed under house arrest. His mail – so central to his work as both a political organiser and as the editor of what was arguably the major Spanish American journal of the time, *Amauta* – was now routinely read and often confiscated. As one of his closest friends, Waldo Frank, noted in his obituary piece for *The Nation*:

> Mariátegui lived in a state of perpetual siege. Often his letters never reached him, his papers were wantonly destroyed; in a hundred petty ways life was made miserable for him and work almost impossible.[1]

Already limited in mobility and dependent on visitors and correspondence for social, intellectual, and, in connection to *Amauta*, commercial exchange, this growing harassment made it impossible for him to function as an intellectual, political organiser, and human being.[2] As Mariátegui states in a letter from November 1929: 'They are trying ... to suffocate me in silence'.[3]

---

1   Frank 1930, p. 704.
2   I have taken most factual information regarding the harassment and struggles faced by Mariátegui during his last days from Flores Galindo 1980, pp. 91–110.
3   Mariátegui 1994, p. 673.

Mariátegui's travails were not only caused by the government's increasingly repressive measures. The political networks so carefully built by the Peruvian socialist were breaking down. As we saw, the APRA, until then a loose anti-imperialist association, had been transformed by its founder Haya de la Torre into a national political party – Partido Nacionalista Libertador[4] (National Liberating Party) – in 1928 with the immediate goal of taking power in Peru whether by election or revolution. John M. Baines (for once) accurately notes that

> Prior to 1928 Mariátegui had been skeptical about the usefulness of form-ing a political party ... His experience in Europe made him cautious about organizing for political action without first having clearly determined the ends for which that action intended.[5]

Mariátegui always believed that organising and educating were indispensable activities for even the most radical political movement. For him, creating a political party before having significant mass support for its radical propos-als implied putting the cart before the horse. However, Mariátegui answered Haya's actions by prematurely founding the Peruvian Socialist Party. Despite its Marxist statement of principles, the Socialist party was at first marginal-ised by the Comintern and, after his death, transformed into another cookie cutter Communist party. Mariátegui's response to this set of events – political repression, the break-up of the Peruvian Left, worsening health – was to decide to emigrate to Argentina. Underlying this planned relocation obviously was Mariátegui's concern with getting better treatment for his ailments. However, throughout his writings, he actually stresses the need to continue publishing *Amauta*. In fact, already in 1927, after his imprisonment and during the tempor-ary banning of his magazine, Mariátegui had written to Samuel Glusberg, who in addition to being a publisher was his main contact in Argentina, informing him that

> If I cannot get the closing of *Amauta* reconsidered, I will endeavour to prepare my trip to Buenos Aires to establish the magazine there, which has an extensive circulation base in Spanish America.[6]

---

4 The APRA actually used two names in its founding documents: 'Partido Nacionalista Liberta-dor' and 'Partido Nacionalista Peruano'. See 'José Carlos Mariátegui and the Culture of Politics' in this study.

5 Baines 1972, pp. 124–5.

6 Mariátegui 1994, p. 304.

As the quotation evidences, towards the end of his life, as the possibility of active politics faded, cultural politics became Mariátegui's main concern. In this chapter, I analyse the potential consequences of this frustrated trip.

1 Buenos Aires and Mexico City as Cultural Meridians

As part of his contribution to the 'Intellectual Meridian Debate',[7] the pan-Hispanic polemic triggered by Spanish poet Guillermo de Torre's suggestion in his 1927 article 'Madrid, meridiano intelectual de Hispanoamérica' that the Iberian capital be considered the necessary cultural centre of the Spanish-speaking world, Mariátegui wrote in his article 'La batalla de *Martín Fierro*' (The Battle of *Martín Fierro*):[8] 'The gravitational fields of the Spanish American spirit are necessarily Mexico City, in the north, and in the South, Buenos Aires'.[9] For Flores Galindo, Mariátegui's writings are characterized by

> a counterpoint between vanguard art and *indigenismos*, between the West and the Andean world, between the vindication of heterodoxy and the exaltation of discipline, between what is national and what is international, between Mexico (the native side of Latin America) and Buenos Aires (the port to Europe).[10]

But as the quotation from Mariátegui implies, the counterpoint mentioned by Flores Galindo was not only between the locations most identified with respectively the indigenous and the local and the modern and cosmopolitan poles of the region's culture, but also between two intellectual and, one must add, publishing centres.

Laura Mulvey and Peter Wollen have noted the importance of Mexico during the 1920s as a cultural mecca for artists worldwide. The British critics write of a 'Mexican Renaissance': 'an extraordinary surge of energy in the arts, which attracted foreign visitors and admirers'.[11] (Among these 'visitors and admirers' one can mention Katherine Anne Porter, Tina Modotti, Edward Weston, Sergei Eisenstein, and D.H. Lawrence).[12] For Mulvey and Wollen, Mexico City was one

---

7   I have dealt with this debate in *The Spaces of Latin American Literature* (pp. 33–47).

8   *Martín Fierro* was a major Argentine cultural journal that included collaborations by Jorge Luis Borges, Oliverio Girondo, and other major poets and writers of Buenos Aires.

9   Mariátegui 1980h, p. 118.

10   Flores Galindo 1980, p. 12.

11   Mulvey and Wollen 1989, p. 82.

12   Additionally, as Jesús Chavarría notes, in addition, to a becoming an artistic mecca, 'Mex-

of the privileged locations – the others are Moscow (constructivism, futurism), Berlin (dadaism), and Paris (surrealism) – where political and artistic revolu-tion were interwoven.[13] The works and names of the great painters Frida Kahlo, Diego Rivera, and José Clemente Orozco, of the composers Carlos Chávez and Silvestre Revueltas, and of the novelist Mariano Azuela, can serve as examples of this cultural rebirth and of the fusion of politics and culture that character-ised Mexican art and letters in the 1920s and early 1930s.

In fact, Mariátegui in 1928 praised Mexico terms that predict those used by Mulvey and Wollen in the 1980s. In one of the first reviews of Azuela's *The Underdogs* (*'Los de abajo'*), he writes:

> The painting, sculpture, the poetry of Mexico are the most vital of the continent. Those [arts] of other Spanish American countries present ... suggestive and exemplary individualities and movements, but those of Mexico have the vital force of an organic and collective phenomenon. They are distinguished by their popular origin and imprint.[14]

Earlier in the same review, he had gone as far as to claim 'Mexico has the key to the future of Indian America'.[15] One can add that Peru is clearly part of this 'Indian America'.

Mexico had apparently succeeded in creating an 'organic' culture rooted in its popular social and historical traditions. What he says about *The Underdogs* is applicable to other Mexican masterworks: 'Azuela has created integrally from Mexican materials. Not in vain his country's revolution is so rich in matter and spirit'.[16] Mexico's high culture is thus presented by Mariátegui as a development of these popular traditions and experiences, rather than, as was generally the case in Peru, as based on their rejection. Mexico was, therefore, an example for the Andean country to follow. As we have seen, Mariátegui's canon is mainly constituted by writers such as Mariano Melgar, Ricardo Palma, and, especially, César Vallejo who attempted to make national art out of popular traditions. But of these, only Vallejo is presented as being fully successful in creating high art from what according to Mariátegui were not only local, but actually indigenous, sources.

---

ico City ... in those days was virtually a mecca for the international left' (Chavarría 1979, p. 101).

13   Mulvey and Wollen 1989, p. 82.
14   Mariátegui 1980h, p. 85.
15   Mariátegui 1980h, p. 84.
16   Mariátegui 1980h, p. 88.

Although Mariátegui would always stress the compatibility between nation-alism and cosmopolitanism, he saw Mexican culture as closed off to foreign influences. As he writes in 'La batalla de *Martín Fierro*', when comparing the two Latin American candidates for 'cultural meridian':

> Mexico [City] is physically a bit closed and distant. Buenos Aires, more connected to the other centers of South America, possesses more mater-ial conditions to become a metropolis.[17]

This distance is described as 'physical', but it is obviously also cultural. A few months after 'La batalla de *Martín Fierro*', in a letter to Glusberg that belongs to the cycle of communications dealing with his possible relocation to Buenos Aires, Mariátegui again compares the two great metropolises:

> Mexico [City] and Buenos Aires are the great centers of Latin Amer-ica. But Mexico [City] is too far from South America and it does not yet have the aptitude to feel, in these [literary, cultural] things, a continental nationalism.[18]

Complicating the counterpoint proposed by Flores Galindo, for Mariátegui, Buenos Aires, and by implication Argentina, present a constellation of traits often seen as contradictory, including cosmopolitanism, pan-Latin American-ism, and a clearly defined sense of national identity. But, as we have seen,[19] for Mariátegui, nationalism is only a necessary stage in the development of a true identity that would be both national and international, and free from both local bias and neocolonial influences.

In 'La batalla de *Martín Fierro*', Mariátegui points out what is, perhaps, the key requirement for a Latin American 'cultural meridian': 'In the city that aspires to coordinate and direct us we need to find, if not a revolutionary spirit, at least a liberal tradition'.[20] The obvious intention of Mariátegui's require-ment was to contradict de Torre's claim for Madrid as a 'cultural meridian', since Spain was governed by Miguel Primo de Rivera's quasi-fascist regime. However, while Mexico during the first half of the 1920s could make claim to a 'revolutionary spirit', in his articles of late 1929 and early 1930, Mari-átegui argues that the promise of the Revolution had become exhausted. In

---

17   Mariátegui 1980h, p. 118.
18   Mariátegui 1994, p. 576.
19   See the chapter 'Mariátegui's Cosmopolitan Nationalism' in this study.
20   Mariátegui 1980h, p. 118.

his 1930 'Al margen del nuevo curso de la política mexicana' (To the Margins of New Mexican Political Situation), he attributes this exhaustion to the specific development of Mexico's internal class dynamics that led to the backwards movement in Mexico during the period following the death of Obregón, the turn to the right of Portes Gil and Ortiz Rubio, which is also manifested in the suspension of democratic rights previously granted to the radical left.[21]

Mexico, therefore, no longer fulfilled the minimum political requirements for a 'cultural meridian' and, one can add, for the publication of a relocated and renewed *Amauta*.

On the other hand, according to Mariátegui, Buenos Aires satisfied all the political and material (economic) requirements for a cultural meridian. The River Plate country was governed by Hipólito Yrigoyen, the mild reformist who had during his earlier tenure as president promoted universal male suffrage and labour laws. Among the 'material conditions' pointed out by Mariátegui in his 'La batalla de *Martín Fierro*' was the existence of a vibrant book industry: '[Buenos Aires] is already a great literary market. An "intellectual meridian" is to a great degree no other thing'.[22] In his 1929 letter to Glusberg, Mariátegui again returns to the topic, but this time relating specifically to the possibility of publishing *Amauta* there: 'Buenos Aires is a city of the necessary category to sustain a Spanish American literary journal that affirms sufficiently our own literary meridian'.[23] Moreover, returning to the comparison with Mexico City, Mariátegui argues: 'Materially, Buenos Aires has much greater capacity for business'.[24]

Furthermore, Mariátegui posits a connection between the state of social structuration and his health. With unusual pathos, Mariátegui writes about his planned trip to Buenos Aires:

> Contact with a healthy and strong country will do me much good spiritually and physically. In Buenos Aires this convalescence, which the weakness of Lima has delayed, will be complete.[25]

---

21   Mariátegui 1980h, p. 68.
22   Mariátegui 1980h, p. 118.
23   Mariátegui 1994, p. 576.
24   Mariátegui 1994, p. 576. He, however, then adds: 'I am amazed that a great editorial house, at least as important as any major Spanish publishing house, has not appeared there [in Buenos Aires]' (Mariátegui 1994, p. 576).
25   Mariátegui 1994, p. 695.

In this quotation from a letter dated 19 December 1929, only five months before his death, the strength of Buenos Aires – obviously economic, political, and cultural – is presented as a potential salve for Mariátegui's physical woes. Here the body politic and Mariátegui's physical body have become intertwined. Mariátegui's rosy view of Buenos Aires was buttressed by the fact that Argentina had experienced an economic boom in the 1920s. Both the possibility of getting better treatment for his ailments and of continuing publication of *Amauta* – though now with greater communicative resources at hand – were based on Argentina's and Buenos Aires's prosperity. As David Rock notes:

> By 1929 Argentina had kept pace with Canada and Australia ... Per capita incomes in Argentina continued to compare favorably with most of Western Europe, and the standards of living rose again, while illiteracy fell. Large segments of the population enjoyed prosperity and well-being.[26]

At least in appearance, Argentina belonged to what would later be called 'the First World'. Therefore, by moving to Buenos Aires, Mariátegui hoped to improve both his chances for physical recovery and improve the visibility and dissemination of *Amauta*.

However, as critics have noted, Argentina's prosperity was built on unstable foundations. Mauricio Rojas has described the Argentina before 1930 in terms that would have surprised the Peruvian Marxist:

> We have a ramshackle model of industrial growth which became wholly untenable when its absolute prerequisite, a dynamic export sector, disappeared. Argentina the prosperous would one day, like Kafka's Georg Samsa, awake transformed – into a country on the edge of the abyss.[27]

The dynamism of the export sector would, of course, be the first economic casualty of the Great Depression that ransacked the world's economies in 1929. Not only the country's economy, but also the liberalism of Argentina was built on much shakier ground than Mariátegui believed. Federico Finchelstein, for instance, writes about the authoritarian dimensions of Argentine liberalism, which made it prone to be displaced (as exemplified, for example, by the Patagonian genocide and the extensive use of the army to resolve internal conflicts).[28] Finchelstein also argues that

---

26   Rock 1987, p. 191.
27   Rojas 2002, p. 49.
28   Finchelstein 2010, p. 65.

The attack against liberalism was also an outcome of liberalism's own success. It was the actual success of modernization, and the complex and messy social and economic realities that emerged with it, that prompted a reaction against liberal Argentina and its order.[29]

As a result, on 6 September 1930, almost six months after the death of Mariátegui, liberal Argentina woke up transformed into the dung beetle known as the dictatorship of 'fascist sympathiser' General José Félix Uriburu.[30] However, one must also note that regardless of these flaws, the economic, political, and cultural crisis that would metamorphose Argentina from a liberal Latin American success story to a country plagued by right-wing coups lay still in the future, if only by a few months. Be that as it may, Argentina's political liberalism and the superficial success of the country's cultural and economic modernisation help understand not only its flourishing print media, but also its opening to diverse perspectives, including those from other countries in Latin America. And it was the diversity and freedom that characterised the country's newspapers and magazines that made Buenos Aires so appealing to Mariátegui.

Mariátegui had, after all, thrived as a journalist not only before his trip to Europe and his espousal of Marxism, but also afterwards, even after the Leguía regime had begun to harass him. A case in point is that sixteen out of the eighteen essays and articles published during the last months of his life – from 1 January to 26 March 1930 – were published in *Variedades* and *Mundial*, the two best-known Peruvian general interest magazines at the time, run by central figures of the conservative cultural establishment.[31] (The remaining two articles were published in *Amauta* and, perhaps surprisingly, in the Mexican newspaper *El Nacional*). Given Mariátegui's success in working within a hostile political and cultural environment, he had reason to believe that he would achieve a similar professional success in a less repressive Buenos Aires. In fact, Alberto Gerchunoff, the author of *The Jewish Gauchos of the Pampas* (1910), and one of Argentina's most respected journalists, wanted the Peruvian Marxist as a collaborator in a new publishing venture.[32] Additionally, Glusberg and

---

29   Finehelstein 2010, p. 65.
30   Finchelstein 2010, p. 50.
31   *Variedades* was directed by writer Clemente Palma and *Mundial* by Andrés Avelino Arámburo. Both magazines supported the Leguía regime and, in fact, would close soon after its fall. However, contradicting the government, they kept publishing Mariátegui until his death. On Clemente Palma, see the chapter 'José Carlos Mariátegui: From Race to Culture'.
32   Mariátegui 1994, p. 321. Gerchunoff, together with Glusberg, Horacio Quiroga, and Leopoldo Lugones, had been among those who signed a letter of protest against Mariátegui's imprisonment in 1927; see Rouillón 1984, p. 376.

Frank had involved patrician Argentine intellectual and cultural patron Victoria Ocampo to help finance a relocated *Amauta*.[33] One can also add that, at least according to family lore, Mariátegui, despite being self-taught, had been offered a university position in Buenos Aires.[34]

But in addition to this cultural liberalism, Argentine 'openness' can also be linked to the fact that the Southern cone country had long maintained close cultural and commercial exchange with Peru and the other Andean countries. In fact, as Elizabeth Kuon Arce et. al. point out,

> The route that united the geographic space between the city of Cuzco, the former capital of the Inca Empire, to the city of Buenos Aires, in the first half of the twentieth century, and that is still being used, can be traced back to the XIV (sic) century, when the Inca Empire was at its height.[35]

Similarly, one of Mariátegui's closest friends, the well-known indigenista Luis Valcárcel noted in his characteristically febrile prose:

> Due to an unavoidable destiny – imposition of the earth, will of the gods – South-Peru looks towards the Atlantic, our compass needle points towards the Plata. From Cuzco, over High-Peru [Bolivia], we extend our arms ready to embrace the cordial arms offered from the austral cosmopolis. The expansion of rapid communications towards the Republic of the Highlands [Bolivia] will benefit South-Peru, bringing us to Bolivia, Brazil, Argentina, Uruguay and Chile.[36]

For the *indigenista*, the old Inca and colonial connections and contacts between the Peruvian Andes and Argentina were, thanks to the improvement in communications, not only being renewed but also expanding.

According to Valcárcel, the links between Peru and Argentina were not limited to planes, cars, and automobiles – though the first means of transportation was still in its infancy. They included a commonality based on race and culture. For him, the rebirth of indigenous consciousness represented by *indigenismo*

---

33 On Gluberg's and Frank's attempt at helping relocate *Amauta*, see Tarcus 2011.

34 A. Mariátegui 2014.

35 Kuon Arce et. al. 2009, p. 16. One must note that the actual heyday of the Inca Empire was the early fifteenth century.

36 Valcárcel 1972, p. 129.

is not about the involvement in the Mestizo-European compact of isolated aboriginal individuals: it is about the mass of people living in subhu-
man conditions, ten million distributed in Peru, Bolivia, and Argentina.[37]

For Valcárcel and, as we will see, for Mariátegui, Argentina does not represent in
populational, racial, or cultural terms the antithesis of Peru. For them, Argentina is not a Euro-American country, while Peru would be an Indo-American
one. Instead, Argentina itself is seen as, at least in part, indigenous, and, therefore, as belonging to a cultural community that includes the Peruvian Andes.
Thus, for artists and writers in Cuzco in the 1920s, and one can add, those of
other Andean regions 'Buenos Aires would become a referent to establish close
links and to define an intellectual vanguard'.[38] In fact, as Kuon Arce et. al. point
out, for many in Cuzco, Buenos Aires represented a cultural centre with which
it was possible to establish a less hierarchical relation than with Lima.[39]

For Mariátegui, moving to Buenos Aires would have permitted him to continue participating in Peruvian cultural life and, perhaps, even to have a more
direct impact in at least some parts of the Andes. As he notes:

> I'll work to prepare my trip to Buenos Aires in order to establish the
> magazine there. [It] has a widespread circulation base in the Americas
> and a solid success in Peru, where the considerable importation of Argen-
> tine magazines would permit to distribute it on a large scale.[40]

Paradoxically, Buenos Aires represented both an opening to the world – in
Flores Galindo's words 'a port to Europe' – and an entrance to a pan-Andean
space that included Cuzco, the intellectual center of *indigenismo*.[41] The Andean
passion for Argentine culture was, at least to a degree, reciprocated by a *porteño*
interest in Andean topics that, from Mariátegui's perspective, could be seen
as responding to a putative Pan-Latin American identity. As Kuon Arce et. al.

---

37   Valcárcel 1972, p. 26.
38   Kuon Arce et. al. 2009, p. 16.
39   Kuon Arce et. al. 2009, p. 16.
40   Mariátegui 1994, p. 304.
41   One can add, that as Flores Galindo notes, this Andean resistance against Lima was also
      expressed politically as resistance to Mariátegui and other radicals established in Lima:
      'The Cuzco [radical] group had an independent and antagonistic rhythm regarding Lima'
      (Flores Galindo 1980, p. 94). This *cuzqueño* independence led to the appearance of 'sig-
      nificant differences' – vis à vis Mariátegui's cultural and political projects – that 'began
      precisely where the largest socialist group existed, that is in Cuzco, the most important
      link, but also the weakest in the chain organized by *Amauta*' (Flores Galindo 1980, p. 94).

note, during the 1920s and 1930s there were several exhibitions in Buenos Aires by Peruvian artists, including Felipe Cossío del Pomar and Enrique Camino Brent.[42] The positive reception of Mariátegui's writings on the part of Argentine intellectual across the whole political spectrum, such as Glusberg, Horacio Quiroga, Gerchunoff, and, Leopoldo Lugones, is but another example of this interest in Peruvian culture.

2   Mestizo Argentina

In his 'Author's Note' to his *Seven Essays*, Mariátegui refers to a central, though, for some, problematic figure in Argentine history:

> I have served my best apprenticeship in Europe and I believe the only salvation for Indo-America lies in European and Western science and thought. Sarmiento, who is still one of the creators of *argentinidad* [Argentine-ness], at one time turned his eyes toward Europe. He found no better way to be an Argentine.[43]

That Mariátegui, who believed in the need for Peru to incorporate, even be based on, indigenous culture and population, would find a forerunner in Domingo Faustino Sarmiento has been a source of scandal for many. After all, Sarmiento was, among many things, a Eurocentric ideologist and, when President, a proponent of the eradication of Argentina's indigenous population. For instance, Katherine Gordy notes about this surprising connection:

> Given Mariátegui's theoretical contributions via the critical encounter of Peruvian reality with European ideas, it is bizarre that when seeking to find Latin American predecessors to his project, he would evoke the name of the unabashedly Eurocentric nineteenth-century Argentine liberal reformer Domingo F. Sarmiento.[44]

But the reason for the Peruvian's admiration for Sarmiento should be clear from the quotation. Like Sarmiento, who adopted liberalism, a new European doctrine in the nineteenth century, Mariátegui has embraced Marxism, a newer European doctrine. Mariátegui identifies in Sarmiento a shared concern with

---

42   Kuon Arce et. al. 2009, p. 313.
43   Mariátegui 1971, p. xxvi.
44   Gordy 2014, p. 2.

creating nationhood by means of new political ideas. As in the case of Sarmiento, Mariátegui's alignment with European thought is presented as compatible with a concern for one's nation. One can add that this imbrication between European Marxism and Latin American reality and identity is at the core of the achievement of *Seven Essays*.[45]

However, behind the analogy proposed by Mariátegui is his belief that, as we have seen, Argentina, unlike Peru, represents a successful, functioning, modern, and unified nation. Writing about both countries, he notes that

> It was inevitable that our motley ethnic composition should affect our literary process. Literature could not develop in Peru, as it did in Argentina, where the fusion of European and Indian produced the gaucho. The latter has permeated Argentine literature and made it perhaps the most clearly defined in Spanish America.[46] The best Argentine writers have found their themes and characters in the popular strata.[47] Santos Vega, Martín Fierro, Anastasio el Pollo were all folk heroes long before they became literary creations.[48] Even today, Argentine literature, which is open to the most modern and cosmopolitan influences, reaffirms its gaucho heritage. Poets in the vanguard of the new generation proclaim their descendance from the gaucho Martin Fierro and from his brave[49] family of folksingers. Jorge Luis Borges, saturated in Westernism and modernism, frequently adopts the accent of the countryside.[50]

Even if Mariátegui would show throughout his work a profound scepticism regarding *mestizaje* (racial mixture) as a solution to social issues, he admires

---

45   Elizabeth Garrels, who is also scandalised by Mariátegui's admiration for Sarmiento, makes an important point: 'both Mariátegui and Sarmiento were modernizers. Mariátegui believed in modernization with the Indians; Sarmiento without them and against them' (Garrels 1982, p. 46). While it is surprising that Mariátegui would never criticize Sarmiento's genocidal policies, the former's admiration for the Argentine leader resided in a belief in the success of Argentina's modernisation.

46   The English-language version mistranslates 'tal vez la que tiene más personalidad' as 'the most individualistic'. A literal translation would be 'perhaps the one that has most personality'. I have corrected it as 'perhaps the most clearly defined'.

47   The English version mistranslates 'estrato popular' as folklore (Mariátegui 2007, p. 203).

48   Mariátegui is here referring to three of the best-known 'gauchesque' poems: Hilario Auscaubi's *Santos Vega* (1851), Estanilao del Campo's *Fausto, impresiones del gaucho Anastasio el pollo en la representación de la opera* (Faust, Impressions of the Gaucho Anastasio the Chicken at the Opera) (1866), and José Hernández's *Martín Fierro* (1872, 1879).

49   I have corrected the translation. The English version mistranslated 'bizarra' as bizarre.

50   Mariátegui 1971, p. 194.

Argentine literature for its ability, at least in his eyes, to bring about a fusion between indigenous and European cultural elements.

Furthermore, this reconciliation of cultural and historical differences and oppositions, which he considers more difficult in the case of Peru, would seem to permit constant modernisation, as exemplified in Borges who is supposedly both saturated with 'modernity' – a better translation than modernism of the original's *modernidad* – but, at least in Mariátegui's eyes, also exhibits links with popular traditional oral genres. Argentina is thus presented here as having achieved in the nineteenth century what Mexico is described, elsewhere, as having attained in the twentieth: the creation of an art based on local resources.[51] Despite their ideological differences, both Sarmiento's *Facundo* and José Hernández's *Martín Fierro* can be described as characterised by their popular character and imprint. Moreover, Argentine modernity – as exemplified by the description of Borges presented in *Seven Essays* – would build on this earlier cultural *argentinidad* by incorporating the latest world cultural innovations. This fusion of local and international resources, which Mariátegui identifies as characteristic of modern Argentine writers, such as Borges, resembles his own praise of Vallejo as writing avant-garde poetry that expresses an indigenous world-view.[52]

As seen earlier in this study, for Mariátegui, nationality, rather than being an obstacle to participation in world culture, is the means through which individuals can relate and act within the international community.[53] Thus the fact that he sees Argentina as an example of a fully formed nationality – perhaps the only one in Latin America – would precisely explain and permit the development of cosmopolitanism. This point is implicit in the reference to Sarmiento quoted above. It is because for the Peruvian Marxist *argentinidad* has been successfully created, that Sarmiento can be seen as an example worthy of emulation.

---

51   The fact that Argentina was able to (supposedly) create this national culture decades before Mexico, may help explain why, according to Mariátegui, the former was much more open to other national and international cultures than the latter.

52   Mariátegui's privileging of the gaucho as the central symbol of Argentine identity is arguably indebted to Leopoldo Lugones's influential *El payador*, which played a central role in establishing José Hernández's *Martín Fierro* as the core of the Argentine literary canon. Ironically, Mariátegui, who virulently opposed José de la Riva Agüero's 'Elogio al Inca Garcilaso', and its conservative Hispanocentric version of *mestizaje*, was much more sympathetic towards the writings of Lugones (as well as towards his person) despite their occupying a position similar to that of Riva Agüero in the Argentine cultural field.

53   See 'Mariátegui's Cosmopolitan Nationalism' in this study.

3   Motley Crew

As Argentine critics, such as Elizabeth Garrels and Oscar Terán, have commented, Mariátegui's contacts in Argentina were not those that one would have
expected from someone who was a member of the Communist International.[54]
For instance, Terán notes:

> But here … it is meaningful how Mariátegui comes into contact with the
> Argentine cultural field. From the margins and full of misunderstandings.
> He will not approach it through revolutionary Marxism or even Marxism
> as such. His contacts will not lead him in the direction of Aníbal Ponce
> [Argentine Communist intellectual] but in that of publisher Samuel Glus-
> berg, who at the start of their epistolary relationship, mentions what
> seems to him a first misunderstanding: 'The first person who brought you
> to my attention – be surprised – was Leopoldo Lugones'.[55]

The motley nature of Mariátegui's direct and indirect contacts can be evidenced in the fact that Quiroga was vaguely anarchistic, Gerchunoff a liberal,
while Lugones (in the late 1920s) is described by Finchelstein as a 'radical fascist' and even as 'the icon of illiberal politics in Latin America'.[56] However, if
Mariátegui's encounter with the Argentine cultural field is 'full of misunder-
standings', these are only so from a (doctrinaire) left-wing perspective. While
there is no denying that Glusberg, who served as Mariátegui's main contact
with Argentine cultural circles, was not a member of the Communist party –
Horacio Tarcus describes him as 'an independent leftwing intellectual, later

---

54   Elizabeth Garrels, for instance, finds it surprising that Mariátegui admired Jorge Luis
     Borges, Oliverio Girondo and other writers associated with the tony Calle Florida: 'because
     one would have expected that Mariátegui would have taken the side of those who pro-
     posed a politically committed literature, that is, the writers of Boedo' (Garrels 1982, p. 103).
     She correctly notes that this surprising preference on the part of the Peruvian originate in
     his concern shared by these *Martín Fierro* writers 'to combine the autochtonous and the
     cosmopolitan' (Garrels 1982, p. 104). If Florida was a street associated with writers of patri-
     cian provenance, Boedo, both a street and neighborhood, gave name to the radical writers
     who met in its bars and cafés.
55   Terán 1996, pp. 23–4.
56   Finchelstein 2010, pp. 58–68. Mariátegui was fully aware of Lugones's politics. He wrote
     to Glusberg: 'I am politically in the opposite pole of Lugones … But between persons with
     clear and defined positions, it is easy to understand and respect each other, even in the
     midst of the struggle. In particular, when they are struggling against each other' (Mari-
     átegui 1994, p. 273).

Trotskyte and libertarian socialist' –[57] one must note that the Peruvian was fully aware of the Argentine editor's politics. In his letter of introduction to Mariátegui, Glusberg describes himself as 'an absolute nihilist', even if he adds 'in a Turgenevan and revolutionary sense'.[58] Therefore, one cannot but conclude that the key to understanding the relationship between Mariátegui and Glusberg is that it is independent from his politics, if not actually predicated on the Argentine editor's distance from international communism.

4   Defending Marxism

Mariátegui's purported trip to Argentina coincided with the plans to publish *Defensa del marxismo: Polémica revolucionaria*, one of his last books, in Buenos Aires. (Its publication, unfortunately, would not take place until after his death).[59] However, the connection of the book to his relocation – Mariátegui wanted Glusberg to publish the book as a kind of calling card to the Southern Cone cultural establishment – merits brief consideration. Glusberg was not enthusiastic about publishing the book. First, he asked Mariátegui to change its original title – it was to be called 'Polémica revolucionaria' (Revolutionary Polemic) – and noted that he had no 'illusions about sales'.[60] Following Glusberg's suggestion, Mariátegui changed it to the arguably not much more marketable *Defensa del marxismo* (Defense of Marxism), with the original title becoming the subtitle. Despite the political title and subject matter, Mariátegui actually considered the text as having sales potential. He introduces to Glusberg the possibility of publishing in Buenos Aires by noting: 'I have another book with an international topic, like *La escena contemporánea*', noting that this, his first book, 'easily sold 1500 copies'.[61] Contradicting Mariátegui's optimism, his rationale for considering Buenos Aires a potential cultural meridian and even one of the main reasons behind moving to the city, Glusberg replied that he could only expect to sell two hundred copies in the city, and that per-

57   Tarcus 2011, p. 80.
58   Mariátegui 1994, p. 257.
59   In 1934, in Santiago de Chile, Glusberg published a version *Defensa del marxismo* – though with sections omitted and with essays Mariátegui had planned to include in *El alma matinal*, another book he had decided to publish in Buenos Aires. At his death, Mariátegui also left completed his short novel *La novela y la vida: Siegfried y el profesor Canella*, which had been published serially in the magazine *Variedades*, and an incomplete version of *El alma matinal*.
60   Mariátegui 1994, p. 340.
61   Mariátegui 1994, p. 330.

haps it was better to publish it in Spain![62] While Mariátegui continued to insist on publishing *Defensa del marxismo*, he finally gave in to Glusberg's suggestions and began preparing the manuscript of *El alma matinal* (The Morning Soul), which in addition to recent essays, such as 'On Explaining Chaplin', also included some of his early and most Sorelian essays such as 'The Final Battle'. He did not live to complete the text. A version of *El alma matinal* would only be published in 1950 by Mariátegui's widow and children.

In addition to the 'international topic', which Mariátegui considered to be of greater potential public interest than one dealing with Peruvian reality,[63] there may be another reason for his wanting to publish *Defensa del marxismo* in Buenos Aires. When Glusberg, in his attempt to avoid publishing the book, suggested contacting La Vanguardia, the publishing house of the Argentine Partido Socialista, Mariátegui responded: 'I thank and accept your offer to intervene with La Vanguardia in order to have them publish the book. But I am afraid that its conclusions unfavorable to Marxism, even if they do not touch on the practice of Socialist parties, would be a reason why La Vanguardia would not be interested in this book'.[64]

One here runs into the paradox that someone who famously described himself as a 'convinced and declared Marxist' would write a book that could be seen as coming to 'conclusions unfavourable to Marxism'.[65] From the letter, it would seem that rather than a defence, Mariátegui had written a debunking of Marxism. Could it be that Mariátegui's mention of 'unfavourable conclusions to Marxism' is a reference to his consistent criticism of social democracy as understood in the 1920s?[66] There is no doubt that *Defensa del marxismo*, as

---

62   Mariátegui 1994, p. 340.

63   At the same time he was working on editing the texts that would make up *Defensa del marxismo* – most had been published earlier in *Amauta* – he was also finishing writing his one 'organic' monograph: *Ideología y política* (not to be confused with the anthology of articles, essays, and other miscellaneous texts later collected under that title by his sons). The original *Ideología y política*, which would have dealt with a history and analysis of political ideologies in Peru, was lost in mysterious circumstances. On the lost book, see 'José Carlos Mariátegui: The Making of a Revolutionary in the Aristocratic Republic'; also, Flores Galindo 2010, pp. 101–3.

64   Mariátegui 1994, p. 525.

65   Mariátegui 1971, p. 42.

66   This point has been made, for instance, by Fernanda Beigel in *El itinerario y la brújula*: 'Mariátegui said that his book *Defensa del marxismo* could find resistance to its publication by the publishing house La Vanguardia ... due to its "conclusions unfavorable to Marxism". In reality, Mariátegui was referring to the ideas of the II International that delimited the text's field of dispute and constituted the theoretical framework accepted by the Socialist Party' (Beigel 2013, pp. 171–2).

many of Mariátegui's writings, constitutes an attack on the reformist Marxism of the Second International. As part of his review of Henri de Man's *Au de-là du marxisme* (1926),[67] he notes that

> Lasallean reformism harmonized much better with social democracy's goals and the praxis it employed in its process of growth than revolutionary Marxism. Thus all the incongruences, all the distances that de Man observes between the theory and practice of German Social-Democracy are not, therefore, strictly attributable to Marxism except to the degree that one wants to call Marxism something that was no longer such almost from the start.[68]

One could easily consider that this description of Social Democracy as different from Marxism could be offensive to the editors of La Vanguardia, which, after all, was the publishing arm of a party aligned with the (Socialist) Second International, which had the German Social Democratic Party as, perhaps, its most important member. However, Mariátegui's criticism of social democracy in *Defensa del marxismo* is only a development of ideas he had long espoused and thus could only be considered 'conclusions unfavourable to Marxism' if all of the Peruvian's writings were taken as such. Flores Galindo argues that in this passage 'Mariátegui alluded to his unorthodox conclusions, when, for example, he refers to Freud or considers Sorel to be Marx's best disciple'.[69] The problem with Flores Galindo's arguments resides in the fact that Mariátegui consistently presents Freud as complementing rather than contradicting Marx. According to the author of *Seven Essays*:

> Freudianism and Marxism, even though the disciples of Freud and Marx are not yet those with the greatest propensity to understand it and notice it, are related in their distinct dominions not only for what in their theories there was of 'affront', as Freud says, to the idealist conceptualisations of humanity, but for the methods used to confront the problems considered.[70]

---

67   The book is partly articulated around discussions of Henri de Man's *Au de-là du marxisme* and Max Eastman's *The Science of Revolution* (1927).

68   Mariátegui 1981c, p. 24.

69   Flores Galindo 1980, p. 102.

70   Mariátegui 2011, p. 220. I have made several corrections to Vanden's and Becker's translation. Their version misses the reference made by Mariátegui to Freud's 'Resistance to Psychoanalysis' and its description of the 'affront' to 'human self-regard' presented by psychoanalysis (Mariátegui 1980c, p. 91). The original text is: 'Freudismo y marxismo, aunque

In this quotation, Freud is presented as perfectly compatible with Marx. By describing both authors' works as 'an affront' to 'idealist conceptualisations of humanity', he is making a reference to Freud's 'Resistance to Psychoanalysis': an essay published in the first issue of *Amauta*. As we know, in that classic essay, psychoanalysis – the 'psychological affront' – is the third in a series of 'affronts' to 'human self-regard' that included 'the biological affront caused by the theory of evolution and the earlier cosmological affront brought about by Copernicus's discovery'.[71] Mariátegui implicitly presents Marx's work as a fourth humiliation of idealist human self-regard, what could be called the 'social affront'. Moreover, for Mariátegui, the difference between Freud and Marx stems from their field of study rather that from their methods which are equally materialistic and scientific. Thus, not only does Freud's work not undermine that of Marx, but when it comes to their methods – rational, scientific, and materialist – they are one and the same. Freud had earlier been mentioned by Mariátegui – even if briefly – in his 1925 *La escena contemporánea* as part of the 'Jewish Renaissance' together with figures such as Albert Einstein, Georges Brandes, and Mariátegui's future personal friend Waldo Frank.[72] In late 1926, in an article significantly titled 'El 'Freudismo' en la literatura contemporánea' (Freudianism in Contemporary Literature), Mariátegui notes the central presence of Freudian insights throughout much of the best literature of the early twentieth century.[73] Moreover, after 1926, Freud would become an occasional point of reference in his writings.[74] Flores Galindo's argument that Mariátegui's 'conclusions unfavourable to Marxism' refers, in part, to the latter's engagement with Freud in *Defensa del marxismo*, is, therefore, untenable; even if this engagement is more exhaustive than those found in earlier texts.

Flores Galindo's suggestion that *Defensa del marxismo*'s numerous mentions of Sorel could be described by Mariátegui as a criticism of Marxism

---

los discípulos de Freud y de Marx no sean todavía los más propensos a entenderlo y advertirlo, se emparentan, en sus distintos dominios, no sólo por lo que en sus teorías había de 'humillación', como dice Freud, para las concepciones idealistas de la humanidad, sino por su método frente a los problemas que abordan' (Mariátegui 1981c, p. 80).

71   Mariátegui 1981c, p. 91.
72   Mariátegui 1980c, p. 214.
73   Mariátegui 1980a, p. 37.
74   Some of Mariátegui's other mentions of Freud are in 'La nueva literatura rusa' (The New Russian Literature) (Mariátegui 1980a, pp. 161–2), '*Levante, por Blanca Luz Brum* (*Levante*, by Blanca Luz Brum') (Mariátegui 1980h, p. 130), 'George Brandes' (Mariátegui 1980a, p. 120), 'Veinticinco años de sucesos extranjeros' ('Twenty Five Years of Foreign Events') (Mariátegui 1980b, p. 198), 'Elogio de *El cemento* y del realismo proletario' ('In Praise of *Cement* and Proletarian Realism') (Mariátegui 1981b, p. 197), etc.

is even flimsier. As we have seen, Sorel is a central influence on Mariátegui. Moreover, he consistently referred to Sorel even in, or, better said, precisely in, the moments when he actually emphasised his Marxist credentials. For instance, 'Anniversary and Balance Sheet' includes a particularly significant mention of the French *syndicaliste*: 'Marx, Sorel, Lenin, these are the men that make history'.[75] Mariátegui's reference to Sorel in the celebrated *Amauta* editorial in which he affirmed the socialist character of the magazine serves as an example of how for him the presence of the French author did not imply in the least any conclusion unfavourable to Marxism. However, a significant difference must be established between 'Anniversary and Balance Sheet' and *Defensa del marxismo*. The first was a defence of revolutionary thinking and politics in response to his break with the APRA and the attacks from Haya de la Torre and his associates. The latter was to be published after his move to Buenos Aires and his unavoidable abandonment of active politics. Therefore, *Defensa del marxismo* responded, at least in part, to the growing criticisms against his person and ideas among Comintern circles. Furthermore, by publishing the text in Buenos Aires, the city where the Latin American headquarters of the Comintern was located, Mariátegui would have rubbed the regional communist leaderhip's noses, sort to speak, in his defence of Sorel and Freud. *Defensa del marxismo* can be seen not only as a calling card to the local intelligentsia, but also as a statement of defiance to International Communism. *Defensa del marxismo*, on the one hand, restated Mariátegui's revolutionary bonafides; on the other, it also made clear his political independence and difference. In addition to a restatement of his Sorelism – even if, as we have seen, the French author is significantly reinterpreted by Mariátegui[76] – there is in *Defensa del marxismo* a discussion of the issue of orthodoxy and its relation to unorthodoxy, or, what amounts to the same thing, of dogma and heresy, in terms that make this book particularly problematic from the perspective of an International Communism that was already becoming fully Stalinised.

---

75   Mariátegui 2011, p. 130.
76   See 'Mariátegui, Sorel and Myth' in this book.

5   Defense of Heresy

In *Defensa del marxismo*, Mariátegui writes:

> In general, the fortune of heresy depends on ... its possibility of becoming
> dogma, of being incorporated into a dogma. Dogma is here understood
> as the doctrine of historical change. And, as such, as long as change is in
> effect, as long as dogma does not become an archive or code of a past
> ideology, nothing guarantees creative freedom, the germinal function of
> thought, like dogma. The intellectual needs to base her speculation in a
> belief, in a principle, that makes her into a factor of history and progress.
> It is then that creative potency can function with the greatest freedom
> available in a [historical] period.[77]

The dogma in question is precisely the key core of Marxist ideas – 'doctrine
of historical change'. By heresy, Mariátegui means new ideas that, while concerned with Marxist topics and goals, and even accepting their basic premises,
move socialism in new directions. As Osvaldo Fernández Díaz notes:

> Heresy is indispensable to verify the health of dogma, where what is uni-
> versal appears connected to personal experience ... and without dogma,
> heresy is nothing more than purely individual action. In this manner,
> [Mariátegui] conceives the relationship between biography and history.[78]

Thus, despite the religious vocabulary – which, as Fernández Díaz has noted,
is borrowed and developed from Miguel de Unamuno's *The Agony of Christianity* – Mariátegui is here making a secular point regarding the necessity of
continuous non-linear evolution in Marxist thought. Not surprisingly, for Mariátegui, the key heresiarch is Sorel.[79] According to Fernández Díaz's what is
personal and individual in Unamuno becomes collective and social in Mari-

---

77   Mariátegui 1981a, p. 125. There is only a truncated translation of this text in Vanden's and
        Becker's *Anthology*.
78   Fernández Díaz 2010, pp. 16–17.
79   'Sorel achieved an original development of Marxism, since he began by accepting all Marx-
        ist premises, not by repudiating them a priori and en masse' (Mariátegui 1981a, p. 126).
        Although, as we have seen, this is a dubious statement, to say the least, for Sorel does not
        'accept all Marxist premises', the fact is that for Mariátegui, heresy, innovation, originates
        in dogma – the writings of Marx – even if leads to conclusions very different from those
        of the author of *Capital*. One can add that Mariátegui himself would be another heresi-
        arch.

átegui. He quotes from Unamuno's *La agonía del cristianismo* – 'What I am going to present here ... is my agony, my Christian struggle'[80] – and adds:

> As we see, in Unamuno's formulation the possessive pronouns link this experience [of agony] with the individual Miguel de Unamuno, reflecting with this the problematic [of agony] exclusively to his individual, and to a degree, non-transferrable personal experience. Mariátegui's formula, on the other hand, begins by proposing a collective subject.[81]

Unamuno's religious individualism becomes socialised by Mariátegui.

Mariátegui's view of the relationship between dogma and heresy is reminiscent of that proposed by T.S. Eliot between innovation and tradition in 'Tradition and the Individual Talent'. As we know, according to Eliot:

> No poet, no artist of any art, has his complete meaning alone. His significance, his appreciation is the appreciation of his relation to the dead poets and artists ... The necessity that he shall conform, that he shall cohere, is not one-sided; what happens when a new work of art is created is something that happens simultaneously to all the works of art which preceded it.[82]

If for Eliot, this tension between innovation as based on tradition and as reconstituting what is understood as tradition is what gives Western literature its vibrancy, for Mariátegui, it ensures the continued relevance of Marxism as an interpretative method. However, unlike the Western literary tradition, which, regardless of the vibrancy or lack of innovation, it is difficult to imagine as disappearing, Marxism, as an interpretive tool, is presented by Mariátegui as threatened by obsolescence. Heresy is thus necessary if dogma – Marxism – is to avoid becoming ossified. But, even if inherited from Unamuno, the references to dogmas and heresy used by Mariátegui also imply a nudge precisely at an International Communism that was clearly beginning to show the hardening of its ideas into 'an archive of past ideology', and that was beginning to exhibit the attitudes of religious institutions at their very worst.

---

80   Quoted in Fernández Díaz 2010, p. 4.
81   Fernández Díaz 2010, p. 4.
82   Eliot 1990, p. 526.

6   Apologia pro vita sua

Since *Defensa del marxismo* is a defence of both the Marxist tradition and, to use Eliot's words, 'the really new' Marxist interpretations, one can read it implicitly as an apologia for Mariátegui's own writings, which were beginning to be seen as being outside the intellectual frameworks prescribed by International Communism. When he writes about Sorel as 'accepting the premises of Marxism' and, therefore, 'achieving an original development of Marxism',[83] he could be writing about himself, defending both his own appropriation of dogma and the necessary heresies when applying Marxism to new realities and questions. It should now be clear why Mariátegui did not approach Ponce or any Marxist Argentine intellectuals.

There was, of course, the apparently fortuitous fact that it was non-Marxists who had responded positively to Mariátegui's writings – Glusberg, obviously, but also Gerchunoff, Quiroga, and Lugones – rather than Communists. But these non-Marxists were reacting favourably to actual aspects of Mariátegui's thought – his vitalism, his interest in psychology and psychoanalysis, his creative literary and cultural criticism, his care in reading Peruvian reality, etc. – that were of no interest, if not actually rejected, by the growingly dogmatic interpretations favoured by the Communist movement. Furthermore, his *Defensa del marxismo* was as much a restatement of Marxism against critics such as de Man or Max Eastman, the purported raison d'etre of the work, as an attack on the hardening and closing of Marxism taking place at the time.

Mariátegui was, therefore, implicitly placing himself outside the cultural circles of the Comintern with his would-be Buenos Aires calling card. But Mariátegui's disassociation from official Communist politics was already implicit in his decision to leave Lima and continue publishing *Amauta* (which, even after its definition as socialist in 1928, was far from being a doctrinaire or party outlet) in Buenos Aires. That, as seen, he collaborated with Glusberg and Frank, at the time leftists, but not members of any party, is proof that he planned to carry on *Amauta* in a similar manner, if not actually opening the journal to even more diverse opinions.

---

83   Mariátegui 1981a, p. 126.

7   Amauta/Sur

In one of the greatest ironies of Latin American cultural history, while Mari-átegui's death put an end to the project of a Buenos Aires *Amauta*, Ocampo and Frank – Glusberg being dismissed from the editorial board – would go on to found *Sur*, which would become the main venue for the writings of Jorge Luis Borges. Thus, the greatest left-wing journal in the region's history indirectly gave birth to the next major Latin American cultural magazine. Indicative of the political winds blowing in South America, a radical, intellectually open, journal was replaced by a brilliant literary publication, though in politics only moderately liberal.[84]

But how different could a Buenos Aires *Amauta* have been from *Sur*? Obviously, Mariátegui would have incorporated more radical and diverse voices. The *Florida* inclination of *Sur*, to a degree a consequence of its identification with the international avant-garde and modernism, had marginalised from its pages writers such as Roberto Arlt. (*Florida*, in reference to an upper-class commercial street, was the name used to designate upper-class Argentine writers conversant with the latest European trends). However, the fact is that, as we have seen, the Peruvian Marxist was an admirer of many of these Florida authors, such as Oliverio Girondo and, especially Borges. And one can easily imagine, despite Mariátegui's radicalism, this hypothetical Buenos Aires *Amauta* still publishing many of the same names as the early versions of *Sur*. The Stalinist establishment of an official communist aesthetics – which took place in full after Mariátegui's death – destroyed the loose alliance between the avant-garde and the left. The enthroning of socialist realism implied that ever fewer writers were able or willing to produce the kind of artistically and politically radical literature that Mariátegui had so valued. The (over-all) publishing silence of César Vallejo in the 1930s is a possible example of the effects of this turn in Communist aesthetics on an artist who refused to compromise either his politics or his art. Mariátegui would have found fewer (officially) Communist avant-garde writers willing to collaborate with his journal.

Nevertheless, as we have discussed, Mariátegui was fully aware of the liberal character of the society of Buenos Aires and saw in this fact one of the key reasons to relocate. Mariátegui's professional career – as a radical who wrote for mainstream journals, and who, as an editor, published non-political

---

84   On the origins of *Sur* and its links with the would-be Buenos Aires *Amauta*, see Tarcus 2011.

authors like José María Eguren and Martín Adán – implied a constant negotiation between his socialist political beliefs and a cultural establishment that
was only marginally liberal. Mariátegui must have been aware that the alliance
between aesthetic, cultural, and political radicalism, of which he may very well
be the best Latin American example, was rapidly fraying. However, he must
surely have felt capable of continuing in Buenos Aires the balancing act of
being a radical in a liberal cultural environment.

8   Conclusion

As we have seen, Mariátegui's tragically frustrated trip raises many questions.
The difficulty with trying to answer them resides in that, while we know what
transpired in Buenos Aires after his death, we have no way of actually knowing what Mariátegui's intellectual evolution would have been. His writings give
us leads – some of which I have tried to follow – but nothing more. Human
beings often evolve in unforeseen directions. Could one have predicted that
the co-director of the horse-racing journal *El Turf* would only ten years later
have become the most creative and original Marxist thinker of Latin America?

But, despite the unavoidable guessing game involved, the questions raised
by the planned relocation to Buenos Aires helps us better understand the tensions in Mariátegui's thought. One can, obviously, assume that the Uriburu
coup would have led Mariátegui to reassess his idealised view of Argentina.
He would have had to reconsider the country's putative liberalism by means
of a class-inflected localized analysis of the kind he brilliantly applied to Peru
in *Seven Essays*. Would his experience of Italy have helped him better analyse
Argentine *nacionalismo* (Catholic right-wing movement) and its links with and
differences from Italian fascism? One cannot help but add that Peru would
also experience during the 1930s a similar turn to the right, as Leguía was
deposed only to be replaced by the elected rightwing government of Colonel
Luis Miguel Sánchez Cerro and, after the latter's assassination, by the even
more rightist dictatorship of General Óscar Benavides. Likewise, even if we
have the basis for a critique of populism – together with right-wing dictatorships the characteristic political regime in twentieth-century Latin America –
in his response to the transformation of the APRA into a political party, an
Argentine sojourn would have forced him to come to grips with populism in
power.

Moreover, in the case of Perón, he would have experienced a populism that,
unlike the originally progressive APRA, originated in the right and was basic-

ally 'a sui-generis radical reformulation of fascism'.[85] Peronism, as Finchelstein notes, included 'Industrialist policies, social welfare, and authoritarian repression of dissidents, extreme anti-communist policies, and totalitarian ... religious and cultural strategies'.[86] Would Mariátegui have followed his admired Borges into identifying Peronism with fascism – and thus disregarding the differences pointed out by Finchelstein?[87] Would he have anticipated the equally partial reading of later leftists who saw in Peronism an Argentine road to socialism? Or would he have been able to achieve a balanced interpretation of Perón's politics – whatever this may be?

As we have seen, the question that has most concerned *mariateguistas* has been whether the trip to Buenos Aires implied an abandonment of political activity. Caught between the Scylla of a right-wing, if not fascist, international political wave, and the Charybdis of a hardening Stalinist Communist movement, could Mariátegui still have been a revolutionary activist? As Flores Galindo puts it:

> Could one still work for the revolution outside the Comintern? ... Some intellectuals distant from orthodox communism would end up seduced by the bourgeoisie, reconciled with their past. Others, in order to avoid this temptation ultimately abandoned critical thinking, subjecting themselves to strictly following Stalin and Moscow. There were even some, like György Lukacs, who preferred to keep quiet, to hide their thoughts, to keep a prolonged silence, convinced that outside the party there was no salvation ... There was finally the possibility of the solitary intellectual, distant from the Comintern, but still attempting to continue within the revolution, maintaining an alert intelligence, but outside the class struggle, holding on to a collective project in solitude.[88]

The great historian argues against any of these responses. He believes, he wants to believe, that Mariátegui would have been able to provide an original answer to the contradictions of this time; one that would have permitted him to continue acting politically while maintaining his intellectual and organisational independence.[89]

---

85   Finchelstein 2010, p. 165.
86   Fichelstein 2010, p. 168.
87   See 'Mariátegui and the Culture of Politics' in this study.
88   Flores Galindo 1980, p. 109.
89   Flores Galindo 1980, p. 110.

Would Mariátegui's probable turn towards culture have permitted him some kind of political agency? It is difficult to tell. On the one hand, the political slant of *Defensa del marxismo* and the collection of articles *El alma matinal*, the work he ultimately proposed as first Argentine publication, so obviously contradict the rapidly hardening Stalinist orthodoxies that, I believe, one cannot see their purported publication as anything but as criticisms of official communism. On the other hand, Mariátegui's planned collaborations with establishment figures as diverse as Gerchunoff and Ocampo would seem to indicate a willingness to privilege the aesthetic over the political. The failure of even such a brilliant (and major) historical figure as Trotsky to establish a significant independent radical socialist political movement makes the chances for Mariátegui doing the same in Latin America slim at best.

The tragedy of Mariátegui's death is not only the obvious one of a life being cut short at the height of its intellectual powers, but also that we were deprived of his response to the cultural and political fluxes in Latin America during the decades in which his political beliefs and ideas would have been tested to their limits.

CHAPTER 9

Mariátegui and Che: Reflections on and around Walter Salles's *The Motorcycle Diaries*

In 1952, Ernesto Guevara, a young medical student then known under the moniker of 'Fúser', arrived in Lima with his friend and travelling companion Alberto Granado, a recently minted pharmacist with whom he had been travelling throughout the continent. But, without entirely abandoning the wanderlust and curiosity for other cultures and peoples that had fuelled their travels since they had left the city of Rosario in Argentina, Ernesto and Alberto came to the capital of Peru with a more specific purpose: to learn how to best treat leprosy under the tutelage of Hugo Pesce, who was according to Guevara's real-life diaries, an 'expert leprologist'.[1] One must remember that leprosy was still incurable and that the social stigma associated with the disease lent, at least in the popular mind, an aura of sainthood to those dedicated to treating and caring for its victims.[2] Arguably, their interest in leprosy evidences the idealism of both Guevara and Granado.

Thus it was perhaps not surprising that Pesce, in Guevara's words, 'welcomed us with extraordinary kindness'.[3] He procured the two Argentine adventurers lodgings in a hospital and had them over for meals.[4] But the Peruvian doctor's generosity was also intellectual. Years later, Guevara, now known as 'Che', the most charismatic leader of the Cuban Revolution, would send a copy of his *Guerrilla Warfare* to Pesce with a significant dedication: 'To Dr. Hugo Pesce who provoked, perhaps without knowing, a great change in my attitude towards life and society'.[5]

In the popularly and critically successful 2004 film *The Motorcycle Diaries*, based on Guevara's travel diaries with the same title and Granado's *Traveling*

---

1   Guevara 2006, p. 135.
2   Lavonne Neff writes about this connection: 'Nowadays, leprosy ... can be halted with antibiotics, and is virtually unknown in North America and Europe. Once, however, it was considered a fate worse than death. Not only did lepers suffer from a then-incurable wasting disease; they also had to deal with the community's fear of infection. A diagnosis of leprosy turned a person into a pariah ... No wonder saints were often identified by their kindness to lepers' (Neff 2005, p. 31).
3   Guevara 2006, p. 135.
4   Guevara 2006, p. 145.
5   Quoted in Kohan 2000, p. 198.

with Che Guevara, Brazilian director Walter Salles and Puerto Rican screen-writer José Rivera have fleshed out and dramatised the encounter between Pesce and Guevara. There, Pesce, portrayed by the Peruvian actor Gustavo Bueno, is shown handing books from his library to Guevara, played by Gael García Bernal. 'This is Mariátegui. You also have to read César Vallejo', Pesce advises the young Argentine adventurer, as he hands him the books.[6] While Vallejo is not mentioned again in the movie, Mariátegui plays a brief but central role in Salles's and Rivera's depiction of Guevara's political development. Soon after, he is shown on his bed reading Mariátegui's *Seven Essays*. While Guevara reads, one hears the filmic Pesce begin a brief summary of the Peruvian Marx-ist's ideas:

> Mariátegui basically talks about the revolutionary potential of the Indians and peasants of Latin America. He says that the problem of the Indian is the problem of the land. And that the revolution will not be copy or imit-ation but the heroic creation of our people. We are too few to be divided, he says. Everything unites us. Nothing divides us.[7]

The film thus presents a relatively accurate summary of the Peruvian Marxist's most characteristic ideas, though not all of these are found in *Seven Essays*, the book Guevara is shown as reading.[8]

In counterpoint to the voice-over, the film cuts to a montage of stills, appar-ently photographs taken by the filmic Guevara and Granado in Argentina, Chile and the Peruvian Andes – the locations they visited before arriving to Lima. These are images of the poverty and exploitation they have seen during their journey, but also of survival. By juxtaposing Mariátegui's ideas with these pic-tures, the film makes the point that by reading *Seven Essays* Guevara is able to

---

6 Salles 2004. I have provided my own translations of the dialogue from the movie.

7 Salles 2004.

8 The 'problem of the Indian is the problem of the land' summarises one of the basic insights of *Seven Essays*: 'The problem of the Indian is rooted in the land tenure system of our eco-nomy' (Mariátegui 1971, p. 22). As we have seen, the reference to 'copy or imitation, but heroic creation' comes from 'Anniversary and Balance Sheet' (1928), the important *Amauta* editorial published by Mariátegui after his break with the APRA (Mariátegui 2011b, p. 130). The ending phrase 'Everything unites us, nothing divides us' comes from 'Message to the Workers' Con-gress' (1927), where Mariátegui states: 'Nothing divides us. Everything unites us' (Mariátegui 2011, p. 183). The film's summary of Mariátegui's ideas is, therefore, accurate, with the excep-tion that the call for unity was made within the context of an address to a workers' congress. Therefore, rather than a call for Pan-Latin American unity, as the film seems to imply, it is an explicit call for working-class unity regardless of political tendency – be it reformist, anarch-ist, or socialist; see 'José Carlos Mariátegui and the Culture of Politics'.

make sense of Latin America's reality, here portrayed as tragic. Therefore, on the one hand, Mariátegui's ideas help Fúser become Che: an activist true to the region's history and society. On the other, through Che, Mariátegui is presented as a point of origin for the region's revolutionaries, from the Cuban revolution to, one imagines, the present.

However, the movie does not show Guevara engaging in or defending actual acts of political violence.[9] Instead, he is portrayed as discovering in his trip the underlying commonality of Latin America and the need for political action predicated on the region's unique traits. This is made clear in the film when Guevara – in response to a surprise party given for his birthday – toasts the doctors and nurses of a leper colony in the Peruvian Amazonia. After expressing his gratitude to his hosts and, perhaps surprisingly, to their country, the filmic Guevara adds:

> We believe, and after this trip even more firmly than before, that the division of America in uncertain and illusory nationalities is a complete fiction. We constitute one mestizo race from Mexico to the Straits of Magellan. Therefore, attempting to free myself from any provincial trace, I toast Peru and a united America.[10]

However, in a letter to his mother, included in the book *The Motorcycle Diaries*, Guevara ironically comments that this 'quintessentially Pan-American speech' – longer and more earnest in the text than in the movie – was 'inspired by the booze' consumed during the party.[11] The self-deprecation of Guevara's interpretation of his speech is completely absent from the movie. The surprise, pride, and emotion reflected on the filmic Granado's face – portrayed by Rodrigo de la Serna – cues the spectator that this is a central moment in Guevara's evolution. The change is further evidenced when, after the party, the transformed Guevara swims across the river, disregarding Granado's concern about the wild animals 'that would eat you raw',[12] in order to say farewell to the

---

9   The one scene in the film in which Guevara seems to defend revolutionary violence takes place after Granado tells him he had the idea of marrying a descendant of the Incas and founding an *indigenista* political party. They would, according to Granado, 'reactivate the revolution of Túpac Amaru'. Guevara curtly replies: 'A revolution without firing shots? You're crazy' (Salles 2004). This scene takes place before Che's encounter with Mariátegui's works.

10 Salles 2004. One must note that, with only very superficial variations, the toast presented in the film corresponds to that found in the *Diaries* (Guevara 2006, p. 149).

11 Guevara 2006, p. 154.

12 Salles 2004.

lepers whose housing was on the other side of the river. Fúser, the sympathetic *pícaro*, the compassionate adventurer, who began the journey in Rosario, has been transformed into the heroic, perhaps even saintly, Che.[13]

Che, in the movie is, therefore, radical and egalitarian – he is concerned with the plight of the indigenous, the poor, and the marginalised – but, at the same time, still 'quintessentially Pan-American'. (Pan-American here being understood as 'Pan-Latin American').[14] This stress on Latin American unity is directly connected to Guevara's coming to terms with one of Mariátegui's lessons: 'Everything unites us. Nothing divides us'. While, as is known, a strong sense of Pan-(Latin)Americanism was at the core of the Cuban revolution during its first years – Che's ill-fated attempt at starting a revolution in Bolivia in 1967 is one example – it is, perhaps, not far-fetched to see the movie as also making a nod to the South American Pink Tide – the rise of left-leaning governments in the region. A reborn Pan-(Latin)Americanism was at the core of Hugo Chávez's continental appeal. Che Guevara and, through him, Mariátegui can, therefore, be seen as at the origins of the populisms of Chávez in Venezuela, the then recently elected Néstor Kirchner in Argentina, and, given the year, 2004, one

---

13   By presenting the trip as a moment of transformation, Salles's *The Motorcycle Diaries* is closer to Granado's account of the trip than to Guevara's text. In the prologue to the Spanish original version of the diary, titled *Con el Che por Sudamérica* (Travelling with Che Guevara: The Making of a Revolutionary), Granado writes that after the 'encounter with the "sick old woman"' in Valparaíso, Chile, 'Fúser begins to disappear a bit in order to transform into the future Che' (Granado 2013). Che's travelling companion also notes that the visit to the patients took place on 20 June, while the birthday celebration took place on 14 June (Granado 2013).

14   The reader may wonder why Guevara's discovery of 'Pan-(Latin) Americanism' is ascribed to his contact with Mariátegui's works rather than, for instance, the possible influence of Haya de la Torre who, it must be noted, was a greater presence in the Lima of 1952 than the author of *Seven Essays*. After all, the famous five points of the APRA movement proposed in 1926 by Haya come much closer to summarising a politics primarily based on 'Pan-(Latin) Americanism' than Mariátegui's writings ever do. First Guevara seems to have had no idea of who Haya was. Guevara's ignorance is evidenced by his surprise at the number of policemen surrounding the Colombian embassy (Guevara 2006, p. 138). In fact, the reason for the police presence was that Haya was an asylee there. However, one must also note that by 1940, Haya had evolved from a Pan-(Latin) Americanist into an 'inter-Americanist', who no longer saw the United States as a regional adversary. In Haya's words: 'It is not Pan-Americanism ... that will resolve the problems of coexistence between the two great economic, political, and ethnic groups of the hemisphere. It will be "Inter-Americanism" that presupposes ... the coexistence of an America [that is] "countryside and raw material" with an America [that is] "industry and capital", respectively structured into corresponding groups of states capable of balancing their relations into effective and lasting good neighborliness' (Quoted in Manrique 2009, p. 37). Haya's updated ideas would probably not have been of interest to the rapidly radicalising Guevara.

assumes also of Brazil's Luiz Inácio 'Lula' da Silva, who was expected to be politically closer to Chávez than he would actually end up being.[15] Perhaps not accidentally, 2004 is also the year when Chávez unveiled his Alianza Bolivariana para los Pueblos de Nuestra América (Bolivarian Alliance for the Peoples of Our America), better known as ALBA, 'an initiative designed to encourage greater trade, solidarity and exchange between nations standing outside of the usual market-based strictures'.[16] These leaders stressed continental unity with, at least nominally, a concern with the indigenous, the poor and the marginalised.

The film thus implicitly presents Mariátegui as the intellectual inspiration for Guevara's pan-Americanism. However, the text the film presents as proposing this continental unity – 'Everything unites us. Nothing divides us' – comes from Mariátegui's 1927 'Message to a Worker's Congress'. Addressing union members and workers of diverging political tendencies – anarchist, reformist, and very few communists – Mariátegui stressed the need for 'proletarian unity':

> Theoretical disagreements do not impede agreement on a program of action. The workers' united front is our objective. In the work of building it the vanguard workers have the obligation to set an example. In the work for today, nothing divides us; everything unites us.[17]

Although in other of his works Mariátegui stressed his belief in the basic commonality of Latin American countries,[18] the actual context of the phrase used in the film is that of a traditional Marxist – though not necessarily Leninist – call for workers to unite.[19]

---

15 While Hugo Chávez had been in power since 1998, Kirchner and Lula took power in 2003. The rise of the Pink Tide would continue with the assumption of office of both Evo Morales and Michelle Bachelet, in 2006, and Rafael Correa, in 2007. One should, however, distinguish, on the one hand, between Chávez, Kirchner, Morales and Correa, whose economic policies were redistributionist, and Lula and Bachelet, who despite their radical credentials, believed in market solutions to social problems.

16 Kozloff 2008, p. 54.

17 Mariátegui 2011, p. 183.

18 For an example of Mariátegui's radical 'Pan-Latin Americanism', see his 'The Unity of Indo-Hispanic America'. There, connecting the 1920s with the 1820s that saw Latin America's struggles for independence from Spain, he writes: 'Now as then, a revolutionary spirit unites Indo-Hispanic America. Bourgeois interests are competitive or rival; the interests of the masses are not. All of America's new men are in solidarity with the Mexican Revolution, its fate, its ideals, and its people. Timid diplomatic toasts will not unite these peoples. In the future, the historic choices of the multitudes will unite them' (Mariátegui 2011, pp. 448–9).

19 The famous twenty-one conditions for admission to the Communist Party clearly indic-

1   Hugo Pesce as Mediator

In *The Other South: Faulkner, Coloniality and the Mariátegui Tradition*, Hosam
Aboul-Ela finds in Salles's *The Motorcycle Diaries* proof for the influence of the
Peruvian Marxist not only on the evolution of future Argentine revolutionaries,
but on Latin American radical thought:

> A very different source of testimony for Mariátegui's general currency dur-
> ing the 1950 and 1960s is Brazilian Walter Salles's cinematic account of
> the young Ernesto 'Che' Guevara's coming to consciousness while read-
> ing Mariátegui in a climactic scene of the film *The Motorcycle Diaries*.[20]

Ironically, a fiction film is presented as proof for the widespread dissemination and influence of his works. Behind this belief in the overall truthfulness
of Salles's portrayal of Guevara's encounter with Mariátegui's ideas is the fact
that Pesce had been a friend and close collaborator of the author of *Seven
Essays*. Together with the union leader Julio Portocarrero, he had represented
the fledgling Partido Socialista at the First Latin American Communist Congress
in Buenos Aires in 1929, and had even co-authored with Mariátegui the important 'The Problem of Race in Latin America'.

Given this personal relationship it is not unreasonable to assume that Pesce
introduced Mariátegui to Guevara, thus guaranteeing a kind of Marxist apostol-
ic succession in the continent. Others have made this connection. For instance,
Azurra Carpo writes, 'In Lima, he meets Hugo Pesci [sic], who introduces him
to the thought of José Carlos Mariátegui, a Peruvian thinker very close to the
intellectual finesse of Antonio Gramsci'.[21] Enrique Krauze flatly states: 'Pesce
gave him some of Mariátegui's writings'.[22] More measured, Néstor Kohan pro-

---

ated in its second entry that: 'Every organisation that wishes to affiliate to the Communist
International must regularly and methodically remove reformists and centrists from every
responsible post in the labour movement (party organisations, editorial boards, trades
unions, parliamentary factions, co-operatives, local government) and replace them with
tested communists, without worrying unduly about the fact that, particularly at first,
ordinary workers from the masses will be replacing 'experienced' opportunists' ([Com-
munist International] 1980).

20   Aboul-Ela 2007, p. 39.
21   Carpo 2006, 238.
22   Krauze 2011, p. 300. It may be of interest that Krauze's original in Spanish is more expans-
ive than the English translation, perhaps reflecting Mariátegui's greater reputation as a
thinker in Latin America: 'Pesce introduced him to the works of Mariátegui and Guevara
was seduced, not as much by the Marxist ideas, but rather by his unique approach to the
Indian, to the communist property of the first owners of the land, and to the [idea of] race
as the promise of a new civilization' (Krauze 2012, p. 323).

poses, 'It's very probable that in that moment [of his visit to Lima] he had had direct contact with the works of José Carlos Mariátegui, Pesce's intellectual father'.[23]

There are, however, a number of difficulties with the film's explicit linking of Che and Mariátegui that, at least, undermines its value as 'testimony'. The first is that this intellectual encounter is made up by screenwriter José Rivera and director Walter Salles. In the movie's two source texts – Che Guevara's *Motorcycle Diaries* and Alberto Granado's *Travelling with Che Guevara* – there is no mention of Mariátegui. Moreover, while Guevara praises Pesce as a doctor and as a man, there is only a very indirect reference to his politics in *Motorcycle Diaries*. In a letter to his father included in the book, Guevara describes Mariátegui's former collaborator as playing 'in the same position as Lusteau'.[24] This a misspelled allusion to Félix Lousteau, who played on the left wing for the classic River Plate soccer teams of the late 1940s and early 1950s.

Alberto Granado provides a more clearly political portrayal of Pesce, as well as of his influence on Che, in *Travelling with Che Guevara*:

> Fuser [sic] dubbed him the Maestro, and he really is one. In every conversation we had with him we learned something, whether it was about leprosy, physiology, politics or philosophy. Through him we not only discovered César Vallejo, that great poet who spoke with the voice of the Inca race ... Politically he is a Marxist and has great sensitivity, as well as great dialectical ability in discussion and in dealing with problems.[25]

As in the movie, Pesce is presented as influencing Guevara intellectually, but the only Peruvian author mentioned in Granado's text is Vallejo. This stress on poetry, one must note, is consistent with the intellectual references mentioned in Guevara's *The Motorcycle Diaries*. He was clearly more interested in poetry than in politics at the time. While neither Marx nor Lenin (nor, obviously, Mariátegui) are mentioned, Guevara refers to Federico García Lorca, Pablo Neruda, and the Venezuelan writer Miguel Otero Silva.

It is only in the introduction to the English edition that Granado mentions Mariátegui. There he notes that Pesce 'introduced us to the most authentic of Peruvian poets, César Vallejo, as well as to José Mariátegui [sic], a true Marxist of Latin American origin, with whose philosophy Ernesto and I fully identi-

23   Kohan 2000, p. 198.
24   Guevara 2006, p. 156.
25   Granado 2014, p. 124.

fied'.[26] This statement, which dates to 2003, is, however, framed by a reference to the movie *Motorcycle Diaries*:[27]

> But once again life has gone beyond my wildest dreams and here I am, fifty years after that trip, when luck, fate, or whatever you want to call it affords me the opportunity of seeing a youthful reincarnation of myself at twenty nine – in the person of the Argentine actor Rodrigo de la Serna, who relives episodes that took place in the last century and that are being re-created by Walter Salles for the film *The Motorcycle Diaries*.[28]

Thanks to Salles's film, Granado found himself 'again in Lima, a city that taught Ernesto and me so much, through the person of Dr. Hugo Pesce'.[29] Therefore, Granado remembered Mariátegui, who is not mentioned in either his or Guevara's 'original' recounting of the trip, only after seeing the movie. Given the vagaries of memory, one could argue that – regarding Pesce's role as a mediator for Mariátegui's influence on Che – the main, perhaps only, 'source of testimony' is a moment in a fiction film made thirty-seven years after the Argentine revolutionary's death and fifty years after the event recounted.

Of course, I am not questioning the fact evidenced by the text of Che's personal dedication of *Guerrilla Warfare* that Pesce was an influence on Guevara and may very well have played a role in his evolution from traveller and sensitive observer to revolutionary. Pesce was, in his own right, a lucid and charismatic figure. Not only did he help redefine the criteria used to classify leprosy internationally,[30] but was also one of the key leaders of the Peruvian Communist Party in the 1930s and beyond. He was General Secretary of the party between 1932 and 1933.[31] The fact that he was able to achieve prominence as a medical expert during a time of political reaction – in 1952, Peru was governed by the dictatorship of general Manuel A. Odría – was not only evidence of his talent and reputation, but also of his ability for personal and political manoeuvring.

A clue as to why neither Guevara nor Granado, at least in his original text, mention Pesce as introducing them to the ideas and works of Mariátegui, can

---

26 Granado 2014, p. xv.
27 Although Salles's *Motorcycle Diaries* was premiered in 2004, Granado participated as a consultant during the filming and, therefore, must have seen earlier versions of the film.
28 Granado 2014, p. xiii.
29 Granado 2014, pp. xv, xiii.
30 Burstein 2003, p. 173.
31 Anonymous 2011, p. 7.

perhaps be found in his militancy in the Communist Party. As one of the two delegates of the (Peruvian) Socialist Party to the Buenos Aires Latin American Communist Conference of 1929, Pesce, together with Julio Portocarrero, had ably defended Mariátegui's political theses regarding the revolutionary potential of indigenous populations, the pluriclassist constitution of the [Peruvian] Socialist Party, and, more generally, the need to adapt political activity to specific cultural and historical realities rather than blindly follow the dictates of the Communist International. However, by the time they returned to Peru, both had unexpectedly become 'proponents of the official positions' of the Comintern.[32] Thus, it is not surprising that Pesce, despite maintaining friendly relations with the Mariátegui family, would become Secretary General of the Communist Party precisely during the period when the process of *desmariateguización* was at its height.[33] As Beigel notes,

> The criticisms made by the Comintern, that were leveled in Peru, South America, and Europe during 1932, gave way to a second phase that began with a more virulent attack against the current founded by Mariátegui within Peruvian Marxism, and ended with the full condemnation of *mariateguismo.*[34]

To my knowledge, there is no record of Pesce, then or later, defending the intellectual and political legacy of his once friend and mentor. Perhaps his willingness to follow party discipline, even as he developed a brilliant professional career, helps explain how he managed to survive the labyrinthine trajectory of international communism. Although a relative thaw towards Mariátegui had taken place within the Communist Party during the 1940s, it was based on the

---

32   Flores Galindo 1980, p. 97. The reasons why Pesce and Portocarrero abandoned Mariátegui
       and his positions are unknown. Flores Galindo writes: 'It was in effect that month [February 1930] that Pesce and Portocarrero returned and ... they had become proponents of the
       official positions: were they persuaded after the Congress? ... It is possible that they experienced pressure during and after the meeting based on the opinion that it was impossible
       to be a revolutionary outside the International. It was not a worthless argument. What
       is a fact is that after their return, Pesce and Portocarrero's positions did not diverge from
       the positions proposed by Buenos Aires [the location of the Latin American office of the
       Comintern] that were already dominant in the [Peruvian] Socialist Party' (Flores Galindo
       1980, pp. 97–98).
33   Javier Mariátegui, son of the author of *Seven Essays*, wrote in an homage to Pesce from
       1994, but only published in 2014: 'Even though I knew him as a child, I had, years later,
       the privilege of being first his student and then his fellow conversationalist. I visited him
       Friday or Saturday evenings' (Mariátegui 2014, p. 78).
34   Beigel 2003, p. 162.

necessary identification of Mariátegui's ideas with those of Lenin and even Stalin. This distortion of the Peruvian's thought is exemplified by Jorge del Prado's 1943 'Mariátegui – marxista-leninista': 'It is surprising how similar is the definition of Leninism proposed by Mariátegui – when formulating with principles of our [Communist] Party in 1928 – to that provided by Stalin in his *Foundations of Leninism* from 1925. Despite [*Foundations of Leninism*] having been published four years earlier, Mariátegui could not have known [*Foundations of Leninism*] since it was only in 1931 that translations into Spanish – or any of the other languages he spoke – became available.'[35] One must note that not only is Mariátegui transformed into a precursor of Stalin, but, in this quotation, the name of the political party founded by Mariátegui – Socialist Party – is transformed into Communist Party, thus erasing, after the fact, an obvious point of friction between the author of *Seven Essays* and International Communism. However, not even this distorted recuperation of Mariátegui as a version of Lenin and Stalin in a Peruvian minor key is to be found in Pesce's own writings, in which 'his intellectual father' is only the most marginal of presences.[36] As we have seen, it would only be with the Cuban revolution – and the need it generated among scholars and radicals to find precedents for an event that seemed for many to come out of nowhere – that Mariátegui was rediscovered. This search for precursors led to Mariátegui becoming acknowledged ex post facto as the 'first Marxist' of Latin America and as a major influence on the region's later radical movements. Moreover, as Beigel notes, the awareness of the distance between Mariátegui and 'Marxism-Leninism', even if purged from its Stalinist accretions, would only begin to take place in the 1960s, when 'many were able to leave behind their prejudice and rigidity in order to overcome 'sanitary cordons' and finally accede to an *indigenista*, Marxist, and nationalist Amauta [Mariátegui]'.[37] Ironically, while the evidence that Mariátegui helped transform Fúser into Che is conjectural at best, there is no doubt that Che – and the revolution he helped bring about – played a central role in the rediscovery of Mariátegui's actual ideas.

That said, Guevara's visit to Lima not only coincided with this timid and distorted rediscovery of Mariátegui taking place within Communist circles, but also with an event that would play a central role in the full return of the Per-

---

35   Del Prado 1980, p. 75.

36   For instance, the anthology of Pesce's writings – *Hugo Pesce. Pensamiento medico y filosófico* – only mentions Mariátegui in passing – no text is quoted nor page given – in his book *Lenguaje y pensamiento: Aspectos en el antiguo Perú*, originally published in 1968 (Pesce 2005, pp. 290, 293).

37   Beigel 2003, p. 203.

uvian's writings and figure: the revitalisation of Editorial Minerva. With the publication of *El alma matinal* (The Morning Soul) in 1950 and of *Seven Essays* in 1952, the works of Mariátegui started to become available again in Peru.[38] This makes the moment Pesce gives Guevara a copy of Mariátegui's book plausible, even if, as we have seen, it is actually the product of the filmmakers' imaginations. But the pathos of the situation – Mariátegui's widow and children republishing the mostly forgotten works of their long-dead husband and father – would have probably called the attention of the young Argentine travelers.[39]

However, Pesce is not the only individual who could have brought Mariátegui to the attention of Guevara. As Paulo Drinot notes, 'According to the memoirs of Hilda Gadea, Guevara's first wife and former APRA militant, she, not Pesce, introduced Guevara to Mariátegui's writings'.[40] One year after his visit to Lima, Guevara met Gadea – who despite her left-wing activism was then still a member of the APRA party – in Guatemala, during the brief progressive government of Jacobo Arbenz. (He would marry Gadea in 1955 and divorce her in 1959). According to Gadea, soon after meeting, Guevara expressed interest in visiting Europe. In response to this desire, she 'advised him to read José Carlos Mariátegui to learn how to study Europe. We talked about Mariátegui's works, *El alma matinal* and *Seven Essays on Peruvian Reality* [sic]'.[41] The possibility that Guevara could have read *El alma matinal* and *Seven Essays* is again given verisimilitude by the fact that, as we have seen, these are precisely the two works by Mariátegui that the Editorial Minerva had reissued by 1953. It may be significant that Mariátegui is presented by Gadea as a guide to understanding European culture, rather than as a beacon for a Latin American revolutionary, as he is in Salles's film and in most accounts of Che's putative encounter with his predecessor's works. Curiously, Gadea is here giving a positive spin to the APRA accusation that Mariátegui was a Eurocentrist. While not the main underlying reason for the book's writing – as we have seen, national topics were at the

---

38   Between 1930 and 1950, all editions of Mariátegui's books were printed outside Peru by publishers not aligned with the Communist movements. The only exception was a very small printing by Editorial Minerva of *Seven Essays*, then run by his brother and widow.

39   Paulo Drinot is correct when he argues: 'In Walter Salles's film, *The Motorcycle Diaries* (2004), Pesce gives Guevara a copy of Mariátegui's *Seven Interpretative Essays on Peruvian Reality* (first published in 1928), and Guevara is portrayed reading this book on several occasions, as if to suggest that his reading of Mariátegui hastened his political awakening. Yet Guevara makes no reference to the book or to Mariátegui in the diaries' (Drinot 2010, p. 94).

40   Drinot 2010, p. 95.

41   Gadea 2008, p. 27.

centre of Mariátegui's writings, at least, since the end of 1924 – he had expected *Seven Essays* to put the lie to this increasingly disseminated canard. As he wrote in the 'Author's Note' to his classic work:

> There are many who think that I am tied to European culture and alien to the facts and issues of my country. Let my book defend me against this cheap and biased assumption.[42]

Gadea does not mention, however, if Guevara ever read the works, or, if he did, what his reaction was.

Additional evidence of a probable connection between Mariátegui and Guevara – now fully identified and identifiable as Che – is the publication by the new revolutionary Cuban government of an anthology of the Peruvian's writing – *El problema de la tierra y otros ensayos* – in 1960, and, in 1963, of a complete edition of *Seven Essays*.[43] This was, of course, the period of Che's greatest political influence. Che, however, never mentioned Mariátegui in any of his speeches or writings.

2   **From Mariátegui to Che**

Despite the lack of textual evidence, many scholars have posited the influence of Mariátegui on Che. This putative intellectual connection received the official imprimatur of the Cuban government in 1975 when the Central Committee of the Cuban Communist Party published a pamphlet that claimed that the 'two great men of the American continent' had

> dedicated their thoughts, their actions, and even their lives to the most intransigent revolutionary cause against colonialism, imperialism, and international neocolonialism. Both constitute the most elegant expression of the tradition of struggle for the complete independence of our continent.[44]

Whether Che had actually read Mariátegui, the fact is that, as Marc Becker notes, there are numerous points of contact between both Marxists: they both would propose an 'open, voluntarist Marxism based on rural, peasant-based

---

42   Mariátegui 1971, p. xxvi.
43   See Becker 1993, p. 86.
44   Quoted in Becker 1993, p. 80.

movement rather than urban, working-class movement found in orthodox Marxism'.[45] More important, while both Second International social democrats and Stalinists believed in an immutable order of socio-economic stages that had to be necessarily traversed by all societies – a belief that would paradoxically condemn Latin American radicals to strive to buttress capitalism and liberal democracy – Mariátegui and Che argued for the possibility of establishing a socialist Latin America. Moreover, for some, Che, like Mariátegui, imagined an egalitarian future radically different from the grey reality that characterised actually existing socialism. As Michael Löwy notes, after acknowledging the impossibility of verifying whether Che had read Mariátegui:

> His [Che's] ideas on the construction of socialism are an attempt at 'heroic creation' of something new, the search – interrupted and incomplete – for a distinct model of socialism, radically opposed in many respects to the 'actually existing' bureaucratic caricature.[46]

As we have seen, 'heroic creation' is the phrase coined by Mariátegui for the transcultural socialism he envisioned.

However, one could also list numerous divergences between both Marxists. For instance, nothing is further from Mariátegui, who envisioned socialism as the end result of a long-term programme of political debate, punctual policy action, radical union activism, and collaboration among diverse progressive sectors, than Che's *foco*, that is, the belief that armed action by a small guerrilla group in the countryside could start a revolution in a Latin America that was a political cinder box.[47] Of course, Mariátegui would have agreed with Che's criticism of those 'who sit down to wait until in some mechanical way all necessary objective and subjective conditions are given without working to acceler-

---

45   Becker 1993, p. 76. One must note, however, that while Mariátegui undeniably revaluated the role of indigenous cultures, institutions, and, of course, population as necessary components of any radical Peruvian movement, he did not disregard the importance of urban sectors for any significant progressive political change. As he wrote in his 'Reply to Luis Alberto Sánchez': 'The vindication that we argue for is that of work. It is that of the working classes, without distinction between coast and highlands, Indian or cholo' (Mariátegui 2011, p. 176).

46   Löwy 2007, p. 119.

47   According to Che Guevara: 'the Cuban Revolution contributed three fundamental lessons to the conduct of revolutionary movements in America. They are: 1. Popular forces can win a war against the army. 2. It is not necessary to wait until all the conditions for making revolution exist; the insurrection can create them. 3. In underdeveloped America the countryside is the basic area for armed fighting' (Guevara 1997, p. 50).

ate them'.[48] Nevertheless, the basic political methodologies proposed by both Marxists are significantly different. It is true that Mariátegui was not opposed in principle to revolutionary violence. Writing about Gandhi, he argues that:

> Revolutionaries of all latitudes have to choose between using violence or suffering it. If one does not want spirit and intelligence to be under the control of force, we must decide to place force under the control of intelligence and the spirit.[49]

He, however, did not discount the need to gain public support – one is tempted to say hegemony – as his cultural, political, and labour organising activity show. Unlike Che, Mariátegui did not believe that the exclusive or even the primary way to accelerate social change was through armed action.

Furthermore, one must distinguish between Che's stress on the countryside as the location for revolutionary action – 'the immense participation of the country people in the life of all the underdeveloped parts of America' –[50] with Mariátegui's radical *indigenismo*. Unlike Che, who writes about a generic country people in his writings about guerrilla warfare – in principle, the same in Cuba, Peru, or Bolivia – Mariátegui's concern with locality is rooted in the specific characteristic of Peruvian Quechua Andean culture and its institutions, such as the *ayllu* (agrarian commune). If Mariátegui was concerned with the relationship between political change and cultural tradition, Che, in *Guerrilla Warfare*, generalises his experiences as a guerrilla leader during the Cuban Revolution into 'fundamental lessons to the conduct of revolutionary movements in America'.[51] For the Argentine revolutionary, all of Latin America was basically the same. A case can be made that Che's disregard for local cultural reality is already evidenced in *The Motorcycle Diaries*. There are several moments when the young Guevara stresses his inability to communicate with indigenous people during his visit to the Peruvian Andes. For instance, the young Guevara writes about 'the silent Indians'; also complaining about the 'wary Indians [who] barely dignified our questions with a response, offering only monosyllabic replies'.[52]

---

48   Guevara 1997, p. 50.

49   Mariátegui 1980c, p. 199. One must note that this qualified paean to violence belongs to the very first period of Mariátegui's Marxist period (1924) and does not reappear in his more mature later works.

50   Guevara 1997, p. 51.

51   Guevara 1997, p. 50.

52   Guevara 2006, p. 101.

Fifteen years later, as he prepared for his last revolutionary attempt in Bolivia, Che would try to avoid repeating his earlier experiences in the Andes and studied Quechua. Unfortunately, the language spoken in the region of Bolivia where he tried to establish his *foco* was Guaraní.[53]

3 The New Man

Perhaps the main point of contact between both Mariátegui and Che was their belief in the possibility of the creation, to use a phrase used by both Marxists, of 'the new man'.[54] This new man and, obviously, woman is, in Kohan's words, a 'new type of subjectivity without which any revolutionary project would fail'.[55] For Che, the new man and woman implied the 'development of a consciousness in which there is a new scale of values. Society as a whole must be converted into a gigantic school'.[56] The end purpose of this process of re-education 'is not a vision of reward for the individual. The prize is the new society in which individuals will have different characteristics: the society of communist human beings'.[57] Guevara correctly notes that, unlike the frequently held belief in individualism as intrinsic to humanity and the market as its natural economic manifestation, the individual, as commonly understood, is a social construction. In his words: 'In rough outline this phenomenon [creation of the new man and woman] is similar to the process by which capitalist consciousness was formed in its initial period'.[58] Just as capitalism had created a society of individualists seeking their personal gain, socialism had to create human beings who identified their personal improvement with that of society as a whole.

One finds a similar stress on the creation of new men and women in Mariátegui's writings, and, in particular, in his posthumously published *Defensa del marxismo* (mostly composed of articles published in 1928 and 1929). In this text, he notes,

> The ethical function of socialism ... should be sought not in grandiloquent Decalogues, nor in philosophic speculations that by no means constitute

53   James 2001, p. 224.
54   Mariátegui concludes 'El alma matinal' (The Morning Soul) with a brief reference to the 'new man [who] is the man of the morning' (Mariátegui 1981b, p. 13).
55   Kohan 2000, p. 141.
56   Guevara 2013, p. 217.
57   Guevara 2013, p. 218.
58   Guevara 2013, p. 217.

a necessity in Marxist theorizing, but in the creation of a producer's moral by the very process of anti-capitalist struggle.[59]

For the author of *Seven Essays*, it is through the 'anti-capitalist struggle' of the working class, which, one must note, does not include acts of violence, but rather is based on their specific class activity, that the moral and subjective changes take place: 'The shop, the factory, affects the worker psychologically and mentally. The union, the class struggle, continues and completes the work that is begun there'.[60] He further defines the new subjectivity being generated by the workers' activities in factories and unions with a quotation from Piero Gobetti:

> Whoever lives in a factory has the dignity of work, the habit of sacrifice and fatigue. The rhythm of life is based strongly on the spirit of tolerance and interdependence that accustoms one to punctuality, to rigor, to continuity.[61]

Tolerance, interdependence, sacrifice, and rigor are among the defining traits of this new subjectivity. One could easily accuse Mariátegui here of idealising factory life and labour unions. He may very well have been influenced by his early witnessing of such landmark inaugural moments in the organisation of Peruvian working-class activity as the successful struggle for the eight-hour work-day.[62] This was also a period that saw a flourishing of working-class cultural activity that, as Flores Galindo notes, included 'the existence of a theater, music, and poetry on proletarian topics, created by the workers themselves'.[63]

---

59   Mariátegui 2011, p. 201.
60   Mariátegui 2011, p. 203.
61   Quoted in Mariátegui 2011e, p. 204.
62   On Mariátegui's support for the early working-class movement and the struggle for the eight-hour work day, see 'José Carlos Mariátegui: The Making of the Revolutionary in the Aristocratic Republic' in this study.
63   Flores Galindo 1980, p. 22. Mariátegui was well acquainted with these worker cultural activities, not only due to his early personal experience as a worker, his continued connection with worker organisations, his labour organising or by his brief editing of *Labor*, a magazine dedicated, as its name indicated, to labour activity and organising, but also by his having been one of the judges of the Concurso Poético de Vanguardia (Vanguard Poetic Contest) organised by the workers of Vitarte, an industrial neighbourhood in Lima, in 1927. (The other judges were Jorge Basadre, a young intellectual and soon to be the country's most respected historian, and the worker and future Aprista union leader Arturo Sabroso) (Flores Galindo 1980, p. 129).

As Gonzalo Espino Relucé notes in his introduction to an anthology of poetry written by workers, *La lira rebelde proletaria*:

> The cultural production by workers must be examined as an alternative phenomenon to the official manner of making culture during the Aristocratic Republic ... Workers, attempting to go beyond their conditions of exploitation and misery, move towards the creation of a proletarian consciousness, and, in this process, produce an intense cultural action as an intrinsic and indispensable element.[64]

Given this substratum of change in the consciousness of workers and in their relationship with cultural production, it may not be surprising that Mariátegui notes: 'If socialism should not be realized as a social order, it would be enough as a work of education and elevation to be justified in history'.[65] Evolution in subjectivity is of greater importance than political change.

Despite their common concern with the construction of new subjectivities, the differences between both thinkers should by now be obvious. For Mariátegui, it is modernity – linked to the actual sites of capitalist production, the organisation of and by the workers, and their struggle to supersede capitalism itself – that ultimately leads to the construction of a new producer's moral and, therefore, of new men and women. For Che, it is only after the establishment of socialism that the development of the new man and woman is possible. Moreover, Mariátegui also believed in the possibility of helping shape new progressive subjectivities through cultural and political intervention and activity. Alas, neither knew that the construction of socialist new men and women would be undermined by the cultural and institutional changes unleashed by late capitalism.

4   Mariátegui as a Founder of Discursivity

It has not been my purpose to deny the actual influence of Mariátegui on Latin American politics or his historical importance. I agree with Mónica Bernabé's description of Mariátegui as a Foucauldian initiator of discursive practice: 'an author who opens the space to something different from herself'.[66] Mariátegui, even if within a more limited intellectual geography than Marx or Freud, would

---

64   Espino Relucé 1984, p. 23.
65   Mariátegui 1980, pp. 204–5.
66   Bernabé 2006, p. 107.

have, in Foucault's words, 'produced ... the possibilities and rules for the formation of other texts'.[67] From this perspective, the author of *Seven Essays* 'established an endless possibility of discourse'.[68]

Foucault's ideas unwittingly echo Mariátegui's own writings on tradition. According to the *Oxford Dictionary of Difficult Words*, the first definition of tradition is 'the transmission of customs or beliefs from generation to generation, the fact of being passed on in this way: *every shade of colour is fixed* **by tradition** *and governed by religious laws* along-established custom or belief that has been passed on in this way: *Japan's unique cultural traditions*; *[*in singular*] an artistic or literary method or style established by an artist, writer, or movement, and subsequently followed by others: *visionary works **in the tradition of William Blake***'.[69] Continuity and fidelity to origins are at the core of conventional notions of tradition.

In his 'Heterodoxia de la tradición' (Heterodoxy of Tradition), Mariátegui, on the other hand, stresses heterodoxy as a necessary aspect of any living tradition. In his words,

> Tradition, on the other hand, is characterised by its refusal to being captured by formula ... tradition is heterogenous and contradictory ... In order to reduce it to a unitary concept, it is necessary to be content with its essence, ignoring its diverse crystalizations.[70]

Like Foucault, he sees a discursive practice, that is, a discursive tradition, as characterised by the opening to endless possibility. He would thus not have necessarily been surprised by the fact that contradictory movements and authors have claimed him as a source; although one can obviously assume that he would have been vehemently opposed to some that have taken his name.

We have already seen that, regardless of the bad faith involved, by the 1940s the Peruvian Communist Party had begun claiming him as not only their founder – something that was not denied even at the height of *antimariateguismo* – but as an intellectual source. Although he actually founded the Peruvian Socialist Party, this appropriation of Mariátegui as a Marxist-Leninist-Stalinist could lay claim to those isolated moments and passages such as when, in 'Programmatic Principles of the Socialist Party', it is stated that:

---

67   Foucault 1998, p. 217.
68   Foucault 1998, p. 217.
69   Hobson 2004, p. 441. Stress in the original.
70   Mariátegui 1981d, p. 118.

The practice of Marxist socialism in this period is that of Marxism-Leninism. Marxism-Leninism is the revolutionary method in the stage of imperialism and monopoly. The Peruvian Socialist Party takes it as its method
of struggle.[71]

However, as we have seen, this statement – probably influenced by the felt need
to join the Comintern – is part of a proposal that, in other aspects, deviated
from Communist orthodoxy, not least in the party's actual name. Moreover,
while the authorship is frequently ascribed to Mariátegui, the fact is that it was
necessarily the result, not only of a compromise with the realities of international communism, but also of a negotiation with the other founding members
of the party.[72]

The 'endless possibility of discourse' found in Mariátegui can be best evidenced if one looks at three important political movements in Peru during the
1980s. Founded and led by Abimael Guzmán, the brutal Shining Path had early
on taken the phrase 'Por el Sendero Luminoso de José Carlos Mariátegui (On
the Shining Path of José Carlos Mariátegui)' as its guiding motto.[73] However, as
Iván Degregori notes, as the years go by 'Bit by bit, the references to Mariátegui
disappear. "Presidente Gonzalo" becomes "the greatest living Marxist-Leninist-
Maoist", the "Fourth Sword of Marxism"'.[74] Mariátegui is progressively demoted
from inspiration to remote precursor. Moreover, the name Shining Path was
rarely used by members of the movement, who preferred to call it Partido
Comunista del Peru (Communist Party of Peru).

There were also significant differences between the Shining Path and its
putative source. The Shining Path took Guevara's privileging of action over
persuasion to its extreme, thus contradicting Mariátegui's stress on creating
popular support for revolutionary change. Moreover, unlike Mariátegui, for
whom connecting socialism to local tradition is a primary concern, the Shining Path's 'official documents entirely omit the ethnic dimension or directly
reject Andean cultural reevaluation as "folklore" or bourgeois manipulation'.[75]
Instead of the careful consideration of Peruvian reality, Degregori sees in the
Shining Path 'a hyperrationalist movement', in its belief in its ideology as cap-

---

71   Socialist Party 2011, p. 238.
72   On Mariátegui's political activity, see 'José Carlos Mariátegui and the Culture of Politics'.
73   According to Becker, at first Guzmán 'based his ideological statements on Mariategui's
     analysis that Peruvian society was simultaneously neo-feudal and neo-colonial' (Becker
     93, p. xii).
74   Degregori 2012, p. 89.
75   Degregori 2012, p. 167.

able of explaining and predicting all phenomena – whether natural, subjective, or social.[76] While often interpreted as a product of Andean culture, the Shining Path ultimately proposed the rejection of any and all local traditions and their replacement with a supposedly socialist praxis rooted in 'Gonzalo thought'.

However, despite the cult of violence that characterised the Shining Path, its embrace of ritual and pageant could be seen as presenting a debased interpretation of Mariátegui's writings on myth and on the relationship between Marxism and religious emotion.[77] As Degregori admits, the Shining Path 'converted science into religion'.[78] Despite the immense ethical differences between them, for the Shining Path, as for Mariátegui, there was a spiritual dimension to political activity. Guzmán channelled his followers' 'spiritual needs' in order to transform them into obedient killing machines.

A movement contemporary to the Shining Path, Izquierda Unida (United Left), the alliance of parties across the radical political spectrum founded in 1980, laid claim to another aspect of Mariátegui's thought: his belief in the necessary unity of all progressive forces. Not surprisingly, 'Alfonso Barrantes, the leader of the Izquierda Unida coalition, also emphasised the importance of studying Mariátegui's thought'.[79] Barrantes would, in fact, become mayor of Lima (1984–86) before the left, including Izquierda Unida, imploded partly as a consequence of the popular reaction against the brutality of the Shining Path – even though Izquierda Unida had been scrupulously democratic – the fall of the Berlin Wall, and the apparent successes of neoliberal policies that began to be implemented with the coming to power of Alberto Fujimori in 1990.

Finally, the early neoliberal writings of Mario Vargas Llosa and Hernando de Soto could be seen as a surprising example of a discursive space other than the socialist one that still developed from Mariátegui's writings. As Efraín Kristal notes:

> Like Mariátegui, Vargas Llosa and de Soto propose their solutions in the name of the poor and for the benefit of all society. Long after having rejected his socialist convictions, Vargas Llosa continues to admire Mariátegui. He even sounds like that first Marxist intellectual in Latin America when he calls for a revolutionary change in the Peruvian political and economic

---

76   Degregori 2012, p. 167.
77   On Mariátegui's appropriation and modification of Georges Sorel's notion of the myth, see
       the chapter 'Mariátegui, Sorel, and Myth'.
78   Degregori 2012, p. 166.
79   Becker 1993, p. xii.

system and when he criticises the negative influence of many intellectuals 'who undermine or destroy the possibilities for political democracy to
work' [in society].[80]

One can add that, in addition to electoral participation, de Soto and Vargas
Llosa have, in a truly *mariateguista* manner, patiently worked for the construction of ideological and cultural hegemony for their ideas in Peru.

But, ironically, given the lack of any textual connection, it would be impossible to include Che Guevara in any discursive field or tradition founded by
Mariátegui.

5   Conclusion: Mariátegui, Che and Borges

There may be, however, an alternative way of contextualising Mariátegui's role
in the politics and thought of the region – and beyond – that would be able
to do justice to the often proposed relationship between Mariátegui and Che.
In order to do so we need to look at the essays of one of Mariátegui's favourite writers, Jorge Luis Borges. In his classic 1951 essay 'Kafka and his Precursors',
Borges writes:

> The word 'precursor' is indispensable to the vocabulary of criticism, but
> one must try to purify it from any connotation of polemic or rivalry. The
> fact is that each writer creates his precursors. His work modifies our con-
> ception of the past, as it will modify the future.[81]

Borges's list of Kafka's precursors is a heterogeneous group that includes eight
century Chinese fabulist Han Yu, Zeno, Kierkegaard, Robert Browning, León
Bloy, and Lord Dunsany. The reason that the constitution of Borges's peculiar
list is possible and logical is that the writings of Kafka have created a new way of
reading. The reader of Kafka thus acquires the capacity to recognise the Czech
author's traits in other authors:

> I had thought, at first, that he was as unique as the phoenix of rhetorical
> praise; after spending a little time with him, I felt I could recognize his
> voice, or his habits, in the texts of various literatures and various ages.[82]

---

80   Kristal 1999, p. 112.
81   Borges 1999, p. 365.
82   Borges 1999, p. 363.

Implicit in 'Kafka and his Precursors' is the fact that the mode of reading created by Kafka would lead one not only to identify precursors, but also successors, among whom one would have to include the Borges of 'The Library of Babel' and 'The Lottery in Babylon'. And, as in the case of the precursors, these successors would not necessarily reflect influence, but, instead, affinity with one or more of the characteristic elements of the central author being considered.

Even if one must ruefully admit that they were more imagined than real, the supposedly unique traits of the Cuban revolution, such as the ability to combine tropical joy and radical political change, or artistic freedom and political mobilisation, led many observers to look for predecessors. But one can also note that after his rediscovery in the 1960s and 1970s, Mariátegui, like Kafka, created, for many, a new set of expectations regarding what it meant to be a Latin American radical. The *Mariáteguian* observer or reader thus brings a new set of criteria to their understanding of politics and theory. Salles's *The Motorcycle Diaries* is an example of how Mariátegui has helped establish the way the political role of Che Guevara is now understood. The stress on Latin American reality – one of the key innovations of Mariátegui's heroic creation of Marxism – is now seen as a necessary component of Che Guevara's politics. It is what makes him in the film a *Latin American* revolutionary rather than merely another deracinated communist.

Mariátegui may not have been an influence on Ernesto Che Guevara but, at least for many Latin American artists and scholars, he has helped shape not only how we understand the Argentine revolutionary, but also what would define any potential Latin American radicalism.

CHAPTER 10

Epilogue: A Tale of Two Quijanos

Perhaps the most influential Peruvian social scientist of the last half century, Aníbal Quijano (1928–2018) is also a widely heard voice in the humanities. His work has become a touchstone for those who, like Walter Mignolo or Sara Castro-Klarén, have looked for Latin American alternatives to a blinkered postcolonial mainstream they consider too indebted to Eurocentric theories and perspectives. As Castro-Klarén argues: 'The imperial English-speaking world, even at the fringe location of its imperial outposts, has considered itself a notch "above" Latin America in the tree of knowledge'.[1] The notion of the coloniality of power – that the division of the world population into races and the establishment of a hierarchical relation among these underlies the world economic system founded with the colonisation of the Americas – should, for many critics in the region, inform all reflection on the postcolonial world and its condition.[2] But, as we saw in the chapter 'José Carlos Mariátegui: From Race to Culture' this concept originated in Quijano's reading of his predecessor.

While a close examination of the totality of Quijano's numerous writings on Mariátegui would, perhaps, be outside the purview of this study, in this chapter I propose to look at the Peruvian sociologist's 'double' 'Prólogo' to the Biblioteca Ayacucho's edition of *Seven Essays*. (One must note that the Biblioteca Ayacucho – an editorial project began in 1974 by the celebrated Uruguayan critic Ángel Rama and Venezuelan writer José Ramón Medina and financed by the Venezuelan government – is composed of those Latin American works judged to be unequivocally canonical). Quijano, who wrote 'José Carlos Mariátegui: Reencuentro y debate' (José Carlos Mariátegui: Reencounter and Debate), the original prologue to the first Ayacucho edition of 1979, incorporated an addendum to the third edition of 2007 titled 'Treinta años despues: Otro reencuentro. Notas para un debate' (Thirty Years Later: Another Reencounter. Notes for a Debate). The development of Quijano's interpretation of Mariátegui, while without doubt the fruit of personal reflection, is, in my opin-

---

1 Castro-Klarén 2008, p. 134.
2 Quijano's influence may actually be spreading outside Latin American and Latin Americanist academia. Even if uncredited, Antonio Negri's and Michael Hardt's 'coloniality of biopower' must be seen as developing Quijano's concept: see Hardt and Negri 2009, pp. 77–82; see Driscoll 2010 for a discussion of the ethical problems in Hart's and Negri's lack of acknowledgment of Quijano's ideas in the development of their 'coloniality of biopower'.

ion, not only indicative of the evolution in the reception of the Peruvian Marxist, but also of the development of radical thought in Latin America and even beyond. Therefore, a brief comparison of both texts – the original prologue and the new 'notes' to that same prologue – permits the reader to evaluate the trajectory of criticism about Mariátegui and the concomitant evolution of theoretical frameworks that have taken place from 1979 to 2007.

1   The 'Reencounter'

Perhaps what first calls the attention of a contemporary reader of 'Reencuentro y debate' is Quijano's optimism regarding the imminence of a radical revolution. Noting the rediscovery of Mariátegui that had taken place during the two decades previous to the Ayacucho edition of 1979, Quijano writes:

> In the Peruvian context it is primarily the … testimony of the reencounter … between a revolutionary movement that is moving forward … and the memory of the man to whom it owes the central contribution to the foundation of its first labor and political national organizations, [the creation of] a still fruitful theoretical matrix, and a revolutionary strategical orientation within Peruvian society.[3]

For the eminent sociologist, not only was it possible in 1979 to identify a clearly motivated 'revolutionary movement', but also to describe it as moving forward.

The unmentioned social context behind these reflections is that of the rise of the left as a significant political force in Peru. In the 1978 elections for the constitutional assembly, which would help reintroduce democratic governance after a (mostly left-wing) military dictatorship of ten years, the different parties of the left garnered 30 percent of the vote.[4] Although, in reality, the winner of the elections, if one can use that term in regard to a constitutional assembly, had

---

3   Quijano 2007a, p. ix.

4   In 1968, the military, led by General Juan Velasco deposed the constitutionally elected President Fernando Belaúnde. The government put in effect a number of left-leaning measures, including nationalisation of the oil industry, land reform, and the participation of unions in the ownership of industry. Velasco, who was ill at the time, was replaced by the more moderate General Francisco Morales in 1975, who would oversee the return to democracy in 1980. While the 'left' supported many of the measures implemented by the regime, there was strong opposition on its part to their reformist nature and to the populist and personalist tone of the Velasco regime. Quijano, for one, was deported in 1973. For a brief summary of Quijano's intellectual and political career, see Assis Clímaco 2014.

been the APRA (with 35 percent of the vote), many on the left saw the receding of the military from politics as a triumph of the radical forces, understood as a class conscious working-class and left-leaning civic movements.[5]

That Quijano interpreted Mariátegui within what he considered to be a revolutionary social and political context is made even clearer later in the text. Quijano compares Mariátegui to those revolutionary thinkers and activists from Asia, Africa, and Latin America 'whose thought and action occupy a great part of the international debate: Mao, Ho Chi Minh, Castro, Guevara and Amilcar Cabral'[6] – a list composed of the revolutionary leaders of China, Vietnam, Cuba, and Guinea Bissau, respectively. Moreover, the sociologist did not see this revolutionary conjuncture as limited to what was then called the 'Third World,' but notes that 'the class struggle is again developing in the very centres of the capitalist world', and 'even in Eastern Europe'.[7] The end of times for capitalism (and state capitalism) was at hand, or so it seemed.

Of course, 1979 also coincided with a major revolutionary success of the Latin American left: the toppling of the Somoza regime by the Sandinistas in Nicaragua. However, the Sandinista revolution, in reality the only military revolutionary triumph after Cuba in 1959, would be the last hurrah of the region's revolutionary left.

Quijano's optimistic (from a radical perspective) evaluation of world politics is, however, debatable. For instance, as Jefferson Cowie notes regarding what the Peruvian sociologist calls the 'class struggle in the very center of the capitalist world', that is, the United States:

---

5   Although the opposition of the mainstream Peruvian left to the military government may seem counterintuitive – given the latter's putative progressivism – it is an established fact. While there had been significant resistance on the part of left-wing intellectuals and movements to the Velasco regime – as exemplified by Quijano's exile to Argentina in 1973 – this resistance increased after 1975, when he was replaced in the leadership of the military junta by the more conservative General Francisco Morales Bermúdez. The numerous social movements of the period included land takeovers, despite the implementation of a land reform by the military government, and the formation of the 'Peasant Confederation of Peru' in the countryside (Degregori 2012, p. 38). However, more importantly, given that the country was already primarily urban, it also included 'workers' organisations and movements, government employees (especially teachers), neighbourhood organisations, feminist groups, and, especially, regional movements – the so-called Defense Fronts (Frentes de Defensa)' (Degregori 2012, p. 39). Carlos Iván Degregori concludes that 'This social effervescence led to the only two national strikes really worthy of the name – in July 1977 and May 1978 – that contributed significantly (and almost without the loss of lives) to the weakening of the military government and the subsequent democratic transition' (Degregori 2012, p. 39).

6   Quijano 2007a, p. x.

7   Quijano 2007a, p. x.

> What many pegged as the promise of a working class-revival in the early 1970s turned out to be more of a swan song by the decade's end. The fragmented nature of the labor protests – by organization, industry, race, geography, and gender failed to coalesce into a lasting national presence … Market orthodoxy eclipsed all alternatives.[8]

The hegemony of neoliberal 'market orthodoxy', represented in the United States by Ronald Reagan and in Britain by Margaret Thatcher, became the true legacy of what had earlier seemed to be a revolutionary moment.

Moreover, Quijano, like many on the left, had been partly blind to the truly epochal nature of 9-11-1973. That was, of course, the date when the Chilean military, led by General Augusto Pinochet, deposed democratically elected socialist president Salvador Allende. The Pinochet coup destroyed Allende's attempt at implementing revolutionary change within the framework of Chile's democratic system. The coup in Chile was at first seen by many as just another rightist or even quasi-fascist military coup, like that of Brazil in 1964 or like the one soon to be set up by the Argentine military in 1976. Thus, the transformative nature of the new Chilean regime was often not fully acknowledged. The lyrics of popular Cuban left-wing *nueva trova* songwriter Pablo Milanés' 'Canción por la unidad latinoamericana' (Song for Latin American Unity) exemplify the optimistic evaluation of the Chilean coup as a temporary right-wing hiccough in the progressive transformation of Latin America and world: 'The birth of the world/was postponed for a moment/It was a brief lapse of time/a second of the universe'.[9] In 1976, Milanés is expressing the vulgar Marxist grand narrative that saw history as unequivocally moving towards communism. This belief was also shared by Quijano and other more sophisticated leftists. They did not realise that Chile had become the laboratory where the radical free-market ideas that would soon be applied as the solution to the economic and social crisis of the 1970s were first put into practice.

Even the class struggle in Eastern Europe, to use Quijano's phrase, was ultimately resolved not only by the destruction of the communist regimes and their replacement by formally democratic regimes, but, in particular, by the implementation of neoliberal economic policies that had been tested in Chile. The irony of this solution to the crisis in Eastern Europe is magnified when one notes that, in the quotation above, Quijano seems to be making an implicit reference to the Solidarity workers' movement in Poland – as a leader of the

---

8 Cowie 2016, p. 18.
9 Milanés 1976. The Spanish lyrics of the song are available at Pablo Milanés's official website: http://www.milanespablo.com/disco/pablo-milanes.

class struggle in 'Eastern Europe'. Not long after, Solidarity's leader, Lech Walesa, would be elected president and oversee the neoliberalisation of his country's economy and culture.

2   Mode of Production

While the frequent description of Marxism as a mode of production narrative is a gross oversimplification, Quijano admires Mariátegui primarily for the acuity of his analysis of the structure of Peru's neocolonial mode of production:

> This focus on the Peruvian economy as a complex and contradictory artic-
> ulation between capital and pre-capital, under the hegemony of the first,
> in the same way as 'feudalism' and 'indigenous communism' are still artic-
> ulated in the [Andean] highlands, both under [the control of] capital,
> affecting not only the logic of economic development, but also, the ways
> of thinking of the [different] classes, is the principal discovery of Mari-
> átegui's investigation, and from which his ideas about the character and
> perspectives of the Peruvian revolution originate.[10]

It is true that Trotsky had already proposed the concept of combined and uneven development, that is, not only the coexistence of more than one mode of production within an economic field, but also the usefulness of pre-capitalist economic structures for the rapid accumulation of capital. However, Mari-átegui saw in the Peruvian interaction among diverging modes of production a (relatively) stable economic and social alloy that helped define the specific economic and social trajectory of the country.

Moreover, as the quotation above exemplifies, Quijano sees this specific neo-colonial combination of modes of production as determining the mentality of Peruvian social classes and, therefore, as defining the specific political tactics and institutions appropriate to promote revolutionary change in the country. Quijano, despite his explicit criticism of the mainstream Soviet interpretation of the evolution of modes of production as necessarily going from feudal, to capitalist, to socialist, buys completely into the notion of an economic base as determining cultural and social superstructure. An example of the determ-inistic character of Quijano's thought at the time can be found in his analysis of the failure of Manuel González Prada to establish a lasting political move-

---

10   Quijano 2007a, pp. lxxxix.

ment in nineteenth-century Peru. Noting the comprador, subordinated, and underdeveloped nature of the Peruvian bourgeoisie, Quijano adds regarding González Prada that

> This is the reason, rather than González Prada's personal traits, as Mariátegui will argue later, that the political movement his immediate followers attempted to set up was frustrated at birth: it did not have the social bases necessary for its development.[11]

Although I find Quijano's analysis convincing, it contradicts the specific reasons Mariátegui gives for the failure of González Prada to establish a successful radical political party – which are of a personal nature. According to Mariátegui: 'His [González Prada's] individualistic, anarchical, solitary spirit was not suited to the direction of a vast collective enterprise'.[12] More important, it is opposed to a central aspect of Mariátegui's thought: his opposition to economic determinism.

From his belief in the importance of literature and, more generally, cultural products in creating the kind of ideological support needed for the maintenance or rejection of neocolonial and capitalist social systems, to his stress on the role of the will in promoting political change, Mariátegui's thinking rejected the kind of economic determinism proposed by Quijano in the 1979 'Reencuentro y debate'. Influenced by Nietzsche and especially Sorel – the latter a presence criticised by Quijano –[13] Mariátegui decried *avant la lettre* the economism present throughout 'Reencuentro y debate'.[14] Even if Quijano ultimately celebrates Mariátegui's stress on political practice, made possible precisely by his use of 'theoretically spurious elements', and his concomitant rejection of the supposedly orthodox positions of the Comintern,[15] the fact remains that, at best, the author of *Seven Essays* is presented as making an analytical silk purse out of a theoretical sow's ear.

---

11   Quijano 2007a, p. xxviii.
12   Mariátegui 1971, p. 208.
13   See 'Mariátegui, Sorel, and Myth' in this study.
14   For instance, in his *Defensa del marxismo*, Mariátegui states 'Marxism, where it has shown itself to be revolutionary – that is where it has been Marxist – has never obeyed a passive and rigid determinism' (Mariátegui 2011, p. 208).
15   Quijano 2007a, p. lxxvi.

3   Mariátegui's Debates

Like Flores Galindo in *La agonía de Mariátegui*, Quijano also looks at the debates the Peruvian Marxist held with the APRA and the Comintern. However, the purpose of the noted sociologist is to present Mariátegui politically if not theoretically as an orthodox Leninist in contrast with Haya's and the Comintern's deviations from what Quijano considers to be the correct interpretation of the ideas of the author of *What Is to Be Done*. Thus, Quijano writes:

> In full accord with Lenin ... imperialist penetration in Latin America is the last stage of capitalism and not its first, as Haya wishes it, in order to establish his originality regarding Lenin.[16]

Throughout the 1979 'Prólogo', Leninism is presented as the guarantee for a true revolutionary position and action. As the quotation makes clear, Haya's theories regarding imperialism – that it signalled the birth of capitalism in Peru – are presented as the product of an attempt at willfully deviating from the right Leninist path rather than as the product of analysis or reflection, no matter how mistaken.

Quijano's also sees Mariátegui's political proposals as an adaptation of the ideas expressed by Lenin, in particular in his classic *Imperialism, the Highest Stage of Capitalism*, to the specific mode of production characteristic of Peru. If Peru is already fully capitalist, even if in a sui generis manner, the ultimate struggle has to be for socialism, not a reformed capitalism. Thus, according to Quijano, Mariátegui saw 'the proletarian direction of the revolution as the touchstone'.[17] For Quijano, Mariátegui, like Lenin and Mao, is, therefore, a proponent of the 'dictatorship of the proletariat'.[18] In fact, in comparison with Mao, 'it is Mariátegui who achieves a clearer and historically verified theoretical precision' regarding his perspective on the 'dictatorship of the proletariat'.[19] Mao is seen by Quijano as, perhaps, the major disciple of Lenin and the true continuator of revolutionary practice.

However, as we have seen, the description of Mariátegui as a strict Leninist is, at best, problematic. Not surprisingly, Quijano makes much of the reference in the 'Programmatic Principles of the Socialist Party' to 'Marxism-Leninism' as the 'revolutionary method of the period of imperialism and monopoly', which

---

16   Quijano 2007a, p. xc.
17   Quijano 2007a, p. cv.
18   Quijano 2007a, p. cv.
19   Quijano 2007a, p. cvi.

the new party 'adopts as its method of struggle'.[20] But the lack of an actual reference to the dictatorship of the proletariat, not only in this text, but throughout
his later writings; the actual paucity of explicit reflection on specifically revolutionary tactics; his rejection of the Leninist condition in the naming of the
party; the opening of this party to a pluri-classist membership, which can be
seen as undermining the stress on the proletarian class composition mentioned in its founding statement of principles; among other deviations from
communist orthodoxy, whether Leninist or Stalinist; all undermine this portrait of Mariátegui as a defender and continuator of Lenin during a time when
the Comintern is seen as falling into Stalinist deviations.

Quijano finalises his 1979 'Prologue' by speculating on what could have
happened had Mariátegui not died young. He imagines him emulating Mao,
who 'followed, with success, a pragmatic policy: belonging and autonomy in
the Third International, under Stalin'.[21] Beyond the objections I have made to
Quijano's facile reading of Mariátegui as a Leninist, here he seems to forget
the exceptional circumstances that made the historical success of Mao, despite
his divergences from Stalin, possible. As we know, the banning of the Chinese
Communist party by the Kuomingtan government led to a civil war beginning
in 1927, which overlapped with the invasion of China by Japan in 1937. Mao was
able to lead the Chinese Communist Party because the chaotic situations did
not permit the Comintern to take full control. By 1949, when the Communist
Party won the civil war, Mao was fully ensconced in power. Regardless of the
evolution Mariátegui's ideas or political practice may have taken had he lived,
it is highly doubtful he would have found a historical context that would have
permitted him to successfully follow a similar policy of simultaneous belonging
and autonomy.

4   Thirty Years Later

As mentioned above, in 2007 Quijano wrote an addendum to the original 'Prologue' titled appropriately 'Treinta años despues: Otro reencuentro. Notas para
un debate', in which he again discusses the works of Mariátegui. What makes
these 'notes' fascinating is the fact that Quijano implicitly rejects some of the
key parameters within which he had earlier read Mariátegui, while also developing in new directions some of his earlier insights about the author of *Seven
Essays*.

---

20   Quijano 2007a, p. cii.
21   Quijano 2007a, p. cix.

Quijano acknowledges the different social and political world that frames his new reflections on Mariátegui. If the 1979 introduction was marked by his belief that the world was experiencing the pangs of revolution, his much shorter 2007 'Notes' is written in the knowledge that the world birthed by the 'explosion of the world capitalist crisis in mid-1973' was built on 'the deepest historical defeat of the workers and … all dominated/exploited/repressed of the world'.[22] Neoliberalism, not socialism, had been the result of the class and social struggles he had identified in 1979. The progressive teleology, which he had so optimistically embraced, had been shown to be but a mirage.

However, one must add that the new narrative proposed by Quijano – of the defeat of workers and other exploited groups at the hands of 'the hypertechnologised levels of capital' –[23] is itself a simplification of what actually happened. If it was a defeat, it was one willed and supported by many of the victims. As Cowie argues regarding the appeal of Reagan for US working-class voters:

> Roosevelt's famous 'Forgotten Man' was becoming a Republican, his enemies less the 'economic royalists,' the class *elites*, against which Roosevelt inveighed in his landslide 1936 victory, than the cultural *elitists* who would look down on the politics and culture of blue collar America. Not all of even the white, male working class joined the New Right, of course, but certainly enough to make a viable coalition on the margins where elections are won.[24]

Neoliberalism could be seen as a free-market wolf in populist sheep clothes, but one must keep in mind that the wolf was aided and welcomed by significant numbers of the working class and 'dominated'.

Even if he does not link it to the rise to hegemony of neoliberalism, Quijano notes that 'historical materialism not only rapidly lost space in the new intellectual and political debate produced by the world crisis … In particular, it lost attractiveness and legitimacy among the new political movements that arose, especially in the 1960s and early 1970s'.[25] Among these political movements, he mentions Paris 1968 and, less convincingly, the anti-imperial struggle in Vietnam. He also notes how 'the growing delegitimisation and conflictivity of the bureaucratic despotism' throughout Eastern Europe and China led to the fall of

---

22   Quijano 2007b, pp. cix, cxxi.
23   Quijano 2007b, p. cxx.
24   Cowie 2010, p. 228.
25   Quijano 2007b, pp. cxiv–cxv.

actually existing socialism.[26] It is symptomatic of the changes in Quijano's view of the world that 'Marxism-Leninism' is now only mentioned in negative contexts: as a rigidly structured dogma, as synonymous of a Eurocentric historical materialism, and as a limited and distorted 'perspective of knowledge'.[27] Gone is the view of Lenin as a guarantor of right revolutionary thought and action.

Quijano, however, still downplays the hegemony achieved throughout the Soviet bloc by free market ideas. For him, the struggle against Communism was led 'by worker movements, students, and intellectuals, called dissidents, fighting against bureaucratic despotism. Some, aiming for a radical democratisation of power ... and others, for a liberalization, at least, of "real existing socialism"'.[28] The fact is that, as we have seen, worker leaders, such as Lech Walesa, and dissidents, such as Vaclav Klaus, the economic adviser to the Czechoslovakian Civic Forum led by the more centrist Vaclav Havel, were unabashed ideological admirers of Ronald Reagan, Margaret Thatcher, and the economic and social policies they supported.[29] Even the legendary Alexander Dubcek, the once leader of the Prague Spring, stated about the British Prime Minister: 'For us, she is not the Iron Lady. She is the kind, dear Mrs. Thatcher'.[30] The depth of neoliberalism's hold among the East European anti-Soviet activists is never acknowledged by Quijano.[31]

But, curiously, Quijano's biggest omission is regarding the evolution of Peruvian politics after 1979. Instead of the emancipatory revolution expected by Quijano and others, Peru during the following decade experienced, on the one hand, the increasingly inept governments of Fernando Belaúnde (1980–85) and Alan García (1985–90) – under the latter's administration, inflation reached

---

26   Quijano 2007b, pp. cxv–cxvi.

27   Quijano 2007, pp. cxiv, cxiv, ccxii.

28   Quijano 2007b, p. cxvi.

29   Walesa wrote about his hero Ronald Reagan a dithyrambic article titled 'In Solidarity' that begins: 'When talking about Ronald Reagan, I have to be personal. We in Poland took him personally. Because we owe him our liberty' (Walesa 2004). Klaus and Havel have both acknowledged the influence of Reagan (see Kengor 2015, p. 89).

30   Dale 1997, p. 122.

31   Johanna Bockman writes about neoliberalism in the waning Eastern bloc: 'Observers soon found that many Eastern Europeans also had a seemingly Reaganite or Thatcherite obsession with free markets. As an exchange student in Budapest, Hungary in Fall 1988 and Spring 1989, I was also bewildered by the supposed socialists who taught us at the Karl Marx University of economics and sounded more like Reagan Republicans than socialists' (Bockmann 2011, p. 1). Bockmann will ultimately attempt to distinguish between socialist free marketeers and neoliberals, but the fact is that radical neoliberal free market policies were implemented throughout Eastern Europe by the generation of leaders who came to power after the fall of communism.

an incredible high of 14,900 percent during the last four months of 1988;[32] on the other, beginning in 1980, the uprising of the Shining Path. Revolution had arrived, but as an orgy of blood. The struggle of the Shining Path to take over the country, and of the military to stop it from doing so, led to nearly 70,000 people being killed. As the Comision de la Verdad y Reconciliacion, the official commission that investigated the uprising and the concomitant dirty war, noted in 2003: 'these figures are greater than the number of human losses suffered by Peru in all of the foreign and civil wars that have occurred in its 182 years of independence'.[33]

As we have seen,[34] despite the often-asserted influence of Mariátegui on the Shining Path, the growth of a cult around Abimael Guzmán, who took up the title of the 'Fourth Sword of Marxism' (after Marx, Lenin, and Mao), led to a weakening of the intellectual links with his predecessor, who, for instance, did not make it to the category of sword.[35] At the time of the writing of 'Reencuentro y debate' (1979), it seemed that the true inheritors of Mariátegui were the radical, but still democratic, Marxist groups that would soon form the United Left. However, by 1990, the Shining Path, now more often self-designated as Partido Comunista del Perú, seemed on the verge of taking power.

Another significant event was the election of Alberto Fujimori as president in 1990. Fujimori won on an anti-neoliberal platform against the well-known novelist (and 2010 Nobel Prize Winner) Mario Vargas Llosa, who had been since the 1980s a staunch defender of free-market solutions to the region's problems. The success of Fujimori in defeating the Shining Path, as well as the less violent Movimiento Revolucionario Tupac Amaru (MRTA), and in taming inflation, led to widespread popular support, even though he disbanded congress and took absolute control of the government in 1992, violated human rights, and, ironically, ruthlessly applied neoliberal corrections to the economy. As Julio Carrion notes:

> In 1995, Fujimori's support among the upper class was virtually identical among the very poor. Over time, however, this coalition dissolved as the upper and middle classes turned against him ... Fujimori's average

---

32   'The annualized rate of inflation between November 1989 and February 1990 was 2, 500 percent, higher than that for August through November 1989, but still below the record annualized levels set during the last four months of 1988 (14, 900 percent)' (Paredes and Sachs 1999, p. 16).

33   Comisión de la Verdad y Reconciliación 2003. 'The most probable figure for victims who died in the violence is 69, 280 individuals' (Comisión de la Verdad y Reconciliación 2003).

34   See 'Mariátegui and Che' in this study.

35   The actual name of the party was Partido Comunista del Perú (Communist Party of Peru).

approval rating among the very poor in 2000 was 17 points higher than his rating among the upper class (53 and 36 percent respectively).[36]

Contradicting leftist expectations, the greatest support for *fujimorismo* is to be found – then and now – among the poor. The end result of the Fujimori regime – in addition to the jailing of the former president for human rights violations, among other reasons – was the embrace of neoliberal policies and free market values by significant sectors of the Peruvian population, including, as we have seen, the workers, the exploited, and the discriminated. (The loss of support for Fujimori among the middle and upper classes was due to his gross corruption of public institutions, rather than an expression of opposition to his economic policies). In fact, since the fall of Fujimori in 2000, all Peruvian governments (Valentín Paniagua [2000–1], Alejandro Toledo [2001–6]), Alan García [2006–11], Ollanta Humala [2011–16]), Pedro Pablo Kuczynski [2016–18], and Martín Vizcarra [2018–] have stayed faithful to the economic policies he inaugurated. [37]

Fujimori thus represented the neoliberal turn in Peru. The success of this transformation is evidenced in an anecdote told by the noted novelist Miguel Gutiérrez (1940–2016):

> I remember that during the mid-90s, I got together with a group of young people of about twenty, whose parents, during their college years, had all espoused left wing positions. To my surprise, all declared themselves to be supporters of Fujimori, principally because of his success in defeating the Shining Path and the MRTA.[38]

Moreover, according to Gutiérrez, they had all embraced a 'radical individualism', which he correctly associates with 'Vargas Llosa's neoliberal and anticommunist preaching' and 'Fujimori's propaganda against traditional politicians'.[39] Even if, like many, they ultimately became disillusioned by Fujimori's corruption, neither they nor large numbers of the population support explicitly left-wing positions.[40]

---

36   Carrión 2006, pp. 129–30.
37   On 23 March 2018, Kuczynski resigned under accusations of corruption. He was substituted by his vice-president Martín Vizcarra.
38   Gutiérrez 2013, p. 2.
39   Gutiérrez 2013, p. 2.
40   Gutiérrez 2013, p. 2. Ollanta Humala, whose Partido Nacionalista Peruano was first seen as analogous to the populist movements led in Venezuela by Hugo Chavez or Evo Mor-

5   Mariátegui, Anti-Eurocentrism, and Modes of Production

If the author of *Seven Essays* is no longer presented by Quijano as a guide for revolutionary political action – revolution is nowhere in sight in the new text and, as we have seen, Lenin, the ultimate paladin of revolution, has fallen into the dustbin of history, or at least been stored in its mouldy attic – he is now seen, in my opinion correctly, as an early critic of Eurocentrism. In this, Quijano is not alone among recent readers. In 2001, Robert J.C. Young, in an attempt at presenting 'Third World Marxists' as precursors to deconstructive postcolonialism, notes: 'Early twentieth-century Latin American Marxists, particularly José Carlos Mariátegui, were the first to raise the problem of Marxism's Eurocentrism'.[41] Quijano, much more convincingly, links this critique of Eurocentrism to the analysis of the specific characteristics of the relationship among modes of production in Peru.

As Quijano writes about Mariátegui's analysis:

> This perspective breaks first with the Eurocentric notion of totality and with evolutionism, which presuppose a unity, both continuous and homogeneous, even if also contradictory, and that move in time in a manner both continuous and homogenous until transformed into another analogous entity.[42]

Mariátegui's analysis of the stable interrelationship among diverging mode of productions contradicts the clear-cut Eurocentric progression – feudalism, capitalism, socialism – and is seen by Quijano as presenting the possibility of a different kind of theoretical understanding:

> It enables us ... to leave behind the general rejection of any version of the idea of totality, as is the case in the old British empiricism and in the new postmodernism, which, in this manner, exclude the issue of power.

---

ales in Bolivia, followed strict neoliberal policies after gaining power. However, during the 2016 election Veronika Mendoza, the candidate for the democratic socialist Frente Amplio, received 18.8 percent of the votes, barely missing the runoff election against Keiko Fujimori, Alberto Fujimori's daughter. Mendoza played a major role in helping Pedro Pablo Kuczynski defeat Fujimori by endorsing the neoliberal economist turned politician. This may have been only a temporary blip in Peru's politics. The congressional elections of 2020, the Frente Amplio, which had split nto two groups, only received 6.21% of the vote. The splinter group Nuevo Peru received 4.77% of the vote (Pereda and Patriau 2020).

41   Young 2001, p. 168.
42   Quijano 2007b, p. cxxviii.

In conclusion, it opens the debate over totality as a field of relations or a unity of heterogeneous, discontinuous, and contradictory elements within the same historical-structural configuration.[43]

Paradoxically, Mariátegui, by undermining traditional Marxist views of totality, is seen as permitting a new way of looking at interrelated cultural, political and historical fields. In the words of another reader of *Seven Essays*, Antonio Cornejo Polar, Mariátegui enables us to see Peru 'as a contradictory totality'.[44] As the quotation makes clear, it is because totality has been reconstructed and, therefore, rescued from its postmodern deconstruction, that the analysis of power and, therefore, of the role of racialisation in the constitution of world economic and social structures is made possible.[45] As Quijano notes:

> Without these movements of theoretical subversion against Eurocentrism ... current investigation would not have been able ... to perceive that the whole pattern of power in the world ... is a specific historical configuration in which one of the constitutive axes is the idea of 'race' as the basis of a whole system of social domination ... and the other is the articulation of all 'modes of production' in one unique structure of commodity production for the world market ... This specific configuration, historico-structurally heterogeneous, is the core of what is today discussed as the coloniality of power.[46]

And the analyses of both axes are seen as prefigured by Mariátegui.

6 Alternative Rationality

The most radical conclusion derived by Quijano from his study of Mariátegui is, surprisingly, given relative short shrift in 'Treinta años después': 'my idea

---

43 Quijano 2007b, p. cxxvii.
44 While Cornejo Polar does not deal directly with Mariategui's analysis of the 'mode of production', he does study the heterogeneous cultural composition of Peruvian society and attributes this basic insight to Mariátegui: 'the conceptual apparatus that is actualized by Mariátegui puts into question and denies the principle of unity of the corpus of Peruvian Literature' (Cornejo Polar 1983, p. 42).
45 However, in practice, the stress on this 'coloniality of power' has often been associated with a dismissal in practice of the need of other social changes. I have dealt with this issue in 'José Carlos Mariátegui: From Race to Culture'.
46 Quijano 2007b, pp. cxxviii–cxxix.

that in Mariátegui's [intellectual] territory many of the central elements of an *alternative rationality*' are present.[47] Among the several texts in which Quijano develops this idea is 'Modernity, Identity and Utopia in Latin America', originally published in Spanish in 1988. In this essay, Quijano again foregrounds the 'mode of production' analysis in order to stress the presence in Latin America of both 'modern' and 'premodern' social structures and the effect this had on Latin American subjectivities.

While this insight regarding an alternative rationality is rooted in his study of Mariátegui, Quijano argues that it was first fully expressed in literature, in particular, in the work of Gabriel García Márquez: 'For by what mode, if not the aesthetic-mythic, can an account be given of this simultaneity of all historical times in the same time?'[48] However, the Peruvian Marxist is presented as evidence for this kind of Latin American (ir)rationality:

> considered today perhaps the greatest Latin American Marxist, Mari-
> átegui was at the same time *not* a Marxist. He openly believed in God. He
> proclaimed that it was not possible to live without a metaphysical con-
> ception of existence, and he felt close to Nietzsche.[49]

One could, of course, remind Quijano that Nietzsche saw himself as a 'good European', but his main point is that Latin American social reality implies a rejection of Western reason in its modern, instrumentalised, and colonialised or colonising version.

Be that as it may, for Quijano:

> The real is rational only inasmuch as rationality does not exclude its
> magic. Juan Rulfo and José María Arguedas, in the privileged seats of
> the heritage of the original rationality of the Lain America, narrated this
> fact.[50]

(These original seats are Mexico and Peru, the locations of the Aztec and Inca civilisations, respectively). Quijano seems to be flirting with the proposal that there is a different Latin American rationality, a position that could be used to justify any type of local custom, no matter how abhorrent, and that, it must be pointed out, was explicitly rejected by Mariátegui when he defended 'femin-

---

47   Quijano 2007b, p. cxxxv (stress in the original).
48   Quijano 1995, p. 211.
49   Quijano 1995, p. 210.
50   Quijano 1995, p. 212.

ist demands' in the article of the same name. Moreover, he also seems to be on the verge of repeating the stereotype of Latin America as actually magical realist, a position that, again, can be used to stress the region's otherness, or, at the same time, promote tourism.[51] Fortunately, Quijano ultimately sees in the region's alternative rationality a way of bringing together in a political and socially progressive way both the European and indigenous traditions:

> from the original Andean rationality, a sense of reciprocity and solidarity; from the original modern rationality, when rationality was still associated with social liberation, a sense of individual liberty and of democracy as a collective decision-making process founded on the free choice of its constituent individuals.[52]

One has to question whether one could have reached this conclusion without the problematic assertion of a magico-realist Latin America.

Informed by Quijano's reflections on alternative rationality and coloniality of power, Castro-Klarén reinterprets Mariátegui's role as intellectual in 'Posting Letters: Writing in the Andes and the Postcolonial Debate'. In this essay, she proposes an Andean tradition that has in Mariátegui one of its greatest avatars, as an alternative and corrective to a Western intellectual perspective that places actual subjects of the global south in a position of inferiority vis-à-vis those of Europe and North America. According to her, mainstream postcolonial thought has incorporated this Western prejudice. For these mainstream postcolonialists, 'coming from Lacan, as they do, mimicry and hybridity imply a sense of lack, fear, suspicion, perennial disencounter and joylessness'.[53] Founded in the sixteenth century by the Inca Garcilaso de la Vega and Felipe Guamán Poma, and developed by Mariátegui and José María Arguedas, the Andean intellectual tradition instead celebrates bi-culturality:

> The bi-cultural colonial subject is a capable subject precisely because he can move from one side to the other, keep them apart, bring them together, cross over, set them side by side in dialogue, struggle for complementarity and reciprocity, or simply keep them at a distance depending on the play of the given moment.[54]

---

51   In 2013, the Colombian government began a campaign to promote tourism to the country claiming 'Colombia is Magical Realism'. See Naef 2018.
52   Quijano 1995, p. 215.
53   Castro-Klarén 2008, p. 156.
54   Castro-Klarén 2008, p. 156.

This passage reminds one of Gloria Anzaldúa's concept of the 'new mestiza',[55] that is, of the culturally hybrid inhabitant of a 'borderlands,' originally localised in the border areas of the United States. But there is a significant difference. Regardless of their specific life experiences, these Andean intellectuals are not presented as either rejecting Western rationality or necessarily as victims of the social and cultural injustices taking place in the borderlands.[56] Their knowledge is not that of the marginalised. On the contrary, for Castro-Klarén, despite their lack of recognition within the Western world – as we know, Guamán Poma remained unknown for nearly four hundred years and Garcilaso, Mariátegui, and Arguedas are far from household names outside Latin America – the bicultural situation is one of intellectual empowerment. These authors have mastered both Western and Andean cultures and are the better for it: 'the four intellectuals ... define the colonial struggle precisely as the capacity to achieve competence in all power/knowledge situations'.[57] One can add that the promise of this view of bi- and multi-culturalism is, as we have seen, the capacity to judge by comparison the limitations of all and any cultural practice and, therefore, develop a true rationality free from Eurocentrism or local bias.

7   Quijano as the Paradigm

I have looked at some length at Quijano's writings on Mariátegui because I see the evolution of his ideas as representative of the mainstream reception

---

55   'The new *mestiza* copes by developing a tolerance for contradictions, a tolerance for ambiguity. She learns to be an Indian in Mexican culture, to be Mexican from an Anglo point of view. She learns to juggle cultures. She has a plural personality, she operates in a pluralistic mode – nothing is thrust out, the good, the bad and the ugly, nothing rejected, nothing abandoned. Not only does she sustain contradictions, she turns the ambiguities into something else' (Anzaldúa 1987, p. 79).

56   According to Anzaldúa, the dwellers of the borderlands are marked by the injustices they experience: 'The prohibited and forbidden are its inhabitants. *Los atravesados* live here: the squint-eyed, the perverse, the queer, the troublesome, the mongrel, the mulatto, the half-breed, the half dead; in short, those who cross over, pass over, or go through the confines of the "normal". Gringos in the u.s. Southwest border consider the inhabitants of the borderlands transgressors, aliens – whether they possess documents or not, whether they're Chicanos, Indians or Blacks. Do not enter, trespassers will be raped, maimed, strangled, gassed, shot. The only "legitimate" inhabitants are those in power, the whites and those who align themselves with whites. Tension grips the inhabitants of the borderlands like a virus. Ambivalence and unrest reside there and death is no stranger' (Anzaldúa 1987, pp. 3–4).

57   Castro-Klarén 2008, p. 157.

of the author of *Seven Essays* from the 1970s to the present. The differences between the 1979 'Reencuentro y debate' and 'Treinta años después' can be seen as exemplifying the paradigm shift that has characterised readings of the Peruvian Marxist. Of course, I am not implying that every single interpretation of the Peruvian Marxist is necessarily similar to Quijano's: the response to Mariátegui is too rich and too varied. However, the theoretical evolution of Quijano's thought is, in my opinion, indicative of the development not only of the interpretation of Mariátegui but, more generally, of the political ideas held by progressive academia in Latin America and abroad.

The view expressed in 1979 in 'Reencuentro y debate' of Mariátegui as a guide to revolutionary politics is not limited to Quijano. It is present, for instance, in Flores Galindo's masterpiece *La agonía de Mariátegui*. Flores Galindo's analysis of the struggles of Mariátegui with both the APRA and the Comintern have as their implicit political context the need the historian felt to develop a truly Peruvian revolutionary politics distant from both populism and Stalinism. Even Roland Forgues's 1994 re-rereading of Mariátegui's works as espousing both socialism and democracy can be seen as continuing and developing this perspective in response to both the fall of the Soviet Bloc and the Shining Path's temporary appropriation of the Peruvian socialist for their blood bath.

Quijano's post-1989 theoretical turnabout can also be seen as representative not only of the changes in the reception of Mariátegui among what remains of the left-leaning intelligentsia, but, more generally, of the evolution of thinking about society during the last thirty or forty years. As has been the wont of recent political theorisations, gone is the emphasis on class, even if a political bite is still to be found in Quijano's writings. Now, instead of as a guide to revolution, the author of *Seven Essays* is primarily presented as a sophisticated critic of Eurocentrism and as a theorist of the role of race in colonial and neocolonial national and international social structures. The study of Mariátegui leads Quijano to identify racism as the structuring principle of the international inequality he names the coloniality of power.

Despite Quijano's criticism of postmodernism, what he offers is a radical, Latin American theorisation that cannot but lead to conclusions similar to those proposed by other radical academic thinkers across the globe. For all, the struggle against racism is the central political battle of our times. However, the question whether this necessary struggle against the ongoing resurgence of racism, as well as the related struggles against patriarchy and gender discrimination, are part of a search for greater economic and social equality is rarely addressed. The last forty years have taught us about neoliberalism's ability to assimilate progressive causes.

8   Conclusion: Mariátegui Unplugged

As I have mentioned throughout this study, the most characteristic contemporary response to Mariátegui in Peru has been that of calling for his thought to be abandoned as a guide. While in principle correct – no thinker should be a guide, though all can be resources for thinking – this response also expressed the neoliberal turn that Peruvian society experienced. The apparent economic and political success of Fujimori and the governments that followed justified the downgrading of Mariátegui to just another historical figure. (Of course, this view of Peru as an unqualified social success implies not taking into account the long-term human, environmental, and social costs of neoliberalism).

However, as the international economic crisis that began in 2008 has spread into a South America that had been mostly immune to its effects, leading to the collapse of the Pink Tide, and to ever growing social turmoil even in those countries that had faithfully embraced market orthodoxy, the optimism that undergirded this rejection of the region's greatest Marxist thinker should be questioned. As Thomas Piketty has proven – although other more leftist critics had made similar points, even if in less documented presentations – one of the principal effects of the neoliberal world that rose from the ashes of existing socialism has been an acute inequality only comparable to the world of the 1920s, that is, the world of the author *Seven Essays*.

It may be useful to remember that the phrase 'Mariátegui unplugged' – used by Marcel Velázquez Castro in his attempt at debunking Mariátegui – can be mainly read in two alternative manners. The first, of course, is as referring to the past tense of 'unplug': 'to disconnect something ... from an electrical source'.[58] In this case, the phrase necessarily implies a putting aside of the ideas of the Peruvian Marxist. The only logical thing to do with an unplugged appliance, let's say a vacuum cleaner or blender, is to put it away. Why should thinkers be any different?

But 'unplugged' as an adjective can also mean 'sung or performed without electrical instruments; acoustic'.[59] Just as the unplugged performances of musicians like Eric Clapton or Nirvana proved to many that their artistry exceeded all and any production trappings, we need to read Mariátegui free from the electric distortion of political dogmas in order to fully understand him.

Even though all readings are unavoidably ideological, I would argue that we are the first generation after his contemporaries to be able to read Mariátegui

---

58   From www.m-w.com.
59   From www.m-w.com.

free from obvious political blinkers. The readers of the 1930s, 1940s and 1950s had to deal with the imprint of Stalinism. Those of the 1960s, 1970s and 1980s were marked by the hopes and disillusions raised by the triumphs and failures of the Cuban revolution and other anti-colonial and revolutionary movements. Those of the 1990s and 2000s could not help but be influenced by the fall of the Soviet bloc and the mirage of neoliberal modernisation. We, today, have seen the failures of all hopes, but also know of the necessity of building a new and better social world as inequality threatens what remains of democratic institutions and environmental apocalypse rapidly approaches. The works of Mariátegui, with all their limitations and surprising insights, remain a necessary resource for these tasks.

Bibliography

Aboul-Ela, Hosam 2007, *The Other South: Faulkner, Coloniality, and the Mariátegui Tradition*, Pittsburgh: U of Pittsburgh P.

Adams, Beverley and Natalia Majluf (eds.) 2019, *Redes de vanguardia. Amauta y América Latina 1926–1930*, Madrid: Artes Gráficas.

Adorno, Theodor 2013 [1970], *Aesthetic Theory*, London: Bloomsbury.

Anderson, Perry 1989 [1976], *Considerations on Western Marxism*, London: Verso.

Angvik, Birger 1999, *La ausencia de forma da forma a la crítica que forma el canon peruano*. Lima: Pontificia Universidad Católica.

Anonymous 1930, 'Ya Ha Firmado', *Time Magazine* 16.10 (September 8), available at: http://content.time.com/time/magazine/article/0,9171,740274,00.html.

Anonymous 1980 [1933 or 1934], 'Bajo la bandera de Lenin. Instrucciones sobre la Jornada de las tres LLL', *Socialismo y participación* 11: 25–33.

Anonymous 2011, 'Secretarios Generales del PCP', *Unidad*, 2011, 16: 7.

Anzaldúa, Gloria 1987, *Borderlands/La Frontera: The New Mestiza*, San Francisco: Aunt Lute.

Appiah, Kwame Anthony 2006, *Cosmopolitanism: Ethics in a World of Strangers*, New York: Norton.

Arendt, Hannah 1970, *On Violence*, San Diego: Harcourt, Brace & CO.

Assis Clímaco, Danilo 2014, *Cuestiones y horizontes: de la dependencia histórico-estructural a la colonialidad/descolonialidad del poder*, by Aníbal Quijano, edited by Danilo Assis Clímaco, Buenos Aires: CLACSO.

Baines, John M. 1972, *Revolution in Peru: Mariátegui and the Myth*, Tuscaloosa, AL: University of Alabama Press.

Basadre, Jorge 1971, 'Introduction', in *Seven Interpretive Essays on Peruvian Reality*, by José Carlos Mariátegui, Austin: University of Texas Press.

Basadre, Jorge 2014, *Historia de la República del Perú 1822–1933. Tomo 14*, Lima: Cantabria, ebook.

Bazán, Armando 1982, *Mariátegui y su tiempo*, Lima: Amauta.

Becker, Marc 1993, *Mariátegui and Latin American Marxist Theory*, Athens, OH: Ohio U in International Studies.

Becker, Marc 2002, 'Mariátegui y el problema de las razas en América Latina,' *Revista Andina*, 35: 191–220.

Becker, Marc 2006, 'Mariátegui, the Comintern, and the Indigenous Question in Latin America', *Science & Society* 70, 4: 450–79.

Becker, Marc 2015, 'José Carlos Mariátegui 85 Years Later', *TelesurTV.net*, available at: http://www.telesurtv.net/english/analysis/Jose-Carlos-Mariategui-85-Years-Later-2 0150415-0029.html.

Beigel, Fernanda 2003, *El itinerario y la brújula. El vanguardismo estético-político de José Carlos Mariátegui*, Buenos Aires: Biblos, 2003.

Beigel, Fernanda 2006, *La epopeya de una generación y una revista. Las redes editoriales de José Carlos Mariátegui en América Latina*, Buenos Aires: Biblos.

Benjamin, Walter 1985 [1968], 'Theses on the Philosophy of History', translated by Harry Zohn, in *Walter Benjamin: Essays and Reflections*, New York: Schocken Books.

Bergson, Henri 1911 [1907], *Creative Evolution*, translated by Arthur Mitchell, New York: Henry Holt.

Berlin, Isaiah 2013 [1979], *Against the Current: Essays on the History of Ideas*. Princeton, NJ: Princeton UP.

Bernabé, Mónica 2006, *Vidas de artista. Bohemia y dandismo en Mariátegui, Valdelomar y Eguren (Lima, 1911–1922)*, Rosario: Beatriz Viterbo.

Biagini, Hugo E. 1999, 'El movimiento estudiantil reformista y sus mentores', in *La Universidad de La Plata y el movimiento estudiantil*, edited by Hugo E. Biagini, La Plata: Ed. U Nacional de La Plata.

Blanchard, Peter 1982, *The Origins of the Peruvian Labor Movement, 1883–1919*, Pittsburgh: University of Pittsburgh Press.

Bockmann, Johanna 2011, *Markets in the Name of Socialism: The Left-Wing Origins of Neoliberalism*, Stanford: Stanford UP.

Borges, Jorge Luis 1999, 'Kafka and his Precursors', translated by Eliot Weinberger, in *Selected Non-Fictions*, edited by Eliot Weinberger, New York: Viking.

Brennan, Timothy, 1990, 'The National Longing for Form', in *Nation and Narration*, edited by Homi Bhabha, Abingdon: Routledge.

Brook, Timothy and Bob Tadashi Wakabayashi 2000, 'Introduction' in *Opium Regimes: China, Britain, and Japan, 1839–1952*, edited by Timothy Brook and Bob Tadshi Wakabayashi, Berkeley: University of California Press.

Bürger, Peter, 1984, *Theory of the Avant-Garde*, translated by Michael Shaw, Minneapolis: University of Minnesota Press.

Burstein, Zuño 2003, 'Hugo Pesce Pescetto', *Revista peruana de medicina experimental y salud pública* 20, 3: 172–3.

Callinicos, Alex 2013, *The Revolutionary Ideas of Karl Marx*, Chicago: Haymarket.

Carpo, Azurra 2006, *In Amazzonia*, Milan: Giangiacommo Feltrinelli Editore.

Carrión, Julio 2006, 'Public Opinion, Market Reforms and Democracy in Fujimori's Peru', in *The Fujimori Legacy: The Rise of Electoral Authoritarianism in Peru*, edited by Julio Carrión, University Park: Penn State.

Carrillo, Teresa 2001, 'Cross-border Talk: Transnational Perspectives on Labor, Race, and Sexuality', in *Talking Visions: Multicultural Feminism in a Transnational Age*, edited by Ella Shohat, Cambridge: MIT.

Castro-Klarén, Sara 2008, 'Posting Letters: Writing in the Andes and the Paradoxes of the Postcolonial Debate', in *Coloniality at Large: Latin America and the Postcolonial*

Debate, edited by Mabel Moraña, Enrique Dussel and Carlos Jaúregui, Durham, NC: Duke University Press.

Céspedes, Diógenes 1995, *Política de la teoría del lenguaje y la poesía en América Latina en el siglo XX*, Santo Domingo: Editora Universitaria.

Chang-Rodríguez, Eugenio 2012, *Pensamiento y acción en González Prada, Mariátegui y Haya de la Torre*, Lima: Pontificia Universidad Católica.

Chavarría, Jesús 1979, *José Carlos Mariátegui and the Rise of Modern Peru, 1890–1930*. Albuquerque, NM: University of New Mexico Press.

Chiappe, Anna 2012 [1969], '... La vida que me diste' (Interview with César Lévano), a *Diario la Primera* 28 February, available at: http://www.diariolaprimeraperu.com/ online/entrevista/la-vida-que-me-diste_106240.html.

Chocano, Magdalena 2011, 'Pulsiones nerviosas de un orden craquelado: desafíos, caballerosidad y esfera política (Perú, 1883–1960)', *Histórica* 35, 1: 141–84.

Comisión de la Verdad y la Reconciliación 2003, 'General Conclusions Final Report', http://www.cverdad.org.pe/ingles/ifinal/conclusiones.php.

[Communist International] no date [1977/1919], 'Minutes of the Second Congress of the Communist International: Seventh Section, July 30 [1919]', translated by Bob Archer, Marxist Internet Archive, available at: https://www.marxists.org/history/ international/comintern/2nd-congress/ch07.htm#v1-p260.

[Communist International] no date [1980/1921], 'The Organisational Structure of the Communist Parties, the Methods and Content of Their Work: Theses', translated by Alix Holt and Barbara Holland, Marxist Internet Archive, available at: https://www .marxists.org/history/international/comintern/3rd-congress/party-theses.htm.

Cornejo Polar, Antonio 1983, 'Literatura peruana: Totalidad contradictoria', *Revista de Crítica Literaria Latinoamericana* 9, 18: 37–50.

Cowie, Jefferson, 2010, *Stayin Alive: The 1970s and the Last Days of the Working Class*, New York: The New Press.

Darío, Rubén 1998, 'El triunfo de Calibán', *Revista Iberoamericana* 64, 184–5: 451–5

D'Allemand, Patricia 2000, 'José Carlos Mariátegui: Culture and the Nation', in *Postcolonial Perspectives on the Cultures of Latin America and Lusophone Africa*, edited by Robin Fiddian, Liverpool: Liverpool UP.

Dale, Ian 1997, *As I Said to Denis –: The Thatcher Book of Quotations*, London: Robson.

De Castro, Juan E. 2002, *Mestizo Nations: Culture, Race, and Conformity in Latin American Literature*, Tucson: U of Arizona P.

De Castro, Juan E. 2008, *The Spaces of Latin American Literature: Tradition, Globalization, and Cultural Production*, New York: Palgrave.

De la Cadena, Marisol 2000, *Indigenous Mestizos: The Politics of Race and Culture in Cuzco, Peru, 1919*, Durham, NC: Duke University Press.

Degler, Carl 1991, *In Search of Human Nature: The Decline and Revival of Darwinism in American Social Thought*, New York: Oxford UP.

Degregori, Carlos Iván, 2012 [2011], *How Difficult to be God: Shining Path's Politics of War in Peru, 1980–1999*, translated by Nancy Appelbaum et. al., Madison: University of Wisconsin Press.

Deguy, Michel 1993 [1988], 'The Discourse of Exaltation: Contribution to a Rereading of Pseudo-Longinus', in *Of the Sublime: Presence in Question*, by Jean Francois Courtine et. al., translated by Jeffrey S. Librett, New York: SUNY Press.

Del Prado, Jorge 1980, 'Mariátegui, marxista-leninista, fundador del Partido Comunista Peruano', in *Mariátegui y el marxismo latinoamericano*, edited by José Aricó, Mexico City: Cuadernos de Pasado y Presente.

Dosek, Thomas and Maritza Paredes 2016, 'Peru Might Elect an Authoritarian President. These Four Maps Tell You Why', *The Washington Post*, 3 June 2016, available at: https://www.washingtonpost.com/news/monkey-cage/wp/2016/06/03/peru-might -elect-an-authoritarian-president-these-four-maps-tell-you-whos-voting-how-and- why/?utm_term=.144d3cf80ec5.

Drinot, Paulo 2010, 'Awaiting the Blood of a Truly Emancipating Revolution: Che Guevara in 1950s Peru', in *Che's Travels: The Making of a Revolutionary in 1950s Latin America*, edited by Paulo Drinot, Durham, NC: Duke University Press.

Driscoll, Mark 2010, 'Looting the Theory Commons: Hardt and Negri's *Commonwealth*', *Postmodern Culture*, 21. 1, available at http://www.pomoculture.org/2013/09/03/looti ng-the-theory-commons-hardt-and-negris-commonwealth/.

Echeverría, Esteban 1999, 'The Slaughterhouse', translated by Ángel Flores, in *The Oxford Book of Latin American Short Stories*, edited by Roberto González Echevarría. New York: Oxford University Press.

Eliot, T.S. 1990, 'Tradition and the Individual Talent', in *Criticism: The Major Texts*, edited by W.J. Bate. New York: Harcourt.

Espino Relucé, Gonzalo 1984, 'Presentación' in *La lira rebelde proletaria: estudio y antologia de la poesia obrera anarquista (1900–1926)*, edited by Gonzalo Espino Relucé, Lima: Tarea.

Fajardo, Luis, 2016, 'Reemplazó Perú a Chile como baluarte del neoliberalismo económico en América Latina?'; *BBC Mundo* 9 December, available at: http://www.bbc .com/mundo/noticias-38033722.

Falasca-Zamponi, Simonetti, 1997, *Fascist Spectacle: The Aesthetics of Power in Mussolini's Italy*, Berkeley: University of California Press.

Febres Cordero, Julio 1894 [1892], 'El nombre de América', in *Actas de la novena reunion Congreso de Americanistas Huelva 1892 Tomo Primero*, Madrid: Tipografía de los hijos de M.G. Hernández.

Fernández Díaz, Osvaldo 2010, 'La agonía de Mariátegui y de Unamuno', available at: http://issuu.com/jotauv/docs/la-agonia-de-mariategui-y-de-unamuno-osvaldo-fer na.

Ferrer Mariátegui, Cecilia 2013, 'Historia de una fotografía inédita', *Boletín Casa Museo José Carlos Mariátegui*, March–April, 2013: 3–4.

Finchelstein, Federico 2010, *Transatlantic Fascism. Ideology, Violence and the Sacred in Argentina and Italy, 1919–1945*, Durham, NC: Duke University Press.

Flores Galindo, Alberto, 1980, *La agonía de Mariátegui. La polémica con el Komintern.* Lima: Desco.

Flores Galindo, Alberto, 1988, *Tiempo de plagas*, by Alberto Flores Galindo, Lima: El caballo rojo.

Flores Galindo, Alberto, 2010, *In Search of an Inca: Identity and Utopia in the Andes*, Cambridge: Cambridge University Press.

Forgues, Roland 1995, *Mariátegui: una utopía realizable*. Lima: Editorial Amauta.

Forgues, Roland 2009, 'Mariátegui y lo negro: antecedentes de un malentendido' in *José Carlos Mariátegui y los estudios latinoamericanos*, edited by Mabel Moraña and Guido Podestá, Pittsburgh: Instituto Internacional de Literatura Latinoamericana.

Foucault, Michel 1998 [1969], 'What is an Author?', translated by Josué V. Harari, in *Aesthetics, Method, and Epistemology*, by Michel Foucault, edited by James D. Faubion, New York: The New Press.

Frank, Waldo 1930, 'A Great American', *The Nation* (18 June): 704.

Gadea, Hilda 2008, *My Life with Che: The Making of a Revolutionary*, New York: Palgrave Macmillan.

García-Bedoya, Carlos 2007, 'El canon literario peruano', *Letras*, 78, 113: 7–24.

García Calderón, Francisco 1907, *Le Perou Contemporain. Etude Sociale*, Paris: Dujarric et cie.

Garrels, Elizabeth 1982, *Mariátegui y la Argentina: Un caso de lentes ajenos*, Gaithersburg, MD: Hispamérica.

[General Confederation of Peruvian Workers] 2011 [1929], 'Manifesto of the General Confederation of Peruvian Workers to the Peruvian Working Class (1929)', in *José Carlos Mariátegui: An Anthology.*

González, Mike 2019, *In the Red Corner: The Marxism of José Carlos Mariátegui*, New York: Haymarket. GooglePlay file.

González Prada, Manuel 1975, 'Memoranda', in *Pensamiento Político de González Prada*, edited by Bruno Podestá, Lima: Instituto Nacional de Cultura.

González Prada, Manuel 2003a [1924], 'Our Indians', in *Free Pages and Other Essays: Anarchist Musings*, Oxford: Oxford UP.

González Prada, Manuel 2003b [1888], 'Speech at the Politeama Theater', in *Free Pages and Other Essays: Anarchist Musings*, Oxford UP.

Gordy, Katherine A. 2014, 'No better way to be Latin American: European science and thought, Latin American theory?', *Postcolonial Studies*, 16, 4: 1–17.

Graciano, Osvaldo 2008, *Entre la torre de marfil y el compromiso politico. Intelectuales de izquierda en la Argentina (1918–1955)*, Bernal: U Nacional de Quilmes Ed.

Granado, Alberto 2013 [1986], *Con el Che por Sudamérica: Nueva edición con prólogo de Alberto Granado Duque*, Buenos Aires: Marea, Kindle file.

Granado, Alberto 2014, *Traveling with Che Guevara: The Making of a Revolutionary*, translated by Lucía Álvarez de Toledo, New York: New Market P.

Guardia, Sara Beatriz 2017, 'Ciudadanas a votar. 60 años de sufragio femenino en el Perú', *Revista Historia de las Mujeres*, 18,162, available at: https://www.cemhal.org/anteriores/2017_2018/5_4_Ciudadanas_SB.pdf.

Guevara, Ernesto 'Che' 1997 [1960], *Guerrilla Warfare*, Lanham, MD: Rowman & Little-field.

Guevara, Ernesto 'Che' 2006, *The Motorcycle Diaries: Notes on a Latin American Journey*, edited and translated by Alexandra Keeble, North Melbourne: Ocean Press.

Guevara, Ernesto 'Che' 2013, 'Socialism and Man in Cuba', in *Che Guevara Reader: Writings on Politics and Revolution*, edited by David Deutschmann, North Melbourne: Ocean Press.

Gutiérrez, Gustavo 1996, 'The Historical Power of the Poor', translated by Robert R. Barr, in *Gustavo Gutiérrez: Essential Writings*, edited by James B. Nickoloff, Minneapolis: Fortress Press.

Gutiérrez, Miguel 2013, 'Hacia una narrativa sin fronteras: Narrativa peruana del siglo XXI', *Libros y Artes (Suplemento)* 64–5: 1–7.

Hardt, Michael and Antonio Negri 2009, *Commonwealth*, Cambridge: Harvard UP.

Haya de la Torre, Víctor Raúl (as Haya Delatorre) 1926, 'What is Apra?', *The Labour Monthly: A Magazine of International Labor* 8.12: 756–9.

Haya de la Torre, Víctor Raúl (as Haya Delatorre) 1936, *El anti-imperialismo y el APRA*, Santiago: Ercilla.

Heilbroner, Robert 1989, 'The Triumph of Capitalism', *The New Yorker* (Jan 23): 98–109.

Higgins, James 2005, *Lima: A Cultural History*, London: Oxford UP.

Hobson, Archie (ed.) 2004, *The Oxford Dictionary of Difficult Words*, Oxford: Oxford UP.

Holloway, John 2010 [2002], *Change the World Without Taking Power*, London: Pluto.

Hunefeldt, Christine 2000, *Liberalism in the Bedroom: Quarreling Spouses in Nineteenth-Century Lima*, University Park, PA: Penn State UP.

Huntington, Samuel 2004, *Who are We? The Challenges to American National Identity*, New York: Simon and Schuster.

Ibérico, Mariano, 1926, *El nuevo absoluto*. Lima: Minerva.

James, Daniel 2001 [1969], *Che Guevara: A Biography*, New York: Cooper Square P.

Jansen, Robert S. [2008], 'Two Paths to Populism: Explaining Peru's First Episode of Populist Modernization', available at: http://www.democracy.uci.edu/files/docs/conferences/grad/Jansen.pdf

Jiménez Borja, José 2005, 'Don José de la Riva Agüero y Osma: notas sobre su vida, obra y estilo', in *José Jiménez Borja. Crítico y maestro la lengua*, edited by Carlos Eduardo Zavaleta, Lima: San Marcos.

Kengor, Paul 2015, in *Reagan's Legacy in a World Transformed*, edited by Jeffrey L. Chidester and Paul Kengor.

Kohan, Néstor 2000, *De Ingenieros al Ché. Ensayos sobre el marxismo Argentino y Latinoamericano*, Buenos Aires: Biblos.

Kozloff, Nikolas 2008, *Revolution! South America and the Rise of the New Left*, New York: Palgrave Macmillan.

Krauze, Enrique 2011, *Redeemers: Ideas and Power in Latin America*, trans. Hank Heifetz. New York: Harpers.

Krauze, Enrique 2012, *Redentores: Ideas y poder en América Latina*. New York: Harpers.

Kristal, Efraín 1999, *Temptation of the Word: The Novels of Mario Vargas Llosa*, Nashville, TN: Vanderbilt UP.

Kropotkin, P. 1906, *The Conquest of Bread*, London: Chapman and Hall.

Kuon Arce, Elizabeth, Rodrigo Gutiérrez Viñuales, Ramón Gutiérrez Viñuales, and Graciela María Viñuales 2009, *Cuzco-Buenos Aires: Ruta de Intelectualidad Americana (1900–1950)*, Lima: U San Martín de Porres, 2009, available at: http://www.ugr.es/~rgutierr/PDF2/LIB%20018.pdf.

Laclau, Ernesto 2005, *On Populist Reason*, London: Verso.

Larsen, Neil 1995, *Reading North by South: On Latin American Literature, Culture, and Politics*, Minneapolis, MN: University of Minnesota Press.

Lenin, Vladimir Ilyich Ulyanov 1927 [1909], *Materialism and Empirocriticism*, translated by David Kvitko and Sydney Hook, London: Martin Laurence.

Lenin, Vladimir Ilyich Ulyanov 1999 [1902], *What is to Be Done?*, translated by Joe Fineberg and Joe Hanna, Lenin Internet Archive, available at: https://www.marxists.org/archive/lenin/works/download/what-itd.pdf.

Llorente, Renzo 2012, 'Georges Sorel's Anarcho-Marxism', in *Libertarian Socialism: Politics in Black and Red*, edited by Alex Prichard, Ruth Kinna, Saku Pinta, and David Berry, New York: Palgrave.

Lomnitz Adler, Claudio 2018, *Nuestra América. Utopía y persistencia de una familia judía*, Mexico City: Fondo de Cultura Económica.

López-Calvo, Ignacio 2014, *Dragons in the Land of the Condor: Writing Tusán in Peru*. Tucson: University of Arizona Press.

López Soria, José Ignacio 1981, 'Notas para el studio del fascismo peruano', in *El pensamiento fascista peruano (1930–1945)*, edited by José Ignacio López Soria, Lima: Mozca Azul.

Löwy, Michael 2007 [2001], 'Neither Imitation nor Copy: Che Guevara in Search of a New Socialism', in *The Marxism of Che Guevara: Philosophy, Economics, Revolutionary Warfare* by Michael Löwy, Lanham: Rowan & Littlefield.

Löwy, Michael 2008 'Communism and Religion: José Carlos Mariátegui's Revolutionary Mysticism', *Latin American Perspectives* 35, 2: 71–9.

Löwy, Michael 2018, 'Mariátegui's Heroic Socialism: An Interview with Michael Löwy', Interview by Nicolas Allen, *Jacobin*, 15 December, available at: https://www.jacobinmag.com/2018/12/jose-carlos-mariategui-seven-interpretive-essays-peru-marxism-revolutionary-myth.

Lukács, Georg 2005 [1936], 'Narrate or Describe?', translated by Arthur Kahn, in *Writer and Critic and Other Essays*, edited by Arthur Kahn, Lincoln, NE: Author's Guild.

Manrique, Nelson 1999, *La piel y la pluma. Escritos sobre literatura, etnicidad y racismo*, Lima: Sur.

Manrique, Nelson 2009, *'¡Usted fue aprista!' Bases para una historia crítica del APRA*, Lima: Fondo editorial de la Pontificia Universidad Católica.

Marger, Martin N. 2015, *Race and Ethnic Relations: American and Global Perspectives*. Stamford, CT: Cengage.

Mariátegui, Aldo 2014, 'Aldo Mariátegui escribe sobre su abuelo José Carlos Mariátegui', *El Comercio* 23 June, available at: https://elcomercio.pe/vamos/columnas/aldo-mariategui-escribe-abuelo-jose-carlos-mariategui-333303-noticia/.

Mariátegui, Javier (ed.) 2014, 'Hugo Pesce, médico y humanista', *Dr. Hugo Pesce Pescetto. Conmemoración del XXV Aniversario de su fallecimiento 1969–1994*, Zuño Burstein Alva. Lima: Ministerio de Salud.

Mariátegui, José Carlos 1971, *Seven Intepretive Essays on Peruvian Reality*, translated by Marjorie Urquidi. Austin: University of Texas Press.

Mariátegui, José Carlos 1976, 'Prólogo a *Tempestad en los Andes*', in *La polémica del indigenismo*, by José Carlos Mariátegui and Luis Alberto Sánchez, edited by Manuel Aquézolo *Castro*, Lima: Mosca Azul.

Mariátegui, José Carlos 1979, *Figuras y aspectos de la vida mundial 1 (1923–1925)*, Lima: Amauta.

Mariátegui, José Carlos 1980a, *El artista y la época*, Lima: Amauta.

Mariátegui, José Carlos 1980b, *Historia de la crisis mundial. Conferencias (Años 1923 y 1924)*, Lima: Amauta.

Mariátegui, José Carlos 1980c, *La escena contemporánea*, Lima: Amauta

Mariátegui, José Carlos 1980d, *Figuras y Aspectos de la vida mundial II (1926–1928)*, Lima: Amauta.

Mariátegui, José Carlos 1980e, *Figuras y aspectos de la vida mundial III (1929–1930)*, Lima Amauta.

Mariátegui, José Carlos 1980f, *La novela y la vida. Siegfried y el profesor Canella*, Lima: Amauta.

Mariátegui, José Carlos 1980g, *Signos y obras*, Lima: Amauta.

Mariátegui, José Carlos 1980h, *Temas de nuestra América*, Lima: Amauta.

Mariátegui, José Carlos 1981a, *Defensa del marxismo*, Lima: Amauta.

Mariátegui, José Carlos 1981b, *El alma matinal y otras estaciones del hombre de hoy*, Lima: Amauta,

Mariátegui, José Carlos 1981c, *Ideología y política*, Lima: Amauta.

Mariátegui, José Carlos 1981d, *Peruanicemos al Perú*, Lima: Amauta.

Mariátegui, José Carlos 1987a, 'Minuto solemne', in *Invitación a la vida heroica. Antología*, edited by Alberto Flores Galindo and Ricardo Portocarrero, Lima: Instituto de apoyo agrario.

Mariátegui, José Carlos 1987b, 'Morfina', in *Escritos juveniles I*, by José Carlos Mariátegui, Lima: Amauta.

Mariátegui, José Carlos 1994, *Correspondencia*, Lima: Amauta.

Mariátegui, José Carlos 2007 [1928], *7 ensayos de interpretación de la realidad peruana*. Caracas, Biblioteca Ayacucho.

Mariátegui, José Carlos 2011, *José Carlos Mariátegui: An Anthology*, translated by Harry E. Vanden and Marc Becker, New York: Monthly Review Press.

Marx, Karl 1975, 'Marx to Vera Zasulich', in *Karl Marx-Frederick Engels. Collected Works Vol. 46*, New York: International Publishers.

Marx, Karl and Friedrich Engels 2012, *The Communist Manifesto: A Modern Edition*, translated by Samuel Moore, New York: Verso.

Masterson, Daniel M. 1991, *Militarism and Politics in Latin America*, Westport, CT: Greenwood P.

Meisel, James H. 1950, 'A Premature Fascist? Sorel and Mussolini', *Political Research Quarterly*. 3, 1: 14–27.

Melis, Antonio 1979, 'Mariátegui, Primer Marxista de América', Mexico City: UNAM.

Mignolo. Walter D. 2012, 'Mariátegui and Gramsci in 'Latin' America', in *The Postcolonial Gramsci*, edited by Neelam Srivastaba and Baidik Bhattacharya, New York: Routledge, pp. 191–212.

Milanés, Pablo 1976, 'Canción por la unidad latinoamericana', in *Pablo Milanés*, Egrem LD 3556, Vinyl.

Moore, Melissa 2014, *Mariátegui's Unfinished Revolution: Politics, Poetics, and Change in 1920s Peru*, Lanham, MD: Bucknell UP.

Mulvey, Laura, and Peter Wollen 1989, 'Frida Kahlo and Tina Modotti', in *Visual and Other Pleasures*, by Laura Mulvey, New York: Palgrave.

Munck, Ronaldo 2013, *Rethinking Latin American Development: Development, Hegemony, and Social Transformation*, New York: Palgrave.

Neff, Lavonne 2005, *Jesus the Healer*, Chicago: Loyola P.

North, Michael, 2013, 'The Making of "Making New"', *Guernica Magazine*, 15 August, available at: https://www.guernicamag.com/features/the-making-of-making-it-new/.

Nouwen, Mollie Lewis 2013. *Oy, My Buenos Aires: Jewish Immigrants and the Creation of Argentine National Identity*, University of New Mexico P: Albuquerque.

Paerregard, Kaersten 2010 [2008], *Peruvians Dispersed: A Global Ethnography of Migration*, Lanham, MD: Lexington Books.

Palma, Clemente 1897, *El porvenir de las razas en el Perú*, Lima: San Marcos, available at: http://cybertesis.unmsm.edu.pe/xmlui/bitstream/handle/cybertesis/338/palma_c.pdf?sequence=1.

Paredes, Carlos E. and Jeffrey Sachs 1991, 'Introduction and Summary', in *Peru's Path to Discovery: A Plan for Economic Stabilization and Growth*, edited by Carlos E. Paredes and Jeffrey Sachs, Washington DC: The Brookings Institution.

Paris, Robert 1973, *La formación ideológica de José Carlos Mariátegui*, translated by Oscar Terán, Mexico: Ediciones Pasado y Presente.

Partido Nacionalista Libertador 1948, 'Esquema del plan de México', in Martínez de la Torre, Ricardo, *Apuntes para una interpretación marxista de historia social del Perú Vol. 2*, Lima: Empresa Editora Peruana.

Partido Nacionalista Peruano 1979, 'El Partido Nacionalista Peruano', *El libro rojo de Haya de la Torre*, edited by Rolando Pereda Torres, Lima: Instituto de Estudios Anti-Imperialistas, pp. 338–54.

Pereda, David and Enrique Patriau 2020, 'Elecciones 2020: La izquierda que se estancó en los recientes comicios', *La República* 2 February, available at: https://larepublica .pe/politica/2020/02/02/elecciones-2020-la-izquierda-que-se-estanco-en-los-recie ntes-comicios-frente-amplio-juntos-por-el-peru-upp-veronica-mendoza-antauro-h umala/.

Pesce, Hugo 2005, *Lenguaje y pensamiento: Aspectos en el Antiguo Perú*, in *Hugo Pesce: Pensamiento Médico y filosófico*, Lima: Ministerio de Salud.

Planas, Enrique 2019. 'Arco Madrid. Mario Vargas Llosa: "Con la muerte de Mariátegui, el Perú sufrió una apagón cultural"', *El Comercio*, 28 February, available at: https:// elcomercio.pe/arcomadrid/mario-vargas-llosa-muerte-mariategui-peru-sufrio-apa gon-cultural-noticia-612018.

Portal, Magda 1930, 'Haya de la Torre y José Carlos Mariátegui', *APRA: Organo del Frente de Trabaladores Manuales e Intelectuales*, 20 October: 4–5.

Portocarrero, Ricardo 1996, 'La genialidad de Mariátegui', *Anuario mariateguiano* 8: 66–72.

Quijano, Aníbal 1993, ' "Raza", "etnia" y "nación" en Mariátegui: cuestiones abiertas', in *Encuentro Internacional Mariátegui y Europa: el otro aspecto del descubrimiento.*, edited by Roland Forgues, Lima: Amauta.

Quijano, Aníbal 1995 [1988], 'Modernity, Identity and Utopia in Latin America', in *The Postmodernism Debate in Latin America*, edited by John Beverley, Michael Aronna, and José Oviedo, Durham, NC: Duke University Press, pp. 201–16.

Quijano, Aníbal 2007a [1979/], 'Prólogo. José Carlos Mariátegui: Rencuentro y debate' José Carlos Mariátegui, *7 ensayos de intepretación de la realidad peruana*, by José Carlos Mariátegui, Carácas: Editorial Ayacucho.

Quijano, Aníbal 2007b 'Treinta años después: otro reencuentro'. *7 ensayos de intepretación de la realidad peruana*, by José Carlos Mariátegui, Carácas: Editorial Ayacucho.

Radek, Karl 2004, 'Contemporary World Literature and the Tasks of Proletarian Literature', Marxist Internet Archive, available at: https://www.marxists.org/archive/radek/ 1934/sovietwritercongress.htm.

Reid, Michael 2019, 'The Wisdom of José Carlos Mariátegui: The Latin American Left Should Rediscover the Peruvian Thinker's Pluralism and Creativity', *The Economist*, 17 April, available at: https://www.economist.com/the-americas/2019/04/17/the -wisdom-of-jose-carlos-mariategui.

Riddell, John 2012, 'Editorial Introduction', in *Toward the United Front: Proceedings of the Fourth Congress of the Communist International, 1922*, edited by John Riddell, Leiden: Brill.

Riva Agüero, José de la 1905, *El carácter de la literatura del Perú independiente*, Lima: Galland.

Riva Agüero, José de la 1962, '[Elogio del] Inca Garcilaso', in *Estudios de literatura peruana. Del Inca Garcilaso a Eguren*, by José de la Riva Agüero, edited by César Pacheco Vélez and Alberto Varillas, Lima: PUCP.

Robin, Corey 2011, *The Reactionary Mind: Conservatism from Edmund Burke to Sarah Palin*, New York: Oxford University Press.

Rock, David 1987, *Argentina 1516–1987: From Colonization to Alfonsín*, Berkeley: University of California Press.

Rodríguez Monegal, Emir 1985, 'América/utopía: García Calderón, el discípulo favorito de Rodó', *Cuadernos Hispanomericanos*, 417: 166–71.

Rodríguez Pastor, Humberto 1995, *José Carlos Mariátegui La Chira. Familia e infancia*, Lima: Sur.

Rojas, Mauricio 2002, *The Sorrows of Carmencita: Argentina's Crisis in Historical Perspective*, Timbro, Sweden: Timbro

Rojo, Grinor 2009, 'Teoría y crítica de la literatura en el pensamiento de José Carlos Mariátegui', in *José Carlos Mariátegui y los estudios latinoamericanos*, edited by Mabel Moraña and Guido Podestá, Pittsburgh: Instituto Internacional de Literatura Latinoamericana.

Rouillón, Guillermo 1975, *La creación heroica de José Carlos Mariátegui: La edad de piedra*, Lima: Editorial Arica.

Rouillón, Guillermo 1984, *La creación heroica de José Carlos Mariátegui: La edad revolucionaria*. Lima: Armida de Picón viuda xde Rouillon e hijos.

Saini, Angela 2019, *Superior: The Return of Race Science*, Boston: Beacon Press.

Salles, Walter, dir. 2004, *The Motorcycle Diaries*, Universal Studios, United Pictures Home Entertainment, 2005, DVD.

Sánchez, Luis Alberto 1969, *Valdelomar o la belle époque*, Mexico City: Fondo de Cultura Económica.

Sánchez, Luis Alberto 1970, 'Prólogo'. in *Las democracias de América Latina/La creación de un continente*, by Francisco García Calderón, Caracas, Biblioteca Ayacucho.

Sánchez Vázquez, Adolfo 2011, 'El marxismo latinoamericano de Mariátegui', in *De Marx al marxismo en América Latina*, by Adolfo Sánchez Vázquez, Mexico City: Itaca.

Sanjinés, Javier, 2012, 'Mariátegui and the Andean Revolutionarism', in *Humanity and Difference in the Global Age*, Rio De Janeiro: Educam, available at: http://www.alati.com.br/pdf/2012/Pequim/15-Conferencia-China-Javier-Sanjines-C.pdf.

Sobrevilla, David 2003, 'Introduction', translated by Frederic H. Fornoff, in *Free Pages and Other Essays: Anarchist Musings*, by Manuel González Prada, Oxford: Oxford UP.

[Socialist Party] 2011 [1928], 'Programmatic Principles of the Socialist Party', translated by Harry E. Vanden and Marc Becker, in *José Carlos Mariátegui: An Anthology*, edited by Harry E. Vanden and Marc Becker, New York: Monthly Review Press.

Sorel, Georges 1972, *Reflections on Violence*, translated by T.E. Hulme and J. Roth, New York: Collier.

Sommer, Doris 1996, 'About Face: The Talker Turns', *Boundary 2*, 23, 1: 91–133.

Spence, Rachel 2019, 'The shortlived but brilliant Latin American journal *Amauta*', *Financial Times*, 8 March, available at: https://www.ft.com/content/9d768e04-3e94 -11e9-9499-290979c9807a.

Tabarovsky, Damián 2007, 'Literatura, éxito y contexto: José Carlos Mariátegui y la construcción crítica', *Perfil*, 8 August, available at https://www.perfil.com/noticias/ cultura/Literatura-exito-y-contexto-20070815-0067.phtml.

Tarcus, Horacio 2011, *Mariátegui en la Argentina o las políticas culturales de Samuel Glusberg*, Buenos Aires: El Cielo por Asalto.

Terán, Óscar 1985, *Discutir Mariátegui*. Puebla, MX: Editorial Universidad Autónoma de Puebla.

Terán, Óscar 1996, 'Mariátegui: el modernismo revolucionario', *Revista del CELEHIS* 5.6– 8: 17–28.

Tola, Raúl 2017, *La noche sin ventanas*, Madrid: Alfaguara.

Unruh, Vicky 1989, 'Mariátegui's Aesthetic Thought: A Critical Reading of the Avant-Gardes', *Latin American Research Review*. 24.3: 45–69.

Valcárcel, Luis. E. 1972 [1927], *Tempestad en los Andes*, Lima: Editorial Universo.

Valdelomar, Abraham 1986, *Obras 1*, Lima: Fundación del Banco Continental para el Fomento de la Educación y la Cultura.

Valdelomar, Abraham 2003 [1917], 'Ensayo sobre la psicología del gallinazo', *Voces (1917– 1920). Edición íntegra. Tomo III*, Bogota: Universidad del Norte.

Valdelomar, Abraham 2011 [1917], 'Norka Rouskaya en el Municipal', *Boletín Casa Museo José Carlos Mariátegui*, (November/December): 3–4.

Vanden, Harry 1975, *José Carlos Mariátegui: Influencias en su formación ideológica*. Lima: Amauta.

Vanden, Harry 1986, *National Marxism in Latin America: José Carlos Mariátegui's Thought and Politics*. Boulder: Lynne Rienner.

Vanden, Harry E. and Marc Becker 2011a, 'Acknowledgments', in *José Carlos Mariátegui: an Anthology*, edited by Harry E. Vanden and Marc Becker. New York: Monthly Review Press.

Vanden, Harry E. and Marc Becker 2011b, 'Aesthetics', in *José Carlos Mariátegui: An Anthology*, edited by Harry E. Vanden and Marc Becker, New York: Monthly Review Press.

Vanden, Harry E. and Marc Becker 2011c, 'Introduction', in *José Carlos Mariátegui: An Anthology*, edited by Harry E. Vanden and Marc Becker. New York: Monthly Review Press.

Vargas Llosa, Mario 1989 [1970], 'The Latin American Novel Today', translated by Nick Mills, *World Literature Today* 63, 2: 266–70.

Vasconcelos, José de, 1955, *La tormenta. Segunda parte de Ulíses criollo*, Mexico City: Jus.

Velázquez Castro, Marcel 2002, 'Los 7 errores de Mariátegui o travesía por el útero del padre', *Ajos &Zafiros*, 3–4: 117–32, available at: http://www.archivochile.com/Ideas _Autores/mariategui_jc/s/mariategui_s0036.pdf.

Velázquez Castro, Marcel 2004, 'Mariátegui Unplugged', *Quehacer* 150, available at: http://www.desco.org.pe/recursos/sites/indice/29/126.pdf.

Viñas, David 2000, *Menemato y otros suburbios*, Buenos Aires: Adriana Hidalgo Editora.

Walesa, Lech 2004, 'In Solidarity', *Wall Street Journal*, 11 June, available at: https://www .wsj.com/articles/SB108691034152234672.

Walter, Richard. J. 2005, *Politics and Urban Growth in Santiago, Chile 1891–1941*, Stanford: Stanford University Press.

Weaver, Kathleen, 2009, *Peruvian Rebel: The World of Magda Portal with a Selection of Her Poems*. University Park, PA: U of Pennsylvania.

Williams, Gareth, 2002, *The Other Side of the Popular: Neoliberalism and Subalternity in Latin America*. Durham, NC: Duke University Press.

Young, Robert J.C. 2001, *Postcolonialism: An Historical Introduction*, Malden, MA: Blackwell.

Index